0709 932200 100

D1645269

Books sho~
Books (not
application,

Date Due

THE NOVELS OF THOMAS LOVE PEACOCK

THE NOVELS OF
Thomas Love Peacock

Bryan Burns

CROOM HELM
London & Sydney

© 1985 Bryan Burns
Croom Helm Ltd, Provident House, Burrell Row,
Beckenham, Kent BR3 1AT

Croom Helm Australia Pty Ltd, First Floor,
139 King Street, Sydney, NSW 2001, Australia

British Library Cataloguing in Publication Data

Burns, Bryan
 The novels of Thomas Love Peacock.
 1. Peacock, Thomas Love — Criticism and
 interpretation
 I. Title
 823'.7 PR5164

ISBN 0-7099-3220-0

Printed and bound in Great Britain
by Billing & Sons Limited, Worcester.

CONTENTS

Chapter I

INTRODUCTION; HEADLONG HALL

The novels of Thomas Love Peacock (1785-1866) have
always been highly regarded by a small, discriminating section of the reading public, and have attracted the admiring but often puzzled attention of a
variety of critics. Peacock's fiction has seemed
virtuosic, dandyish and oblique, a special taste
which few could appreciate and even fewer dare to
judge. Every attempt to fit this fiction neatly
into a tradition, to pin down the bizarre framework
within which Peacock is operating with such undeniable cleverness and aplomb, has foundered in the face
of his remarkable elusiveness of tone, theme and
procedure. No critic of his own time was able to
offer a convincing explanation of Peacock's novels,
and even to-day no satisfying consensus exists. It
is not difficult to laugh at these books, to admire
their wit and intelligence, or to perceive the
pointedness of their satirical jibes at contemporary
folly, but the problem of relating together their
separate elements, of seeing them whole, has remained refractory. Whenever a centre is grasped for, a
stable point of view or moral perspective apparently
discovered, it soon resolves itself into yet another
tantalizing and ambiguous conundrum. Peacock is
obviously concerned with the state of civilization
in his day, especially as this is shown in the arts,
and with the political organization of society. His
characters talk incessantly--it is almost the only
thing that they do--and even a superficial reading
would distinguish the pre-eminence of matters of
literary health and social justice among the endless
topics by which their exotic verbal resources are
encouraged into life. This interest in the realm of
public life, presented in a context of irony, and
giving evidence of clearminded scrutiny as well as
of whimsical elaboration, has guided generations of

1

readers towards a view of Peacock as conservative
satirist, attacking the vices of the present in
terms of the virtues of the past. This interpretation is unarguably appropriate to many of the most
striking and successful aspects of the novels. It
accounts for the attacks on a corrupt electoral
system in Melincourt (1817) and the mockery of
Romantic posturing in Nightmare Abbey (1818); it
explains the irony of Peacock's writing, his
sceptical approach to popular controversy, the
caricatural nature of a good number of his characters
and the high comedy of the scrapes in which he ent-
angles them. Above all, it conditions us not to
expect the full, rich creation of a fictional world
which we find in Jane Austen, and points us instead
in the direction of the fable--of Fielding's
Jonathan Wild, for instance, or Voltaire's Candide.
It has led to some excellent criticism, and remains
the necessary starting-place for any thoroughgoing
enquiry into the nature of Peacock's achievement.
But, like other orthodoxies, its effect has been to
blinker as well as to illuminate. It has taught us
to neglect certain aspects of these books and to
over-value others. It has fostered great academic
zeal in source-finding and reference-checking: the
significance of long-dead debates has been unearthed
and exhibited, and precise identifications have been
made between characters and circumstances in
Peacock's novels and authentic archetypes in the
world outside. This has usefully demonstrated the
extent and intimacy of Peacock's involvement with
the public life of early nineteenth-century England
and his scorn for its values, and it has correctly
presented him as a figure who stands sardonically
apart from the conventionalities of the mainstream.
But it has also rather simplified his position. I
think that to see Peacock only, or mainly, as a
satirist is unduly to emphasize the disparaging,
negative side of his work. In fact, his fiction
gives us much more than complaint: its censure is
finely, nervously paired with a compensating
celebration of the private delights of festivity and
love. It is this more positive quality which I hope
to stress, since it seems to me that a just view of
Peacock's writing can only be one that is true to
the joint (if uneasily joint) nature of his inspiration. For me, though with many changes, hedgings
and sometimes regressions, Peacock is a comic novelist as much as a satirist--that is to say, while he
consistently attacks the hypocrisy and misguidedness
he sees around him, he also suggests cheering

alternatives, and always contrives final chapters in
which marriages, feasting and the singing of hearty
songs predominate over gloom.

Peacock turned to verse long before he began
writing fiction, and his poetic production is substantial and often accomplished. However, his
sympathies are narrow, and the orthodoxy of his
taste generally prevents his verse from rising above
a level of acceptable adequacy. Peacock's problem
is a familiar one--the problem of an aspiring young
author attempting to prove himself in the most favoured literary genres of his period. But the poetic
tradition in which he was brought up was decorous
and elegant; even by the time of his first, adolescent attempts at composition its Augustan refine-
ments were nearing the end of their useful life, and
it is hard to believe that anyone could have infused
them with new fire.
Yet Peacock's longest poems, covering a space
of about twelve years, and linking the verse-writing
of his apprenticeship and the novel-writing of his
maturity, retain a certain interest. The first,
'Palmyra', was published in 1806 and then reissued,
in a condensed and fortunately clarified version, in
1812. The poem is something of a literary relic, a
graceful, visually pleasing example of the Pindaric
style which had been popular in the previous
century, and replete with echoes of Milton and Gray.
It presents the ruined city of Palmyra, once splendid and powerful, as an example of the power of
time, and concludes, with melancholy resignation -
          '"Man, and the works of man, are only
               born to die!"'(1).
It is evidently dangerous to give too personal a
reading of a poem such as this, whose theme and
handling could be paralleled in a hundred works of
the eighteenth century. But it does seem to hint at
a writer already oppressed by a fear of mutability.
Peacock's next long poem, The Genius of the Thames,
dates from 1810. It is an orthodox loco-descriptive
piece which owes something to Thomson and to Pope's
'Windsor Forest', and most of all to Milton, but its
real interest is not in the Augustan good manners of
its verse, its 'connoisseur's relish in the amenit-
ies of a settled style'(2). Rather, it throws light
on another aspect of Peacock's unease during this
period, and reveals him turning to Nature and not to
the past for support. However, uncertainties as to
the inevitability of change and decay soon supervene,
and the poem manages to achieve only the most half-

hearted kind of optimism. Peacock's next major
poem, The Philosophy of Melancholy, was published in
1812. It presents itself with some pomp as an
analysis of the pleasures which accrue from an acquiescent contemplation of the 'universal mutability
of things'(3). In fact, The Philosophy of Melancholy is more a series of graceful verse-stories with
a dormant central plan, and offering diversion of an
unexacting sort, than any kind of metaphysical
enquiry. Peacock's apparent disenchantment with the
world reaches its apogee in the unfinished
'Ahrimanes', on which he seems to have been busy
during the four years prior to the publication of
Melincourt. 'Ahrimanes' tells the story of two
young lovers whose lives are blighted by the new
sway among their people of the perverse cult of
Ahrimanes, which has supplanted the kindly worship
of Oromazes:

> '"First Oromazes--Lord of peace and day--
> Dominion held o'er nature and mankind.
> Now Ahrimanes rules, and holds his way
> In storms: for such his task by her
>   [Necessity] assigned,
> To shake the world with war, and rouse
>   the powers of mind"'(4).

In this poem Peacock finds no possibility of escape
from the futility which he sees everywhere around
him. But something like an accommodation of this
dilemma, and certainly a culmination of Peacock's
poetry, was achieved with the publication of
Rhododaphne in 1818. Rhododaphne is traditional in
form and powerful in effect; its vision of a classical past is impressive alike for its beauty and its
nostalgia:

> 'In ocean's caves no Nereid dwells:
> No Oread walks the mountain-dells:
> The streams no sedge-crowned Genii roll
> From bounteous urn: great Pan is dead'(5).

By the end of this rich and moving work, the only
thing the poet has discovered as a barrier to chaos
is the love of two young people, with its associated
values of simplicity and naturalness. I think it
would be too schematic to deduce a simple growth in
certainty between 'Palmyra' and Rhododaphne, and a
resolution of doubt in this last of Peacock's major
poems. Indeed, melancholy and regretfulness seem as
strongly felt in his later as in his earlier writings. But it does appear reasonable to note the
persistence of Peacock's concern for a present-day
world perceived in terms of unease and impermanence,
and where no trustworthy pointers towards individual

happiness are to be found.

The gloomy fatalism of these poems contrasts startlingly with the briskness and wit of Peacock's novels. There are a number of explanations for this. Although two of the poems overlap with the writing of Headlong Hall (1815), Melincourt and Nightmare Abbey, their overall mood belongs to a previous period of Peacock's life: the period of a young man's restlessness, casting about for an occupation and making ambitious efforts to secure fame in the world of letters. They have about them the pretentiousness of an adolescent, world-weary pessimism and a youthful exaggeration in the manufacture of apocalypse. The poetic genres that Peacock employs immediately entrap him in a system of conventions which requires both despondency and melodrama; equally, it often lures him towards the panacea of some Christian apotheosis in which he had no genuine belief at all. It hardly seems surprising, then, that these poems should be so different from the fiction which followed them. Their value is that they give us evidence as to Peacock's early views and proof that he was not by nature fitted for verse. At least, he was not fitted for most of the verse that he attempted. But at about the same time that his first novel was germinating in his mind, he tried his hand at a more congenial kind of poetry. This is represented by Sir Hornbook (1813), an allegorical ballad humorously detailing the parts of speech and their use, and Sir Proteus (1814), an attack on the arrogant indiscipline of modern writers. These slight pieces are jeux d'esprit whose ingenious skill and free-ranging play of mind set them apart from works like 'Ahrimanes'. Sir Hornbook, with its expressive dramatic effects and jaunty progress, seems refreshingly vivid and entertaining:

'Sir Verb was old, and many a year,
All scenes and climates seeing,
Had run a wild and strange career
Through every mode of being'(6).

Sir Proteus is a satirical ballad employing the irony, grotesquerie of incident and rhetorical exaggeration which were simultaneously put to use in Headlong Hall, and then fully developed in Peacock's later books.

With the exception of the two ballads I have just been discussing, and a small number of other, similar poems which intersperse his career, it is hard not to see Peacock's poetry as a prolonged false turning, an attempt to achieve success in a

medium for which he was temperamentally unsuited.
It has competence, interest and skill, but it is
wrong; and it shows that if Peacock was ever to
make progress with his writing, it would have to be
in prose, not in verse.

Peacock did not immediately turn from poetry to
fiction. Like many young men of his time, he was
fond of the theatre, and his library included plays
which range from Aeschylus through Restoration
comedy to ephemeral spine-chillers by M.G. Lewis and
sentimental farces by Richard Cumberland. Much
later in his life, in the first of a series of
essays on the classical theatre, published in
Fraser's Magazine in 1852, Peacock remarks that 'the
drama has been the favourite study of this portion
of our plurality, and has furnished to us, on many
and many occasions, a refuge of light and tranquillity from the storms and darkness of every-day
life'(7). Intrinsic taste, therefore, must have
suggested the drama to Peacock as a suitable exercise of his talents, and he cannot have been unaware
that a popular play might well make the fortune of
its author. So, intermittently between about 1805
and 1813, Peacock wrote three complete plays, and
jottings towards four more also survive. But it
must be seen as an index of Peacock's good sense
that he issued none of these works himself, and that
the only dramatic piece that appeared under his name
is his translation of part of the Italian play,
Gl'Ingannati; one of the sources of Twelfth Night.
     Probably the first in date of Peacock's plays,
and the least in achievement, is the Ossianic melodrama, 'The Circle of Loda'. It is a leaden and
derivative work, its violent, Nordic story told in
mechanical verse, and never rises above contrivance.
     An obvious alternative after the failure of
'The Circle of Loda' would be something familiar and
humorous, and closer to the plays which were then
successful on the London stage. Accordingly, Peacock tried his hand at farce, a form which would
evidently be attractive to a writer who loved 'exaggerated description and boisterous action'(8), and
produced 'The Dilettanti' and 'The Three Doctors'.
In both of these works it is plain that Peacock
feels much more at home than either in his poetry or
in the closet-drama of 'The Circle of Loda'.
     'The Dilettanti' is a farce of a conventional
kind, somewhat crudely put together. It tells the
story of a narrow-minded businessman, Mr Comfit,
whose fashionable young wife has filled his house

with 'a whole cargo of dilettanti'(9). He suspects
that his wife may be having an affair with one of
these dilettanti, and adopts a disguise to discover
the truth. The misapprehensions we might expect
follow comically in the train of Mr Comfit's ruse,
and it is only after confusions involving every one
of the characters that order is restored and the
Comfit family resumes the calm tenor of its life.
Even from this brief summary one can gain some
notion of the lack of originality of this play:
almost all of its elements are derived from Sheridan
or from the rich store-house of Restoration comedy.
Only the dilettanti, a posturing group of amateurs
devoid of the talent which might justify their para-
sitic existences, have a hint of freshness. But
there is one thing about 'The Dilettanti' which
excuses its discussion in any study of Peacock, and
that is its prose: from Comfit's neatly turned
first speech, which begins the play on a note of
liveliness and vernacular energy--'Am I really old
Gregory Comfit, the plodding man of business, that
was once fortunate enough to have a wife without a
particle of taste in her whole composition? Ah!
those were happy times! But she took it into her
head to pop off the perch, and I took it into mine
to marry a girl, and be cursed to me!'(10)--through
the resourceful badinage of the low-life characters
and the rhetorical vapourings of the dilettanti, its
fluency and variety never flag.
	'The Three Doctors' is a more assured piece of
writing than 'The Dilettanti', and seems likely to
be later. The story concerns the attempts of a
number of suitors to gain the hand of Caroline Hippy,
the only daughter of a hypochondriac father who has
inherited a Welsh estate and is now attempting to
put it to rights. Caroline rejects the landscape
gardener Marmaduke Milestone, Esq, whom her father
has chosen for her, and remains faithful to the
charms of her first lover, O'Fir, with whom she
eventually runs off to be married. 'The Three
Doctors' is lighter and more operatic than either of
its predecessors. Its lyricism and fine touch also
make it much more pleasing, and it is the only one
of Peacock's works for the theatre which one can
imagine having any chance of success on the stage.
Individual scenes, though thin, are entertaining
enough and the wit seems already moving towards the
ironic spruceness of Peacock's developed style. As
in 'The Dilettanti', the crotcheteers here point
forwards to the novels: they are energetic robots
with particular and recognizable voices and fashion-

able enthusiasms, and perfectly attuned to comic
action. In this play, given its intrinsic success
and also its many links with the novel which comes
after it, we can have little doubt that Peacock has
found the techniques which suit him best.

A first impetus to Peacock's delighted movement
towards the novel must have been given by his discovery of the vigour of his prose and of the comic
effects to be gained from rapid action, and both of
these he owes primarily to his experiments in the
drama. A second was the influence of Shelley, whom
Peacock met in 1812 and who became a close friend.
Everything about Peacock's early life leads one to
see him as a man of acuity and uncertainty. I think
that his doubts were given sharpness and authority
in the course of his relationship with Shelley, and
that it was this relationship which encouraged the
underlying unorthodoxy of Peacock's feelings to rise
to the surface with more confidence than before.
The correlative of this new freedom is the desire
for a different form of expression, perhaps wider in
scope, and certainly less formulaic and constrained,
by which to communicate with a large public.
The novel was an obvious recourse. Indeed,
with both poetry and the drama behind him, Peacock
had nowhere else to turn. But he now knew the
dangers of any unthinking adherence to literary con-
vention. His verse and his plays are vitiated by
their standardized format and traditional effects;
Peacock therefore looked critically at the fiction
of the day, found it largely unsuited to the iconoc-
lastic purposes uppermost in his mind, and decided
instead eclectically to establish a form which was
appropriate to his individual needs and hampered by
no existing canons of decorum. A number of features
of Peacock's writing can of course be paralleled in
other novelists, but not all of them, nor even most
of them. He follows no definite line in English literature: in some respects he is like Swift, in some
like Sterne, in some like the authors, particularly
Bage and Holcroft[11], who flourished in the uneasy,
politically explosive aftermath of the French Revo-
lution--but in general he is like none of them.
Partly this points to an independent turn of mind,
newly invigorated by contact with Shelley; partly,
to rebellion against the authoritarian aegis of the
accepted styles of his period; partly, to requirements for the novel form which no existing work
quite accommodated. One may reasonably ask for some
definition of these requirements, since they prompt

the originality of a book such as Headlong Hall. I
think that the first, and probably the most important, of Peacock's desiderata is that his novels
should be works of dialectic, not of statement: that
they should suggest, hint and tantalize; that they
should play off conflicting views without reaching
ponderously for the definitive. In addition, they
should include both polemic and romance, without
allowing one to overwhelm the other. Finally, their
tone should be comic, and they should in the end,
while giving due weight to innumerable causes for
complaint, be able to present a cheerful and even
celebratory view of human nature. Peacock desires,
then, a tentative and freewheeling sort of novel,
and has high ambitions in terms of the breadth and
refractoriness of his materials. It is unsurprising
that he generally moves outside fiction altogether,
therefore, and, particularly, outside English fiction, in his search for the techniques and stratagems from which his own books might be formed.

The records of Peacock's library show him to
have been well read in English literature and in the
classics and to have had a taste for curiosa in all
languages. He makes references in his novels to
Homer and Aeschylus, Vergil and Horace, Shakespeare
and Milton, the expected hall-marks of excellence to
which any cultivated person might allude, and which
he often sets in ironic apposition to the literary
hacks of the present day. But his personal predilection seems to have been for some of the lesser-
known writers of antiquity and for comedy of high
eccentricity or extravagance. He is, accordingly,
entirely cognizant of the standards of worth set by
the major figures of literature, but, like many avid
readers, is especially responsive to the heterodox
pleasures of works which are remote from the mainstream. It is to these latter works, in a spirit of
adventurousness and discrimination, that Peacock
frequently turns when he sets himself the task of
adapting the novel to meet his individual needs.

In the classics, Peacock's preference for Greek
over Latin is everywhere obvious, and it seems plain
that he regarded Homer as the greatest of all poets.
But, except in so far as he sets the criteria of
naturalness and beauty by which all art is to be
judged, Homer has left no direct mark on Peacock's
books. Two other Greek writers, however, certainly
have. Aristophanes, the first, strikingly exemplifies the robust satirical humour and the interest in
opinion to which Peacock is so strongly attracted.
Aristophanes's plays demonstrate the vital effect of

comedy in releasing mankind from the rigidities of
everyday life, and provide an entertaining rationale
for Peacock's own encouragement of 'freedom of
conscience and freedom of inquiry'[12]. If
Aristophanes gives Peacock a grounding in the uses
of comedy, it is Plato who suggests the structure
which his fiction might adopt. Unusually at this
time, Peacock was familiar with Plato's dialogues,
and must have found them a dazzling model for the
argumentative pliancy and questioning flow of
thought at which he aims himself, though in a less
strenuous way. Apart from Aristophanes and Plato,
Peacock's Greek enthusiasms seem quaint and periph-
eral. He often talks of Nonnus, the obscure
Alexandrian author of an immense epic poem on the
escapades of the god Dionysus, the Dionysiaca; he
mentions Athenaeus, who anthologized the literary
gossip of his period in his single surviving work,
the Deipnosophistae, or 'Sophists at Dinner'; he
refers to the satirist Lucian, in whose sharp dialogues he could find much of the fantasy, and the
irony directed against complacency, which also
characterize his own novels. It would be hard to
detect firm links between these three figures, and I
shall not attempt to do so. Only, I think it is not
by chance that they are all writers of a time of
decadence: if they have vigour, it is the vigour in
reproof of the censorious Lucian, and in principle
they content themselves with the decorative oddity
and anodyne languor suitable to the literature of a
silver age. So, if Aristophanes and Plato give
Peacock impetus towards comedy and a dialectical
approach, these authors perhaps teach him the time-
passing skills, the compensations for the absence of
heroism, which are indispensable to the artists of a
declining world.

Peacock's interest in Latin literature seems to
have concentrated on figures rather distant from the
centre. By far the most significant is Petronius,
author of the Satyricon, the scandalously amusing
picaresque novel in prose intermingled with verse of
which only a small portion unfortunately remains to
us. What Peacock takes from Petronius is not the
loosely episodic plot, with its stories of pleasing
rogues wandering around Italy and getting into
erotic and financial scrapes, nor does he attempt
the vivid realism of the Satyricon's scenes of low
life. But there is an undoubted chime between the
two writers: one, the cultivated elegantiae arbiter
of the sophisticated court of Nero, the other, the
sceptical, pleasure-loving spectator of an existence

in which he could see little that was pure or true.
What relates Petronius to Peacock is a sensibility
in which cynical pragmatism and sensuous delight
take precedence over religious faith, and ideology
is always regarded with unease. Both are surrounded
by folly and double-dealing, and have the unenviable
job of finding some measure of liberty and happiness.
Both turn away from public life and seek compensation in the joys of the body, in feasting, and most
of all in love (though the forms that this takes in
Petronius, and the specifically sexual nature of its
impediments, have no parallel in Peacock).
Marilyn Butler points out that the basis of
Peacock's classicism is 'liberal, intellectual and
humanist'[13]. But it is also pagan: it offers a
realm in which the body as well as the mind may be
opened up to freedom. The latter-day European
writers to whom Peacock is indebted show many of the
same traits. The first is Cervantes, the main
source in the novel of a comedy derived, like
Peacock's, from the gap between the world of books
and the more refractory world we actually experience.
Cervantes is most important for his satire against
foolish idealisms and heads turned by romance, and
for the fact that, like Peacock, he maintains sympathy at the same time that he points out error.
Even more important than Cervantes, however, is
Rabelais, described approvingly by Peacock as 'one
of the wisest and most learned, as well as wittiest
of men, [who] put on the robe of the all-licensed
fool, that he might, like the court-jester, convey
bitter truths under the semblance of simple buffoonery'[14]. This comment neatly defines the role of
the artist in the comedy of opinion jointly practised by Rabelais and Peacock, and establishes the
framework within which they write: giving pleasure,
first of all, and arousing healthy laughter wherever
possible, but also concerned to show up falsehood
and to expose mankind to scrutiny. Rabelais represents the culmination of the tradition of learned
wit, in which the foibles of the cultivated are
humorously set against earthly delights of love and
revelry, and where the body always seems a surer
guide to satisfaction than the mind. It is evident
that Peacock thought carefully about Rabelais, and
that he saw himself as following at some distance in
the large footsteps of this master. The influence
of Voltaire, adduced by Peacock himself, has often
been noted, and there are many similarities of
detail between the writings of the two men. But in
some respects more interesting is the link between

Peacock and Voltaire's contemporary, Diderot. I am
not concerned here with the considerable extent and
significance of Diderot's philosophical and controversial work, but rather with his novels, and especially with Jacques le fataliste. Formally, this is
eccentric and apparently haphazard; its relevance
from the point of view of any study of Peacock lies
in its combination of free-wheeling humour and the
anatomy of opinion, and it shares Peacock's sense of
the clash between man as a creature of the senses
and man as a thinker and fabricator of philosophies.
In both writers a contingent kind of comedy is
derived from the frequent collision of the brisk un-
expectedness of the actual with the tidy, predeterm-
ined plans of the ideologue, and it is characteristic of each that this should encourage the reader to
an impression of the agreeable possibilities which
are available when man is liberated from the strait-
jacket of orthodoxy.

A glance at the records of Peacock's library
will show the catholicity of his taste for English,
as for other, literature. He read Shakespeare and
Milton, but was also acquainted with a variety of
lesser, sometimes pot-boiling works, as well. There
are some English books, such as Gulliver's Travels
and Jonathan Wild, which clearly contributed to the
novel as it was practised by Peacock, and which have
a similar, fabling concern with the remoulding of
popular beliefs. But I think, beyond these generic
bonds, that little really connects Peacock with
Swift or Fielding. The major English influence on
Peacock is that of the comedies of Shakespeare,
which seems to me to go far beyond the relationship
that one would expect between works of the same kind
and in the same language. The presence of Shakespeare's mature comedies underlies almost every
element of Peacock's books, particularly in their
common emphasis on the healthful affect of natural
surroundings, their explicit or implicit pastoralism, their rich sense of young women as agents of
sanity and the impression that they give of the
festive strengths that are hidden beneath the world
of affairs. In addition, there are numerous allus-
ions to Shakespeare in all the novels. A second
figure to whom Peacock often refers is the satirical
poet, Samuel Butler, author of Hudibras, whose
ironic energy and commonsensical standpoint probably
gave encouragement to the novelist's burlesque verse
and also contributed something towards the vigour of
his fiction. Of his predecessors in the English
novel, Peacock owes most to Sterne. Peacock's

comedy is intrinsically Sterne-like in its use of
the hobby-horse, its more or less guarded appeal to
sentiment, but also, most of all, in its playing off
of a disputatious surface against a beckoning inner
life of feeling. Like Rabelais, too, both novelists
are operating in a context of learned wit whose
impact is to lessen the role of public activity and
to encourage a sense of the overriding importance of
the individual.

Peacock was also fond of philosophy and of mon-
ographs on the growth and uses of language--the
latter not at all surprising in an author so greatly
disturbed by the mishandling of words in the
spheres of controversy, journalism and politics.
This reading contributed nothing to the shape of
Peacock's fiction, though several of the philosophical works that he mentions are in dialogue form,
but must have given strength to the inherent scepticism of his thought. Most of the philosophers whom
Peacock read are now little known, and it does not
seem necessary to interpret them in detail. But
their overall position, or at least the general
tenor of their minds, is not irrelevant to the
understanding of Headlong Hall and its peers. In
their different ways, all are speaking for a
critical revaluation of accepted views, for a
clearer, fuller, less hide-bound perspective on man:
pretty well exactly, in fact, for the values which
motivate Peacock's own novels.

The writers whom I have been discussing all
seem to have contributed something, either formally
or thematically, to the conception of Peacock's
books. But, with the exception of the essay on
'French Comic Romances' contributed to the London
Review for 1835, Peacock makes no direct comment on
the authors who had given indications towards the
sort of fiction he wished to write. Thus, although
he talks of Nonnus and Diderot at different times in
different novels, he never explicitly says what he
owes to them, or to any other writer. I must,
therefore, stress the tentativeness of the linkages
I have proposed and the impossibility of proving
their strength. I have also, deliberately, omitted
comment on the extraordinary selection of authors,
ranging through Chaucer, Boccaccio, the elegant,
slight and quite un-Peacockian Marmontel, to even
the most minor novelists of his own day, who have
been advanced as Peacock's ancestors. It seems to
me that the task of considering influence is quite
complicated enough, without including so many
figures of such uncertain or tangential relevance.

In the end, then, except for the listing of
Aristophanes, Petronius, Rabelais, Swift, Voltaire
and the Fielding of Jonathan Wild which Peacock himself constitutes as the class of comic fiction 'in
which the characters are abstractions or embodied
classifications, and the implied or embodied opinions the main matter of the work'(15), and where his
own books certainly belong, we can have no sure
guide as to the sources of Peacock's fiction.

But, if we take a duly cautious conspectus of
the writers I have mentioned, a number of shared
interests emerge. There are of course exceptions,
and it is not feasible for these often disparate
figures to be crisply marshalled into a single
tradition. The first overall prepossession seems to
be with comedy, and with comedy as an instrument of
education as well as a main-spring of delight: as
Peacock notes, 'An intense love of truth, and a
clear apprehension of truth, are both essential to
comic writing of the first class'(16), and the duty
of the novelist is to communicate this truth in a
provocative but entertaining way. Secondly, many of
the authors are concerned to foster some sense of
human vitality and resilience, though this may
amount to little more than the fact of their joint
comic approach to man's problems. Lastly, a surprising number of them are formally mixed or innov-
ative, and, from Petronius through to Sterne, often
combine the effects of different genres, and poetry
and prose. These prepossessions are central to the
Peacockian conversation novel, and it seems unlikely
that Peacock did not derive some kind of support
from the example of the predecessors I have noted;
however, the assimiliation of such various qualities
into a new form is the considerable achievement of
Peacock alone.

By about 1815, Peacock had largely exhausted,
but had learned from, two of the most immediately
appealing literary modes available to him. He had
definitively given up the drama, except in so far as
he could adopt some of its techniques in his fiction.
His last important poem, Rhododaphne, was published
in 1818, and the occasional verse which he continued
to write until nearly the end of his life was no
more than slight and gentlemanly.

The main influence in Peacock's life at this
time was that of Shelley. Peacock's views, as we
may see from his writings, were unsettled and lacked
clarity of focus. They were stirred and given shape
by Shelley's outspoken attacks on what he saw as

false and oppressive in the world around him. From
1812 to 1818, when Shelley departed for Italy, Pea -
cock was exhilaratingly in touch with a profound
intelligence of a radical kind--an intelligence,
moreover, whose scrutiny was from the first directed
at the roots of society's power, its religion and
its political establishment. Discussion with
Shelley can only have confirmed the doubtfulness
with which Peacock regarded the Christian faith and
the entrenched partiality and hypocrisy of the beau
monde. Peacock was never an uncritical member of
Shelley's circle, and had no truck with some of its
wilder enthusiasms, but it certainly provided the
special impetus which led him towards the enquiring
sort of novel at which he excelled, and of which the
first instance is Headlong Hall, published in the
December of 1815.

For Peacock, at this time, disturbance was not
confined to feelings about the public realm; his
private life too was in some disarray. He had no
established occupation or regular source of income,
though in 1815 he began to receive a pension from
Shelley. He thought of founding a school in Westmoreland, considered emigration, and had a number of
shadowy affairs; in 1815 he was arrested for debt,
after a relationship with a supposed heiress, and
imprisoned. It was evidently a turbulent period,
and it seems reasonable to suppose that this would
produce an even stronger desire than before for
literary success and for some kind of recognition.
Thus we have Headlong Hall, a work whose rich and
singular ancestry I have described, and which inaug-
urates a new genre in English fiction.

The first sentence of the book is fresh and
disconcerting: 'The ambiguous light of a December
morning, peeping through the windows of the Holyhead
mail, dispelled the soft visions of the four insides, who had slept, or seemed to sleep, through
the first seventy miles of the road, with as much
comfort as may be supposed consistent with the
jolting of the vehicle, and an occasional admonition
to remember the coachman, thundered through the open
door, accompanied by the gentle breath of Boreas,
into the ears of the drowsy traveller' (p.5).
Almost every novel of the eighteenth century
includes a coach ride somewhere, but none is like
this. The tone seems impossible to pin down, hover-
ing between ironic acerbity and the coy pathetic
fallacy of 'peeping'. The syntax contributes to the
uncertainty, suspending clauses rather sharply

apart, giving an air of separateness, not of
cohesion. The allusion to Boreas reminds us of a
classical past in which the present is strangely
implicated, and establishes the subtle paralleling
of then and now from which Peacock's writing derives
much of its insidiously judging character. The
effect is unnerving, and we are deprived of the
secure grasp for which we might hope.

As the chapter progresses, and fantasy and
verbal idiosyncrasy are given free rein, we soon realize how far we are to be led from any simple or
naturalistic presentation of events: 'This name
[Headlong] may appear at first sight not to be truly
Cambrian, like those of the Rices, and Prices, and
Morgans, and Owens, and Williamses, and Evanses, and
Parrys, and Joneses; but, nevertheless, the Head-
longs claim to be not less genuine derivatives from
the antique branch of Cadwallader than any of the
last named multiramified families' (p.6). Peacock
makes no attempt in this witty catalogue to pretend
that we are reading an authentic record of the gen-
ealogical integrity of a prosperous Welsh family:
his intention is that we should laugh, and that we
should appreciate the comical, fabling nature of his
writing. As in all his books, we move away from the
everyday world and into a sphere which is freed from
obligations to verisimilitude. The preposterous
derivations and family histories, the ironies ('unlike other Welsh squires, he [Squire Headlong] had
actually suffered certain phenomena, called books,
to find their way into his house', p.7), the non-
chalant simplesse in the handling of the characters
and story, all immediately assure us that this is to
be a work of romance, not of realism. Whereas Jane
Austen and Scott build up the heroes and heroines of
their novels into convincing figures, and try to
ensure consistency and probability in their actions,
Peacock manipulates the elements of his fiction
with insouciant abruptness and verve. Personality,
and the sense of fact and of a social world which
are necessary to naturalistic fiction, are jettison-
ed. Indeed, the complicated etymologies slyly
offered, especially that of Mr Jenkison, 'according
to the strictest principles' (p.9), may be seen as
jokes at the expense of precisely that kind of
annalistic zeal which sometimes makes Scott, for
example, rather dry reading. For the undermining
absurdity here is that while the derivations may
proceed with impeccable authority, it is on the
unlikely--rather, impossible--basis of Englishmen
having names drawn from the classical Greek. We may

be certain, therefore, that direct observation of
the world is not to be found in this book, and that
the techniques suitable to its different genre will
eschew the quiet merging and flow, the inconspicuous
ordonnance, of novels closer to actuality. Peacock
is quite as aware of what he is doing as Diderot,
who notes in Jacques le fataliste that 'Il est bien
évident que je ne fais pas un roman, puisque je
néglige ce qu'un romancier ne manquerait pas d'emp-
loyer'(17). However, though Headlong Hall repudiates many of the effects of the mainstream novel,
what it neither repudiates nor lacks is liveliness:
it is odd, in some ways it is restricted, but it is
not boring.
    Almost all of the activity in the book has an
air of overt aesthetic purpose: we are never permitted to believe that the standards of outside life
can straightforwardly apply. This is a limitation
of scope, but also a liberation. We are freed from
immediate duty to the real world of our moral,
political and social problems. Indeed, Peacock even
relieves himself of responsibility for his own
characters: 'I left them to speak for themselves;
and I thought I might very fitly preserve my own
impersonality, having never intruded on the personality of others, nor taken any liberties but with
public conduct and public opinions' (p.1). There is
a mood of festivity: refreshment and illumination
are the aims, and we enjoy a holiday from everyday
cares. But the book does not content itself with a
frivolous refusal to engage in debate. Like its
successors, it deals with the substrata of life, and
little with superficial details of behaviour. We
cannot make much of the inner nature of Mr Foster
and his friends, as they show themselves in this
first chapter; but, as compensation, we soon perceive the importance of questions as to the opposing
values of past and present, and the links between
society and some more wholesome state, and it is to
these questions rather than to matters of character
or plot that the novel will address itself. Headlong Hall is a work of sophistication, but in a
pared, indirect and fabling mode which has no time
for the creation of a full novelistic canvas.
There are flaws in Peacock's execution of his
scheme, but, even from the first few pages of the
book, one can see that it is bold and ingenious.

    The most striking of Peacock's stratagems in
Headlong Hall is his irony. It seems to be everywhere, and lurks, a threatening but intangible

presence, behind even the most innocuous remarks:
for instance, 'The sun was now terminating his
diurnal course, and the lights were glittering on
the festal board' (p.38). This briefly sets the
scene for dinner, and that is unproblematic; but,
we ask ourselves, are we also to detect irony behind
the pedantry and cliché of 'terminating', 'diurnal
course' and 'festal board'? Perhaps: Peacock is
meticulously spruce, and rarely lapses into slackness or inattention. But if the sentence is ironic,
then at what target is its irony directed?--it can
hardly be the fact that it is evening, and that the
table is prepared for dinner; nor the dinner itself.
The only possibility seems to be that Peacock is
indicating doubts as to this hackneyed style of
writing itself--but how obliquely! In this case, as
in many others, one is left adrift, deliberately, I
think, unable quite to accept such writing as
straightforward, but equally unable to pin down its
undertone of disquiet. This is disorienting: its
effect is to prevent us from exercising any clarity
of literary judgement. The singularity of Peacock's
use of irony in Headlong Hall may be felt when it is
contrasted with Fielding's in Jonathan Wild: there,
the control of our sympathies and the standpoint of
the author are not for a moment in doubt. But, in
the Peacock novel, irony is more diffused and random: almost nothing escapes its faint (or pronounced) qualification. As a result, the writer's
position vis-à-vis his material is often hard to
grasp, and the reader seems doomed to an insecurity
which is both particular (in the comments on the
crassness of the literary market-place, for example)
and also general (in the aura of misgiving that
surrounds most of the activities of most of the
characters).

This ambiguity in its irony does not appear
unconsidered, nor does the book at all give the
impression of confusion. Quite the contrary:
command is signalled by each keen phrase and shapely
paragraph. Instead of confusion, we feel a comic
frustration which educates us in the folly of
expecting things to be simple, tidy or systematic.
Though there is justice in Manganelli's remark that
Peacock 'adombra in certo modo una condizione di
esistenzialismo ironico'(18), we should not over-
emphasize its implication of a very modern kind of
disengagement. Peacock is prone to feelings of
decline, and has a powerful apprehension of the
difficulties of perceiving the truth and the complex, hybrid nature of experience, but he also has a

belief in the resilience and soundness of human life.
He demonstrates this belief in the prominence that
he gives to love and to the healthful influence of
young women on young men, and in his rich celebration of the sociable pleasures of the dinner-table,
of music and of the countryside. So Peacock's
irony, while omnipresent in the texture of his
writing, conveys no impression of hopelessness.
There is a basic affirmation and even warmth. The
irony makes us wary of accepting the orthodox or the
apparently undesigning, but it is not cold or bitter.
And behind the puzzling surface there is a concern
for the truth, and for the awakening of dormant
virtues, which is not less vigorous for the non-
committal nature of its presentation.

It is thus that the materials of gloom are
transformed into comedy, by the Peacock whom
Spedding acutely characterized as 'a questioning,
not a denying spirit'(19). Peacock's is an art of
subterfuge, maintaining an embattled good humour
despite his awareness of man's vulnerability. Overall, the favoured targets of Peacock's subversion
are false authority and prescriptive system; he
regularly sets up contrasts between the blinkered
obsessiveness of his crotcheteers and the freedom
and happiness of the existence from which their
hobby-horses effectively exile them. There are of
course particular notions which Peacock explores in
each of his books, as well as the general unease
which runs through them all. In Headlong Hall he is
involved in the question of whether or not the world
is deteriorating, and with the narrowness and pass-
ivity of the cultivated elite whom he assembles as
its representatives. However, although his regard
seems unfaltering, and his prose has the formal
distinction of deliberate art, Peacock does not
commit himself to an equivalent sharpness of point
of view. Everything is elusive, dialectical, tentative, and there have been surprisingly various
readings both of individual Peacock novels and of
the features of his work as a whole. The lack of a
firm perspective warns us that we should not praise
or condemn without great care. Peacock's method,
spry, visual and uncommentated, both exposes the
absurdities of his characters, and also permits us
forbearance. The crotcheteers are foolish, and we
can hardly fail to feel sceptical about the many
bees in their bonnets, but they are never explicitly
reproved; each always has his say, and is allowed a
few frenzied, entertaining moments in the spotlight
before a companion takes his place. The effect is

finely to combine sympathy with critical awareness:
as Olwen Campbell says, Peacock 'liked the flavour
of an imperfect world, and the preposterousness of
peccant humanity'[20]. In his handling of argument,
too, Peacock offers no final adjudication of right
or wrong, though a general sense of his feelings may
be more or less apparent. Discussion, therefore,--
about the progress or decay of the world, the
benefits or otherwise of animal food, or the pros
and cons of landscape gardening--proceeds not in
what we like to think of as the normal way, with
some heed being paid to valid points made on both
side of the debate, but as a series of parallel
monologues. No resolution seems feasible, nor is
one forthcoming except by the heart-warming arrival
of beef and burgundy, or the singing of a comic song.
As Lorna Sage remarks, Peacock seems to go out of
his way to make 'mediation or synthesis...seem impossible'[21]. Thus, although arguments are adumbrated
in Peacock's novels, and a wide variety of beliefs
passionately voiced by an equally wide variety of
characters, the author maintains his teasing obliqueness of stance, and we are left with the disconcerting, invigorating circumstance of a work of art
which entertains us greatly, but also refuses to
permit us the security and certainty which we comfortably expect of it.

We are likely to be most taken aback by Peacock's presentation of discussions drawn from topics
of polemical interest in his own day. They are
conducted in language of energy and poise:
> '"Sir," said Mr. Milestone, "you will have
> the goodness to make a distinction between
> the picturesque and the beautiful."
> "Will I?" said Sir Patrick, "och! but I
> won't. For what is beautiful? That which
> pleases the eye. And what pleases the eye?
> Tints variously broken and blended. Now,
> tints variously broken and blended constitute
> the picturesque"' (p.31).

The intellectual good manners of this prose, and its
air of assurance, seem to place it in the eighteenth,
not the nineteenth century. It is precisely Peacock's purpose that we should be swayed by that assurance, and then afterwards come to realize with
what ease the wool may be pulled over our eyes. For
Sir Patrick in fact exemplifies the familiar rhetorical sleight-of-hand by which assertion is made to
do the work of proof. The confidence of his speech,
and the forcefulness of its syntax, carry conviction.

But what he says is logically quite unsatisfactory:
'"That which pleases the eye"' is not at all to be
restricted to '"Tints variously broken and blended"',
and his proposed identity of the beautiful and picturesque is therefore groundless. I do not think we
feel that Sir Patrick is entirely to be disparaged,
or that Peacock must hold some contrary view of the
relationship between beauty and picturesqueness.
Peacock permits leeway; he leaves the reader free.
His risky refusal plainly to indicate praise or
blame produces a generalized scepticism in which
favour and disfavour may be equally hard to perceive.
Even Peacock's decision in Headlong Hall to filter
much of the argument through three well-matched but
obstinately contradictory philosophers, Mr Foster,
Mr Escot and Mr Jenkison, guarantees a full airing
of possibilities but also virtually ensures that no
one view will predominate. This disturbs us by
preventing the resolution we anticipate, and also
suggests that ideology, especially when its base is
so narrow, is unlikely to help us in our dealings
with the real world. So, in Peacock, 'the last word'
is a chimaera, and the attempt to regulate the
diversity of our experience into a cosy pattern
proves simultaneous comic and fruitless. But Peacock gives no doctrine in his turn to replace those
at which he directs the force of his witty subversion. Rather, quietly, he suggests that other realm
of existence which has been neglected by the urgent
singleness of polemicists; an alternative which he
must have regarded, like Butler, as a liberation into common sense as well as into enjoyment:
'He knew what's what, and that's as high
As metaphysic wit can fly'(22).
Lorna Sage has said that Peacock's books amount
to 'a statement of faith in doubt'(23), and that is
exact. Since all sides of argument are ironized,
since there is no agreed conclusion to any dispute,
the whole status of discussion begins to change. It
stimulates flight of imaginative verve, displays of
comic energy, in addition to suggesting evidence and
organizing support or attack. It leads us not only
to ponder judgement, to think for ourselves, therefore; it also seems a show, a juggling-act with
words. What remains with us is an exciting intellectual turmoil quite deprived of finality, and given
a comic rather than a melancholic turn by the certainties that underlie it. It is Diderot, characteristically, who best evokes this circumstance: '"O
vanité de nos pensées! ô pauvrete de la gloire et de
nos travaux...Il n'y a rien de solide que de boire,

manger, vivre, aimer et dormir"'(24).

Peacock specifically encourages, and builds upon, the subtle ambiguousness which I have detected everywhere in Headlong Hall. It is not intended that we should ever relapse lazily into any sureness as to the position of the author, or the true worth of any of the arguments presented to us. What goes on in Headlong Hall is bemusing, alternative and challenging, and it is not by chance that the book's activities are insulated from straightforward contact with the everyday. It is the merit of the form Peacock chooses that it permits the reader a holiday, full of reminiscences of actuality and elaborations of its problems, but freed from any direct weight of responsibility. Peacock was not naturally optimistic, and conditions in his society hardly gave cause for much hopefulness; the comic resilience that he achieves in his fiction is made possible only by the fact of its obliqueness and its distance from the world. We do not have any immediate or piercing sense of the harm that wrong ideas may do, nor are we allowed to see them in the fullness of their implications. But it should not be thought that the ideas which proliferate in Peacock's books are only the quaint appurtenances of the characters by whom they are voiced, and exist only as diverting but insignificant gambits in an irresolvable debate. Certainly this is one impression that one has of them: that they are jokey, and that much of their purpose is to delight us by their inventive oddity. However, the fact that they produce no answers cannot obscure their frequent acuteness and intelligence, or the powerful effect that is produced by their practice in society rather than by their mere vivid exposition at the hands of clever, but safely impotent, dilettanti. Within the brief span of Peacock's novels, the problems of his day, and indeed of all days, can convincingly be limited in compass and counterpointed with a life of love and of the senses of whose strength everyone may be assured. The notions that animate the crotcheteers, however, and the painful circumstances to which they are a response, linger on in our minds. Some of them, certainly, such as the phrenology of Mr Cranium, are of less weight, though they generally have some relevance in terms of a major problem. Many of the discussions, such as those involving the minor figure I have just mentioned, are especially directed towards a local controversy, and are meant principally to illuminate the exaggerations and absurdities of the fashionable or new-fangled. But others, represented in <u>Headlong Hall</u> particularly by the long-standing debate as to the progress or deterioration of civilization by Messrs Escot, Foster and Jenkison, and by the divergence of theory from practice and the unwise tampering with the forms of Nature, formulate arguments which are of importance in a view of the health of any society.

In his excellent essay on <u>Headlong Hall</u>, Peter Garside warns that 'there is a <u>real danger</u> that we accentuate the parodic-contemporary while disregarding the intangible 'other' Peacock'[25]. It has indeed been usual to locate Peacock's primary concern in the social, cultural and political fads of his own times, and it is undeniable that his work is dense with references to the dilemmas, and some of the figures, then most in the public eye. Thus one function of Mr Milestone in <u>Headlong Hall</u> is to dramatize and cast doubt upon current theories of the 'improvements' that might be made by the landscape gardener; Mr Foster may be related to the optimistic philosopher, William Godwin; and Mr Panscope seems a cunning parody of the sort of obscurantist and mystic most saliently represented in early nineteenth-century English literature by Coleridge. Further examples could be adduced from almost every page of the novel. But our experience of <u>Headlong Hall</u> is not at all that of a book whose interest is only in the present-day and polemical. The debates that it presents are sometimes topical, and sometimes wider-ranging. In fact, the principal contrasts in the novel are not between the sensible and the absurd parties in any argument, but instead between modern civilization <u>per se</u> and the simple, healthy values of life. A constant, implied complaint, which never bluntly obtrudes itself on the reader, sets off the greatness of the past, the true beauty of an untainted countryside and the rich satisfaction of a life of the senses, against the incorrigible corruptness of the contemporary public world. So, for instance, there are descriptions of the Welsh landscape in this book whose grandeur is enough to still even the apparently unstoppable chatter of the characters, and evocations of moments of affection, or of cheerful feasting, which transform otherwise indefatigable crotcheteers. When we come to assess the contemporaneity of <u>Headlong Hall</u>, therefore, we should not be misled by <u>its dramatic</u> silhouetting of a number of disputes then much in the air. In his preface to the 1837 edition of his novels, Peacock himself emphasizes the more general aspect of his writings: 'the classes of tastes, feelings, and opinions, which were successively brought into play in these little tales, remain substantially the same' (p.2). Not only is the allusive texture of Peacock's prose much more various than has been supposed: illustrations from the present are not at all more frequent than those drawn from the past. It is of the nature of his art that it should perceive modern poetry in the critical light of the achievements of Homer or Vergil, or the pettiness of time-serving politicians by comparison with the nobility of Athenian democracy. Peacock does not, however, permit even these contrasts to remain unqualified. There are episodes which celebrate the arts and societies of the ancient world at the expense of their modern counterparts, but nowhere is there any unequivocal statement which elevates this preference into dogma. Indeed, although it is a matter of irony throughout the novel that the enfeebled relicts of the present should expend such energy in tracing their ancestors back to the heroic times of 'the Trojan War' (p.105), we are also given a sense of the folly of leading one's life in terms of what was rather than of what is. There are other elements which make for catholicity in Headlong Hall, apart from the broad perspectives of its prose. Almost every discussion moves quietly from a particular phenomenon to some larger issue which may affect many societies and many periods, not just one. So, in Chapter VII, the book's principal antagonists begin with disagreements as to a contemporary scene defined by Mr Escot as 'a complicated picture of artificial life' (p.77), but soon pass on to an analysis of the nature of truth whose relevance is to human behaviour in general, and not merely to its immediate manifestations in an age of uncertainty. In the same way, the method of Peacock's characterization has often been misrepresented as a purely parodic transposition from life into art, so that, for instance, Mr Foster is seen only as a humorous version of Godwin, or Mr Panscope of Coleridge. As I hope to show later, this simplifies the way in which Peacock operates, and very much limits the intended effect of the bright eccentrics who people his pages.

It would clearly be disingenuous to pretend that Headlong Hall can be divorced from intimate reference to the dilemmas of its time, though I have suggested that this aspect of the book is often over-emphasized. It reveals itself not only in polemical dispute, but also in convincing comment on some actual circumstances of life. Of course

Headlong Hall is not a book by Jane Austen, nor does it have the kind of detailed social observation that we find in Nightmare Abbey or Gryll Grange (1861); but there are residual connections between this work and the sort of realistic delineation on which it seems to have turned its back. Peacock is a master of insinuation, and sometimes startles us by perceptions whose ring of authenticity seems conferred by experience. One of the most poignant appears as the conclusion to a grand description of Traeth Mawr in its ring of mountains, its waters soon to be dispersed by the building of an embankment: 'Vast rocks and precipices, intersected with little torrents, formed the barrier on the left: on the right, the triple summit of Moëlwyn reared its majestic boundary: in the depth was that sea of mountains, the wild and stormy outline of the Snowdonian chain, with the giant Wyddfa towering in the midst. The mountain-frame remains unchanged, unchangeable; but the liquid mirror it enclosed is gone' (p.74). Even stylistically, this is remarkable; untouched by irony, with a sadness that seems the mood of its author, it achieves a stillness that moves one to conviction. It gives no impression of an assumed deteriorationism, and is remote from the gloomy crotcheteering of Mr Escot; the voice is Peacock's voice, and the scene whose impending destruction it laments is one that recurs in a number of his books, and always with the same connotations. A lesser instance of this effect is the comment on the entertainments after dinner: 'Miss Tenorina and Miss Graziosa now enchanted the company with some very scientific compositions, which, as usual, excited admiration and astonishment in everyone, without a single particle of genuine pleasure' (p.68). The irony of 'enchanted' here, and the exaggerated phrasing, closely relate this passage to the general tenor of the novel; but its punctuation, which separates out the disillusioned 'as usual' from the rest of the sentence, gives emotional force to a perception that can only have been gained in the real world. Moments such as these are to be found throughout Peacock's fiction, and provide a counterbalance to the impulses towards fantasy and eclecticism which generate so much of its energy. They ensure that Peacock's novels permit us the pleasure of relief from pressing cares, and emancipation into a more festive existence, but do not court the irresponsibility of a flight into a cloud-cuckoo-land entirely divorced from reference either to ideological disagreement or to everyday reality.

For Jean-Jacques Mayoux, Peacock, 'comme tous les vrais esprits comiques, avait une certaine confiance dans la nature humaine'[26]. Clearly, Peacock was not immune to the perplexity of his generation, but, equally clearly, his fiction is devised to accommodate that perplexity. It takes account of the forces which are ranged against truth and joy, but attempts to derive sustenance from the vitality with which all people are endowed. So, although a good deal of the book is taken up with complaint, much of the rest consists of celebrations like those we find in Shakespeare's comedies--eating, drinking, dancing and singing. Continual reminders of man's physical self, and of the delights of sociability and solidarity, counterpoint the intellectual wrong-headedness and apartness of the crotcheteers. Often food will conclude an argument by the power of its irresistible call to those needs which are fundamental to us all. And the complement of eating in this novel, as in life, is drinking. Repeatedly, the power of burgundy or claret is used to reassert a sense of community when disagreements between characters begin to take them too far. In Chapter V, 'The Dinner', for instance, though quarrelling culminates in Mr Panscope's furious 'Lightning and devils' (p.56), unity is soon restored by Squire Headlong's call for bumpers and a glee, in the grand chorus of which everyone sings together:

'Let the bottle pass freely, don't shirk
        it nor spare it,
For a heeltap! a heeltap! I never could
        bear it!' (p.57).
Jolly drinking-songs like this, which frequently signal the end of crotcheteering disharmony in all Peacock's books, serve to join a company in unison and, often, to leave the reader an impression of good humour rather than of bad.

The form of Headlong Hall is adapted to present both complaint and consolation. Only Sterne among previous novelists in English was so well able to derive comedy from unease and to play off a surface of satirical reproof against a less emphasized, but vigorous, undercurrent of celebration. The country-house setting serves to limit responsibility and to prevent the shattering intrusion of mundane standards. In addition, the sharp comic action and the non-committalness of the tone do not allow us to be deeply engaged. We are inspired to think widely around a variety of topics of both general and particular relevance, but we are not inspired to feel passionately about them, nor to conclude that error is inescapable and that mankind has no positive recourses in which to place its trust. 'Pleasure is the end'(27) was the message of Epicurus; it is a fitting epigraph for a work like Headlong Hall, in which gloom can always be lightened by laughter and man is optimistically imaged as a creature of the senses, and therefore open to delight, as much as a vulnerable creature of the intellect.

Peacock's prime antidote to malaise is the power of love. Genuine affection between man and woman is always treated approvingly by Peacock, though irony is directed at the falsities of spouse-hunting in polite society. Love stands for certain wholesome qualities in humanity, and is immediately set against those features of the modern world, and of social living per se, which Peacock most doubts. Its effect is to overturn both the schemes of the crotcheteers and the rigid criteria of class and wealth by which marriage is governed in the beau monde. Its impact is liberating, for it presents characters with an alternative to the hobby-horse which is irresistibly more agreeable, and which frees them from folly. So, at the end, we have a Mr Escot less constrained than before, a figure whose a priori notions have been conquered by the reality of his love for the tormenting Cephalis, and whom we may hope to have been educated in virtue even at this late stage of his life. However, this education is not heavily stressed; Peacock values the power of love, but he cannot honestly point to any grand transformation which will quite alter the fate of his characters. Love and marriage, therefore, produce improvements, but not miracles. Uncertainties remain, as they always will; even the clever, emancipated and volatile women who come increasingly to act as his agents of love and unorthodoxy cannot entirely silence that side of Peacock which is unconquerably anxious.

The second major positive force in Peacock's books is the power of Nature. Mountain scenery, especially if it is Welsh mountain scenery, arouses feelings of awe in Peacock which are just like those we find in the Romantic poets who were his (sometimes scorned) contemporaries. So, when Escot, Foster and Jenkison take a walk in the country, 'their road wound along a narrow and romantic pass, through the middle of which an impetuous torrent dashed over vast fragments of stone. The pass was bordered on both sides by perpendicular rocks, broken into the wildest forms of fantastic magnificence' (p.72).

The significance of such moments is underlined by
their effect; devoid of irony, they move the reader
with a sense of intangible and superhuman force, and
even the three philosophers fall under its sway--
they 'looked on in silence; and at length unwillingly turned away, and proceeded to the little town
of Tremadoc' (pp.74-5). Nature in Peacock is potent
and enduring, and his satire of the present day is
fuelled by a melancholy, contrasting sense of '"the
primitive dignity of...[man's] sylvan origin"'(p.10).
Contact with Nature impresses and soothes, and, particularly in Maid Marian (1822), there is a striking
antithesis between the oppressiveness of life in the
city and the freedom of life in the woods. Nature
acts as a kind of reassurance, therefore, a guaran-
tee that in the midst of flux some things at least
remain trustworthy. However, it offers no direct
path to a better existence. It is rather that it
exists quietly in the background, a vital power
whose often unacknowledged presence reflects ironically on the blinkered lives of Squire Headlong's
guests.

His characters are mainly responsible for our
sense of Peacock's comedy, and therefore of the
fundamental hopefulness of his outlook. Of their
integrity we are never in doubt; each is sharply
particularized by insistence on a single habit of
mind and a small number of qualities of voice and
person. We are not likely to forget that Mr Escot
is a pessimist, Mr Foster an optimist, or Mr
Jenkison a supporter of the status quo, and it is
essential that this should be so. The fact that the
characters are only one thing, and do only one thing,
however, leaves us with no feeling of insufficiency.
In a fable we do not expect the thoroughness of
realization that we find in the naturalistic novel.
Complexity is replaced by a statuesque simplicity;
and the characters remain in our minds because their
energy is not diffused--everything is channelled in
a particular, intense direction. It is wrong to
think of these figures merely as dummies; they are
mouthpieces of opinion, stage-managed with great
dramatic effectiveness and given a brilliant, ambiguous rhetoric, but they are more than this as well.
Although they often say foolish things, they do not
inspire disdain. Sense, perceptiveness, even truth
seem permitted to all of them from time to time, and
the result is that they may become sympathetic, or
dignified. The type of the greedy clergyman is an
obvious butt for an irreligious author like Peacock;

yet Dr Gaster, in <u>Headlong Hall</u>, is accompanied by
none of the opprobrium which Fielding directs at the
gormandizing Parson Trulliber in <u>Joseph Andrews</u>. Dr
Gaster eats a great deal, and consistently subverts
altruistic expectations as to his ecclesiastical
vocation, but his life remains unashamedly vivacious;
though his faults are displayed, it is in a context
of fellow-feeling as well as of judgement. In the
end, what Peacock achieves is a rare blending, in
his creation of character as in the texture of <u>Head-
long Hall</u> as a whole: neither satire in a pure
state nor comedy in a pure state, but a mixture of
the two in which we may recognize an equivocation of
impulse which is typical of all his fiction.

That the crotcheteers are organized around one
central obsession, whether it is phrenology, deteriorationism or the writing of corrupt reviews, and
that they are treated with good humour, is obvious
enough. But a crotcheteer is more than just an
entertaining zealot. Curiously, he is both free and
captive. He inhabits a comic world where he is
largely immune to the intransigence of reality, and
is thus able to contrive his system by speculation
alone: actuality does not concern him. These systems become more bizarre and singleminded as the
book progresses; they prescribe more and more, and
convince less and less. We cease to perceive them
principally as explanation: they are flights of
fancy, unimpeded by the mundane, and they give us an
exhilarating sense of a mind liberated from its
usual limits. This seems to me to be the positive
side to the crotcheteers, the pleasing, inventive
manner in which they conduct the peculiar business
of their lives. Of course, the circumstances that
surround it still provide a muted commentary on the
validity of each of the hobby-horses, and even within individual speeches there is an exaggeration
about which we cannot help but feel suspicious. So,
like Peacock himself, though we may be responsive
towards much of what Mr Escot says, we will draw up
short before the finality of his vision of '"absolute, universal, irremediable deterioration"' (p.102).
But the more overtly critical function of the crotcheteers has in the past, I think, been overstated.
It does not seem to me to be feasible to try to
relate each of them tidily to some controversial
figure of Peacock's own time; except in one or two
cases, Peacock forms his crotcheteers by picking up
hints here and there from life and using his imagination to adapt and reassemble them into new creations. He does not aim for a <u>roman-à-clef</u>. His

interests are wider than that; and he uses whatever
materials come to hand to produce the stereotypes
that he needs for his ambitious panorama of the
follies of his own, and of most other, societies. It
is simply incorrect to say that Mr Panscope, in
Headlong Hall, 'is' Samuel Taylor Coleridge in life;
in fact, as Joukovsky has remarked, 'no single detail
in Peacock's characterization of Panscope can be
construed as a definite allusion to Coleridge or his
works'[28]. It is rather that both Mr Panscope and
Coleridge might be interpreted as fair specimens of
the 'chemical, botanical, geological, astronomical,
mathematical, metaphysical, meteorological, anatom-
ical, physiological, galvanistical, musical, pictor-
ial, bibliographical, critical philosopher' (p.28),
of whose omnicompetence and obscurantism Peacock is
understandably sceptical. We are not tied, therefore, to a view of the crotcheteers merely as
thinly-disguised, particular attacks on the public
figures of Peacock's day; we should see them
instead as representatives of broader-ranging dilemmas, and agents of solace as well as of critical
enquiry. Thus, we note that Mr Cranium's view of
the world is a distorted one, and that he has become
the slave of his system instead of its master; we
recognize the limitations of perspective that an
interest only in phrenology must entail. Mr
Cranium's lecture, especially, is used to poke fun
at the narrowness of his approach to mankind, and
above all at the impossibility of his attempt at a
'definition' of the species. But we are not encouraged to see distortion and constraint as the only
features of his character, nor to consider him
merely as a man trapped within his crotchet. Mr
Cranium offers a doubting comment on the then current fashion for phrenology, and a warning, in the
words of the philosopher William Drummond, a favourite author of Peacock's, that 'To assign causes for
every thing has been the vain attempt of ignorance
in every age'[29]. However, he also offers us
pleasure: we laugh at his eccentricities, and
respond favourably to his energy and ingenuity, and
the comic strengths of his long, apparently closely-
argued speeches. Although he is a minor figure, Mr
Cranium can justly stand representative for his
unruly peers in Headlong Hall--a group whose charm
has too often been slighted, and who have a warmer
purpose than many critics have admitted.

   Unfortunately, Peacock's handling of his crotcheteers does not quite live up to the wit and
freshness of their conception. From an artistic

point of view, monomania has an obvious flaw: it is
always the same. So, though their topics may change,
the perspectives of the characters do not, and we
soon grasp that Mr Escot will always spread gloom,
Mr Foster always look on the bright side of things,
and Mr Jenkison always steer a middle course. Peacock performs literary acrobatics to avoid the
threat of repetitiousness and tedium. Yet still,
our attention sometimes flags. In the first few
chapters not enough of the characters are brought
into play, and the talk becomes mechanical; we
constantly anticipate what is to happen next--
       'Mr. Jenkison thought the scenery was just
       what it ought to be, and required no
       alteration.
       Mr. Foster thought it could be improved, but
       doubted if that effect would be produced by
       the system of Mr. Milestone.
       Mr. Escot did not think that any human being
       could improve it, but had no doubt of its
       having changed very considerably for the
       worse, since the days when the now barren
       rocks were covered with the immense forest
       of Snowdon, which must have contained a
       very fine race of wild men, not less than ten
       feet high'.
This exchange occurs on page 25 of the Halliford
edition of Headlong Hall, and already its only real
point of interest is Mr Escot's last, fascinating
supposition. There is a sort of relentlessness to
the crotcheteering; our impatience grows as characters endlessly reconfirm their obsessions, in speeches whose prolixity is satirized but insufficiently
restrained. There is glee, inventiveness and animation, but not enough. In the later conversation
novels this problem is largely circumvented: Peacock becomes adroit at varying the pace and circumstances of the arguments, there is more action and
more attention to richness of personality, and his
ingredients, especially in Melincourt, are wider in
scope. In Headlong Hall, however, the monotony of a
good deal of the crotcheteering inevitably detracts
from one's overall sense of the book's success.
       Sometimes, Peacock seems almost able to do more
with minor figures than with major ones. His vent-
riloquism is superb, and he captures the brogue of
Mr MacLaurel much better than Scott ever could:
'Really, Squire Headlong, this is the vara nectar
itsel. Ye hae saretainly descovered the tarrestrial
paradise, but it flows wi' a better leecor than milk
an' honey' (p.38). Even the most unimportant

characters are caught with vividness and precision.
Squire Headlong's unwillingly spinsterish aunt, for
instance, is presented with a grotesquerie worthy of
Smollett: 'Miss Brindle-mew was very well contented
with Mr. Jenkinson, and gave him two or three ogles,
accompanied by a most risible distortion of the
countenance which she intended for a captivating
smile' (p.129). Of course, the advantage of these
small roles is plain: they are little exposed, and
the reader is in much less danger of over-familiar-
ity.

The most vocative character in the novel is Mr
Escot, but Peacock does not handle him with skill.
The mode of the book depends on no one view, and no
one person, achieving evident triumph over the
others. Yet Mr Escot often attracts more attention
than seems his due. As early as Chapter V, he
speaks so much more sharply than his adversaries that
he threatens to transform himself into the spokesman
of the author's approval or disapproval:

> 'MR. ESCOT.
> I should be sorry, sir, to advance any
> opinion that you would not think absurd.
> MR. PANSCOPE.
> Death and fury, sir--
> MR. ESCOT.
> Say no more sir. That apology is
> quite sufficient.
> MR. PANSCOPE.
> Apology, sir?
> MR. ESCOT.
> Even so, sir. You have lost your
> temper, which I consider equivalent to
> a confession that you have the worst of
> the argument' (p.56).

It is only the comic interposition of Squire Headlong here, calling for music and harmony, that prevents Mr Escot from overwhelming Mr Panscope and upsetting the book's poise in these matters of opinion.
But Mr Escot will not be subdued; his pessimism
seems almost irresistibly appealing to Peacock, and
although his speeches have a proper leavening of
exaggeration, oddity and long-windedness, they also
offer moving and vigorous support for some ideas
which are far from absurd. In part, this follows
Peacock's usual practice of permitting every character to speak from time to time with conspicuous
verve and conviction, but in part, too, it hints at
his special fondness for this figure above all
others. Again, in Chapter VII, Mr Escot speaks
coolly and with weight: 'I think you must at least

assent to the following positions: that the many
are sacrificed to the few; that ninety-nine in a
hundred are occupied in a perpetual struggle for the
preservation of a perilous and precarious existence,
while the remaining one wallows in all the redundan-
cies of luxury that can be wrung from their labours
and privations; that luxury and liberty are incompatible; and that every new want you invent for
civilised man is a new instrument of torture for him
who cannot indulge it' (p.82). This has much in its
favour--truth, it seems to me, for one thing. It
also accords very well with the libertarian enthusiasms Peacock maintained throughout his life. Yet
to endorse it openly, to allow Mr Escot to emerge as
hero or as the voice of the author himself, would be
to upset the book's fragile balance of ease and unease, its scepticism as to the discovery of the right
and wrong of almost any matter of public moment. So
we are recalled to comedy, and Mr Escot is denied
the last word: the chapter ends instead with 'a
tremendous explosion, followed by a violent splash-
ing of water, and various sounds of tumult and confusion'. This pattern is often repeated, and Mr
Escot, moving towards victory in argument, is drawn
back at the last moment (and sometimes after that).
Increasingly, Peacock reins him in, labelling him
neatly as 'the deteriorationist' (p.91), attempting
safely to inflate his remarks into fantasy. Indeed,
at the end of the novel Mr Escott is even allowed to
change, and we are encouraged to see him as a figure
happily freed by the power of love: as he says, 'I
have danced, contrary to my system, as I have done
many other things since I have been here, from a
motive that you will easily guess' (p.120). But it
is hard to believe that any of the crotcheteers is
capable of so complete a metamorphosis; in fact,
although he admits the slight alleviation of man's
plight by '"The affection...of two congenial spirits,
united not by legal bondage and superstitious imposture, but by mutual confidence and reciprocal
virtues"' (p.151), Mr Escot's final speech returns
to the '"groans...tyranny, disease"' (p.154) of his
earlier, enduring self. Thus, we are told that Mr
Escot is different, but the emphasis is on his remaining the same; and it is not until the fuller
development of his love theme in Melincourt and its
successors that Peacock learns to handle the growth
of his characters with substance.
    There is a striking contrast between Mr Escot
and Squire Headlong; the former is maladroit, the
latter seems a complete success. From the start he

is separated from his guests because his obsessions turn out to have more to do with food and drink than with the elaboration of impractical schemes. His liveliness and good humour are unfailing. He is the prime representative of the Bacchic energies which Peacock wishes healthfully to set against the discussions of the crotcheteers. We notice, too, that it is Squire Headlong who does the arranging of the marriages at the end of the book, thus consummating it as skilfully as it was begun. He is, therefore, not simply a convenient lay-figure equipped with wealth, ambition and an agreeable country house; he is a Rabelaisian master of ceremonies who duly calls for music, reiterates 'Pass the bottle' (p.52) and ensures that claret and roast beef will always be to hand. When he is at his most characteristic, 'capering for joy' (p.90), the embodiment of the novel's anti-authoritarianism, he is a force that liberates and permits, but does not constrain.

In all of Peacock's books women are sane, natural and therapeutic. It is evident that Peacock liked women, admired them, and thought them largely free from the intellectual vices of their menfolk; their influence, and the love they inspire, help produce a welcome return to common sense and breadth of perspective in the men who cross their path. They are instinctive antagonists to crotcheteering, and regularly sing, or play musical instruments, at the cheerful gatherings which signal its defeat (or at least, its remission). The first woman whom we meet in Headlong Hall is the Squire's sister, Caprioletta, who appears as if from heaven, 'beaming like light on chaos, to arrange disorder and harmonise discord' (p.22). Her beneficent power, associated with affection and independence of feeling, must be set against the frivolity of Graziosa and Tenorina Chromatic, the coquettishness of Cephalis Cranium, the dullness of Miss Philomela Poppyseed and the extravagance of Miss Brindle-mew. But it remains our most vivid impression of womanhood in the novel, and continues in the rest of Peacock's works, more fully developed and more emotionally arresting than here, to give support to his comedy and to testify to his uncondescending views of the opposite sex.

Peacock's is a comedy of opinion, not of character, though in some later books, especially Nightmare Abbey and Gryll Grange, he begins to attempt a richer rendition of personality than would be appropriate in Headlong Hall. Nevertheless, despite his clever development of the crotcheteer, Peacock's handling of his characters in this novel is open to a number of

objections. The cast is large and the work is short;
there is little time to do more than firmly link a
name to an obsession, and then to reconfirm this linkage forever after. Also, Peacock does not seem quite able to balance the different positions he allots
to his characters, or certainly to maintain the equilibrium of pro and contra on which the book's critical purpose is dependent; thus, Caprioletta is given
too little to do, and Mr Escot too much. In general,
these faults are corrected by the time Peacock achieves mature control of the conversation novel with the
publication of Nightmare Abbey; but in Headlong Hall
they contribute largely to the sense of thinness and
awkwardness which is the book's major drawback.

We may have doubts about Peacock's characterization; we can have none about his prose. There are
few authors who so often startle and delight us by
the concentration, exactness and wit of their
writing. Almost any page might supply anthology
pieces, whether of playful, amused antithesis--'Miss
Cephalis blushed like a carnation at the sight of
Mr. Escot, and Mr. Escot glowed like a corn-poppy at
the sight of Miss Cephalis' (p.26)--or of argumentative dexterity:
'MR. PANSCOPE.
I am not obliged, sir, as Dr. Johnson
observed on a similar occasion, to
furnish you with an understanding.
MR. ESCOT.
I fear, sir, you would have some
difficulty in furnishing me with such
an article from your own stock' (p.55).
The felicitous glitter of Peacock's style is an
essential feature of the sort of fiction he intends
to create. If we do not have rounded characters in
his books, or much of a story, or any direct view of
society, at least we have language of great poise and
animation. Peacock has been called 'the descendant
of Shakespeare and Sterne'(30); in this respect he
is also the ancestor of Beckett.
There is a further connection between Peacock
and Beckett. Both are masters of rhetoric, yet their
use of that skill is reflexive: it subverts itself.
The prose seems perfect, final, as if defying one to
doubt. Close attention, however, shows it riddled
with contrarieties. This is part of Mr Cranium's
phrenological lecture:"'Here is the skull of a turnspit, which, after a wretched life of dirty work, was
turned out of doors to die on a dunghill. I have
been induced to preserve it, in consequence of its

remarkable similarity to this, which belonged to a
courtly poet, who having grown grey in flattering the
great, was cast off in the same manner to perish by
the same catastrophe"' (p.115). The context here is
of a supposedly scientific discourse, and the demonstration of an infallible system of explaining men's
characters. Mr Cranium's tone is grave and assured,
and his conclusions seem reasonable. But the so-
called argument of this passage will stand no examination at all. In reality, despite its pretensions,
everything hinges on assumption. The skull of a
turnspit may resemble that of a courtly poet and
their lives may have been alike, but that is no proof
that the configuration of one's skull will indicate
the qualities of one's personality. The effect of
such writing is constantly to make one suspicious of
the apparently trustworthy, the apparently true; it
reinforces the irony and jokiness which everywhere
give Peacock's works their power to disturb and to
refresh.

    In a more straightforward way, Peacock is also
capable of images whose bravura and suggestiveness
add greatly to the evocative richness of his prose.
Sometimes, these images are brisk and thrifty: 'next
arrived a post-chaise, carrying four insides, whose
extreme thinness enabled them to travel thus economically without experiencing the slightest inconven-
ience' (p.27). Sometimes, they are poetically
charged:

      '"If we can imagine a philosophical auricula
      falling into a train of theoretical meditation
      on its original and natural nutriment, till
      it should work itself up into a profound
      abomination of bullock's blood, sugar-baker's
      scum, and other <u>unnatural</u> ingredients of that
      rich composition of soil which had brought
      it to perfection, and insist on being planted
      in common earth, it would have all the
      advantage of natural theory on its side that
      the most strenuous advocate of the vegetable
      system could desire; but it would soon
      discover the practical error of its retrograde
      experiment by its lamentable inferiority in
      strength and beauty to all the auriculas
      around it"' (p.19).
The first of these examples has an impressive lucidity and sufficiency; the second is a dazzling
conceit with implications for almost every area of
the novel. And both tend to give a quality of
visual expressiveness to writing which might otherwise seem rather intangible.

Headlong Hall is an experimental work, trying
out the possibilities of its form and familiarizing
its author with the brave new world of fiction.
Occasionally, Peacock stumbles, and quite often
there is stiffness in his handling of unaccustomed
effects. But his prose, developed and sophisticated
in the drama, already has the touch of a master.

Headlong Hall is hardly plotted at all; there
are incidents, and marriages which neatly tie a
number of loose ends, but the story as such has
little significance. We are asked not so much to
see and understand things progressing, as to hold
everything together and simultaneous in our minds.
This is a book which presents us with a different
way of considering the world, rather than one which
leads us through changing circumstances to the resolution of thematic conflicts. In effect, nothing
happens: as Edmund Wilson says, 'Peacock is an
artist the aim of whose art is to achieve not merely
a weaving of ideas but also an atmosphere--an aroma,
a flavour, a harmony'(31). Thus we have almost no
notion of cause and effect; various situations
occur--a walk, a ball, a lecture--but the connections between them are tenuous. What we feel is that
each situation, instead of producing the next, amusing parallels and elaborates upon it. The manner of
the novel is exploratory. In place of the integrated plot-structure of orthodox fiction, we have a
shape which is responsive to other needs: dramatiz-
ing opposed ideas, encouraging a broad, unsettled
perspective on the topics it addresses, acclimatizing the reader to a clash of thoughts, not of personalities. The slightly abrupt pauses, the lack of
smoothness in moving from one subject to another,the
brusque transitions between the chapters, simply
indicate Peacock's lack of interest either in a flow
of realistic narrative or in the maintenance of a
constant grip on the reader's feelings. At the same
time, while admitting that this is a matter of mode,
and adapted to Peacock's needs, one begins to see
dangers. Headlong Hall is short and trenchant, and
we have little difficulty in seeing the book whole.
But in a longer novel such as Melincourt there are
real problems of fragmentariness and confusion.

In thematic terms, Headlong Hall revolves
around certain habits of mind whose vigour seems un-
productive, except that they provide entertainment
for the reader. These habits of mind are principally represented by the impractical systems-making

of the crotcheteers, where the complexities of life
are disregarded in a rush towards single, neat,
encompassing notions: as if unceasing recourse to
the mysteries of craniology were a sufficient answer
to the problem of finding pattern and sense in one's
experience. Taken together, the crotchets provide a
cross-section of the follies of Peacock's time,
especially in the arts, and point sharply to the
wrongheadedness of intellectuals and the consequent
impotence and absurdity of their efforts. Peacock's
method is not to analyse each of these follies in
detail or to suggest more sensible approaches than,
say, the malicious intemperance of so-called review-
ers such as Mr Gall and Mr Treacle, or the simple-
minded optimism of Mr Foster; he instills doubt,
but offers no particular remedies. We are, therefore, unhampered by Utopian visions of responsible
criticism or balanced perspectives; contemporary
complaint takes on a more universal cast. We note
that Peacock's intellectuals seem frequently deluded,
and that the present, with its idealistic hopes of
progress and improvement, exists in an equivocal
relationship with the past. But what we come to feel
most is that crotchets get one nowhere, amusing
though they may be, and that the constraint they
involve is against the best interests of mankind.
Peacock's intention is not to broadcast his views of
the controversies of the day; it is to indicate his
scepticism as to the value of any rigid system which
attempts to accommodate the variousness of life, and
in particular, of narrow obsessions masquerading
under the guise of 'authority' and purporting to
explain what reality is like. Thus the novel gives
us a comic demonstration of the impossibility of
pinning man down; it centres on his energy and intransigence, and the impertinence of schemes to
contain him--above all, those which are based on
speculation and not on a recognition of the hetero-
geneity of existence. While Peacock indicates
qualms about almost every idea or argument voiced by
his characters, and supports no other ideas or arguments in their place, he does seem to support that
whole realm of living which he represents by love,
by feasting, and by the power of Nature. Of course,
an objection we might make to this is obvious: that
Peacock has discredited the whole intellectual ethos
of his period, but has merely put a system of his
own in its place. This is true, though it is not
strongly felt in these terms. Our impression of
what Peacock offers us is not that it is just
another foible, or another tidy prescription achieved

by the convenient omission of all evidence to the
contrary. Instead, it is perceived as a liberation
whose legitimacy is not imposed from without, but
arises from within.

It is in connection with these circumstances
that some of our unease as to Peacock's artistry in
this novel may reach a head. His purpose is insidiously to play off a foolish world of public activity
against another world which is warmer, more natural
and more private. It is hard not to feel that Peacock's satire rather overwhelms the reassurance which
is meant to be its complement. As a result, the book
appears frailer than was presumably intended; its
positive side is too brutally opposed by its extensive, lively array of frivolity and misdirection.
Nor is this the only way in which the author's in-
experience upsets the fineness of the form he has
devised. We have the occasional impression of a
fatal heaviness of touch, an urge towards a fairly
crude kind of proselytization, especially when
Peacock is presenting some situation about which he
has very strong doubts. Mr Escot I have already
mentioned; but here is Mr Milestone discoursing on
landscape:

'You are right, Miss Graziosa: your taste
is correct--perfectly en règle. Now, here
is the same place corrected--trimmed--pol-
ished--decorated--adorned. Here sweeps a
plantation, in that beautiful regular
curve: there winds a gravel walk: here
are parts of the old wood, left in these
majestic circular clumps, disposed at equal
distances with wonderful symmetry: there
are some single shrubs scattered in elegant
profusion: here a Portugal laurel, there a
juniper; here a lauristinus, there a spruce
fir; here a larch, there a lilac; here a
rhododendron, there an arbutus. The stream,
you see, is become a canal: the banks are
perfectly smooth and green, sloping to the
water's edge: and there is Lord Littlebrain,
rowing in an elegant boat' (pp.64-5).

This could not possibly be clearer: it batters the
reader into understanding. One appreciates that the
basis of comic technique is exaggeration, and that
Mr Milestone's speech is the exaggeration into
absurdity of the meddlesome, over-orderly mind of
the landscape gardener. But it makes its point with
such a crass elaboration of examples that we may
come in the end merely to be fatigued. A misjudge-
ment of this sort is not unusual in first works of a

complex kind, but it nevertheless exacerbates our
sense of Headlong Hall as a novel whose elements are
not quite in equilibrium.

Some of the same doubts shadow Peacock's management of the final chapters of his book. By the end
of Chapter XIII, 'The Ball', with its celebratory
song, we feel that the action is moving towards a
climax. The major concerns of the novel come to the
surface in scenes of confident liveliness and accommodating good nature: when Tenorina, for instance,
is approached matrimonially by her host, 'The young
lady proved to be as ready as the squire, and the
preliminaries were arranged in little more than five
minutes' (p.140). The marriages provide a neat,
comic settlement of some of the difficulties which
have most troubled the characters. Summation seems
to be what we are offered, and we might expect to
respond with satisfaction. But the tone is uneasy.
There is an air of enforcement, as if Peacock were
interested in things stopping, instead of being
resolved. The weddings are agreeable, but they are
not grand gestures to ratify the book's hopefulness.
It is rather that this interlude, this collection of
incidents and conversations that composes Headlong
Hall, is over, and ends quietly, with that mingling
of uncertainty and assurance which has characterized
it throughout. Thus the last word is with the easygoing Mr Jenkison, but is preceded by a long diatribe in which Mr Escot presents his own marriage as
the sole consolation to be found in a world '"which
dares to call itself virtuous"' (p.153). There are
no real changes, therefore; it is only that the
optimistic undercurrent of which we have always been
aware emerges at the end to leave us on a sanguine
note. No education has occurred; it is just that a
fuller vision has become possible as the book progresses and matters are exposed with greater sharpness and in more detail. This guardedness, this
feeling that the novel is a staging-post--that it is
not an answer--is perfectly caught by Mayoux when he
talks of what he calls 'cette espèce d'armistice
qu'est toujours un roman Peacockien'(32). But, even
given this explanation, it is hard not to feel that
there is something not quite achieved about these
hasty pages.

One's first point in a concluding assessment of
Headlong Hall must be to re-emphasize its originality: it resembles few other works of fiction, and
seems to spring fresh and new from the particular

situation of its author. Its purpose is to encourage breadth and clarity of perspective, and it
gathers comedy from its conjunction of the exuberance of the human condition with the fruitlessness
of attempts to impose upon it. Artistically its
success is considerable, and one could not deny
Peacock's brio in the management of his effects. At
the same time, there is a tendency to overstatement,
an occasional monotony in the performance of the
crotcheteers and a suspicion that the positives
Peacock offers us are not yet as confident as he
would like them to be. As we see from his later
books, Peacock takes note of these difficulties, and
does his best to remedy them by providing a richer
development of themes, greater fullness of characterization and a more encompassing plot. But Headlong Hall is more than apprentice work; it has
flaws, as I have said, but it remains a remarkably
daring and sophisticated piece of writing.

CHAPTER II

MELINCOURT

Melincourt, the longest and most ambitious of Peacock's novels, followed Headlong Hall with extraordinary promptness. It is an unlikely, sometimes
baffling companion to the earlier work, especially
in its wide scope and in the new elaborateness of its
organization, and it has often reduced critics to
puzzlement. Certain elements of the book, such as
the figure of Sir Oran Haut-ton, the story of Desmond
and the handling of the corrupt election at the
borough of Onevote, have been generally praised, and
there is much to admire in the way of incidental
felicities and fine scenes of comedy or satire. But
there is also much that seems strident, clumsy or
prolix. Here, the form that works sharply and freshly in Headlong Hall is desperately tried as Peacock
impels it simultaneously towards fullness of coverage
and moral commitment. I do not wish to undervalue
the delight one may feel en passant in reading
through this book, and some things in it, such as its
charming, ennobled orang-outang, are as brilliant as
anything in the rest of Peacock. But overall, it
seems to me, these undoubted pleasures do not compensate for the flaws about which even Peacock's contemporaries complained.
     One reason for the misjudgements from which
Melincourt suffers may be found in the conditions of
its composition. Headlong Hall was succeeded by a
winter of 'mere Atticism'(1). Some time may have
been spent reading for a historical work, which Peacock thought would be 'more useful than any I have
yet planned'(2), and in the summer his 'out-of-door
propensities'(3) led him more often to the river than
to his study. It is improbable that he could have
begun Melincourt before July, 1816, and the novel
must therefore have been written 'more or less cons-
ecutively in the eight or nine months preceding its

publication'[4]. Even for an author as decisive as Peacock, this is remarkable. He always wrote rapidly, and none of his books took long to complete; but none approaches the 455 pages taken up by Melincourt in the Halliford edition. I do not think it us unreasonable to suppose that some of the repetitions and confusions that mar the latter part of the novel are due more to haste of composition than to laxity of design. In addition, Marilyn Butler has convincingly proposed that a good deal of material in the last of the three volumes of Melincourt's original issue formed no part of Peacock's intended scheme for the book, but was included in response to unforeseen provocations by the forces of reaction. The first of these, Coleridge's The Statesman's Manual, presents arguments in favour of the religious orthodoxy and political conservatism to which Peacock was most opposed, and appeared in December, 1816. The second was the Tory campaign, at about the same time, to restrict the liberties of an outspoken press which seemed bent on exaggerating unrest into revolution and was certainly no friend to the governmental status quo. So Chapter XXXI, 'Cimmerian Lodge', ironically characterizes the Coleridgean figure of Mr Mystic by collecting choice dicta from The Statesman's Manual, and Chapter XXXIX, 'Mainchance Villa', suddenly applies itself to the dangers of any one-sided muzzling of the press, using the Quarterly Review for October, 1816 as its source-text. However, even given the speed of its writing and the distractedness of its author, the problems posed by Melincourt do not seem resolved. After all, Peacock was meeting no dead-line, and had no fixed occupation to determine what he should do with his time. There is no apparent reason why he should not have worked on Melincourt for as long as was necessary to bring it to the same pitch of stringency as his other books.

An explanation for Peacock's urgency may be derived from the nature of his circumstances during the last few months of 1816 and at the beginning of 1817. Not only was he at the height of his confidence and vitality, and with one accomplished novel already behind him. Also, it seems plain that contact with Shelley had given a more political edge to his feelings about the public life of his period. These conditions set the stage for a work on a large scale, a keen anatomy of the state of the nation in which a committed young writer might demonstrate the full extent of his powers. In other words, just such a work as Melincourt. Two preparatory pieces,

both undeveloped, link Headlong Hall with its
successor and indicate the questioning direction of
Peacock's thought at this time. The fragmentary
'Ahrimanes', which Peacock had begun between 1813
and 1815, was fitfully continued until Melincourt
decided him finally to set it aside. 'Ahrimanes' is
a didactic poem in a grave eighteenth-century mode,
and gives a picture of a world of evil-doing in
which the peace and security necessary for personal
fulfilment are nowhere to be found. Peacock's
presentation of the lost paradise of early man expresses an intense regret for the 'love, and health,
and peaceful thoughts'(5) which alone can satisfy
our basic needs. The distressed fascination with
which this early bliss is contrasted with the present viciousness of the world is the strongest feeling in the poem, and is unmistakably personal in
tone. The prose sketch 'Calidore', which was begun
just before Melincourt, comically follows through
the irreligious implications of the heavier-handed
'Ahrimanes'. It is a witty parable in which Peacock
sets the charming pagan ingénu of his title amid the
so-called Christian decencies of modern-day England
in order to highlight the freedom and naturalness of
the one way of life as against the corruption of the
other. Both these works assert a deep dissatisfaction with the established church and the established
political system, and indicate that Peacock was
moving in the direction of a more radical expression
of his antipathy to the falsities of the contemporary world.

Shelley had introduced his protégé into a freethinking circle alert to the latest progressive
ideas. Melincourt has a powerful sense of the
moment and of being critically in the thick of
things; of all Peacock's works it is the most
immediately concerned and apropos. Far more than
Headlong Hall, it has a young man's headiness and
exuberance. One feels that Peacock's eyes have been
newly opened to the shabbiness of his world, and
that he knows his talents to be appropriate to the
task of exposure and subversion that is required. He
sees about him, as the year 1816 proceeds, increasing evidence of economic and social crisis, and
hopes that his writing can play some educative part
in the conflicts of the time. He is thus prepared
to take risks, to commit himself and show his hand,
as he is nowhere else. He does not husband his
resources; instead, he stretches his abilities to
their limit and sometimes beyond. For the reader,
there is a kind of exhilaration to all this,

especially in the context of an oeuvre as reticent
and well-tended as Peacock's. It seems as if he is
deeply moved, and is girding himself for a major
statement which will call on all his reserves.
Perhaps to its detriment therefore, Melincourt casts
aside the non-committal brevity of its predecessor
and rushes ambitiously towards a thoroughgoing,
partisan involvement in the controversies of its day.
It takes to heart the liberating dictum of Epicurus,
that we 'must release ourselves from the prison of
affairs and politics'(6), and offers us Peacock's
fullest, most daring attack on the follies of the
society he saw around him.

The state of England is at the forefront of our
attention in Melincourt, and social and political
affairs, broadly conceived, make constant demands on
our conscience. Much of the country's framework and
many of its problems are investigated, wittily
discussed and then dramatized for us in pungent,
often self-contained episodes like the Anti-Saccharine Fête or the encounter with Mr Moley Mystic. A
sense of fragmentariness is hard to avoid, especially in the later sections of the book, where incidents and parallels proliferate endlessly, unrestrained by any evident controlling structure. Encyclopaedism and dispersedness need be no disadvantage in
a work of fiction, as we may see in Rabelais or in
Balzac. But even given the alterations in its form,
Melincourt makes a poor showing against the trenchancy of Headlong Hall or Nightmare Abbey. Overall,
the frequent scenes which are nicely done, or superb,
do little to counteract an impression which is mainly of garrulous tourism in a context of moral concern. Kingsley Amis has complained of what he calls
Peacock's 'inordinate capacity for simple diffuseness and repetition'(7), and in general that seems
to me to be wrong; of Melincourt, however, it is
indisputably right.

Redundancy is not the only harmful result of
Peacock's new direction in Melincourt. If Headlong
Hall was rather too fragile, this novel is rather
too stalwart. The reformist tendency of its social
comment, and the Jacobinism of its politics, are
pronounced robustly, at length and with conviction.
The solicitude seems genuine, but sometimes produces
only sermonizing or bluster. Mr Forester, who almost
never stops talking, unhappily combines the severity
of a prefect with the moral righteousness of an old-
style clergyman: 'In every mode of human action
there are two ways to be pursued--a good and a bad

one. It is the duty of every man to ascertain the
former, as clearly as his capacity will admit, by an
accurate examination of general relations; and to
act upon it rigidly, without regard to his own previous habits, or the common practice of the world'
(p.50). Behind declamations like this, and in spite
of the irony with which they are often refreshed,
one senses a fatal urge impelling Melincourt towards
proselytism. The approach to the reader becomes
disconcertingly brusque; opinions are less subtly
veiled and fantasized than they were before, and
Peacock's overtness dispels much of the comedy for
which his books have always been best liked. Though
not invariably, his manner loses poetry and wit. The
bright, alternative worlds of Headlong Hall and
Nightmare Abbey are checked here by an overriding
impression of wrongdoing. Peacock's other novels
are freer; in Melincourt the ambience is close to
reality, and its problems seen too grave for charming games and diversions.

In addition, as Peacock tinkers with the form
of the conversation novel in this book, a necessary
balance is disturbed. It is not quite that solemnity and pressedness take command of a texture which
was previously mobile and taut; it is that a number
of different manners co-exist, and that they resist
assimilation. Melincourt is an intermediate sort of
work, mingling satire, romance and a more everyday
kind of storytelling without ever settling exactly
on its procedures. So, for long periods, social and
political ironies occupy our attention; then the
highly-charged love-affair between Anthelia and Mr
Forester resumes a central role; then, abruptly,
the focus changes yet again. This is more than the
perky disjunctiveness that one finds in all of Peacock's novels; it is a real inability to decide on
the balance and relation of the elements of which
the book is composed. Melincourt is very near to
the incidents and personalities of the outside world,
and the gravity of approach that this involves seems
to upset the vulnerable equilibrium which Peacock
nicely established in Headlong Hall. I think that
Peacock's novels need insulation and eclecticism in
order to succeed; the interest that they generate
comes from the consanguinity of romantic and anti-
romantic urges within them, and the inevitable
tension that this produces. But here, festivity and
joy have a lesser role to play; much of the book is
negative, composed of reprobation or outright attack.
Eating, drinking, music and love, the upholders of
Peacock's optimism and of his trust in man's good

nature, are subdued. Even the relationship between
Anthelia and Mr Forester, although more developed
than its progenitors in Headlong Hall, is under-
stressed and intermittent. We feel, somehow, that a
valuable part of Peacock's special quality is lost
in the course of his experiments in Melincourt; his
discarding of so much of the energy, equivocation
and fineness of touch of Headlong Hall diminishes
the unique value of the conversation novel, and
gives too free a rein to earnestness. Although
there have been dissenting voices, critics have not
viewed this shift with approval; indeed, it is very
hard not to long in Melincourt for rather more of
the vivacity which still links it (if tenuously)
with its sceptical, jokey peers.

In Melincourt, Peacock opens out and domestic-
ates the dinner-table colloquy of Headlong Hall. He
commits himself to a large and various cast of
characters, a considerable range of incident and a
miscellany of demanding technical skills, and seems
determined to do full justice to the panorama of
dishonesty and stupidity that he sees around him. He
attempts moral, philosophical, political and romantic viewpoints on his material; with more or less
success, he weaves in discourses on the nature of
man, attacks on the establishment and its mishandling of its responsibilities and the quest for true
love in which Anthelia and Mr Forester eventually
find fulfilment. This rich project encourages Peacock to great ingenuities and felicities of constr-
uction, especially in his well-considered handling
of the first two volumes of the work (up to Chapter
XXVIII, 'The Chess Dance'). But even by the end of
Volume II, Peacock's control is faltering; his
management of pace, and his direction of our interest as between the different strands of his story,do
not conceal the increasing gratuitousness and
repetitiousness of his writing. Melincourt entraps
Peacock in the quandaries of a complex literary work
of ample dimensions and high ambition. It requires,
in particular, expertise in the maintenance of
pattern and in the careful linking of disparate
materials--precisely the expertise with which a
brief, rather discrete novel like Headlong Hall
could not have equipped its author. In addition,
the elements which Peacock chooses to conflate in
Melincourt are of a refractory and unconsonant
kind. On the one hand there is the cerebral wit of
the anatomy, which operates by irony and analysis,
and turns a cold eye on extravagance of feeling; on

the other, there is the romance which emanates from
Anthelia and proves irresistible to the men who fall
in her way; and, forming a background to both, there
is the critical conspectus of the world and its ways,
sometimes integrated, but more often thematically
isolated from the principal activities of the characters. Given this degree of dilation, it is unsurprising that critics have bemusedly lost sight of the
fundamental shape of Melincourt, and have argued for
its reconsideration as 'a sophisticated beast
fable'[8] or as (in large part) 'Renaissance romance'[9].

In fact, discussion still takes up much space in
Melincourt, as it does in all Peacock's books, and it
remains appropriate to see the work as a conversation
novel, though of a modified kind. But it is more
sententious than we expect from Peacock, and its symposia on the conditions of man in society are accompanied by a plethora of interspersed accounts and adventures and some episodes of unqualified exhortation. It is the adventures, rather than the topics
which they dramatize, that we are most likely to remember; and, as Kjellin says, 'Only in Melincourt is
an action of decisive importance to the plot'[10].
The high points of the book are the figure of Sir
Oran and the charivari of the Onevote election; the
crotcheteers are more stolidly imagined and more exp-
ository than in Headlong Hall or Nightmare Abbey and
it is hard not to feel that too many of the disputes,
crucial though they are to the novel's ideological
purpose, are dull or heavy-handed. In principle,
therefore, what we find in Melincourt is a curious
inversion of Peacock's usual talents; he handles exciting incidents better than philosophizings at the
dinner-table, and exchanges the entertaining fantasy
of his characters and their hobby-horses for a more
propagandist discourse less enlivened by his characteristic, tantalizing wit. But the experimental variety of Melincourt requires a convincing centre and a
coherent, encompassing organization. It is here, I
think, that Peacock fails. Marilyn Butler[11] has
ingeniously argued for what she sees as the underlying symmetry and consistency of Peacock's storyline
in Melincourt. Her evidence is persuasive, though
she marshals the narrative into a formal spruceness
suspiciously more developed than in the other novels.
I am convinced that she has justly perceived Peacock's intentions in this work; but I am not convinced that these intentions are properly realized in
the book we have before us.

Melincourt begins nicely, with an amplitude and

confidence of exposition which is matched only by <u>Gryll Grange</u> among Peacock's works. The important figures are fully and entertainingly given, and their circumstances sketched, amidst a brisk to-ing and fro-ing between Melincourt Castle, Hypocon House (the home of the genial Mr Hippy) and Mr Forester's tastefully refurbished Redrose Abbey. Peacock shows considerable skill both in galvanizing comic situations and in setting up the context of judgement and opinion within which the most important debates in the novel will take place. We see that Anthelia's quest for some nineteenth-century paladin will provide the romantic interest of the book, and that questions of social justice and political virtue will be central to its philosophical concern. It is with deliberate, somewhat lumbering artistry that the group surrounding Anthelia is kept apart from that surrounding Mr Forester until Chapter XV, by which time all necessary information has been supplied to the reader and the action proper can begin. For the ensuing five chapters this develops the qualities and significance of the growing relationship between Anthelia and Mr Forester, introduces the first attempt on Anthelia's person, and provides an interlude of sociability and intimate feeling as a counterpoint to the climactic scenes at the Onevote election. These occupy Chapters XXI and XXII, and vividly embody Peacock's principal political warning in the book. It is at this stage that <u>Melincourt</u>'s previously grand, varied and deft handling of its materials begins to decline. The topics addressed in individual chapters become increasingly selfcontained and heterogeneous. It seems as if one element in Peacock's design, the political, has been sufficiently expressed, but that he has lost sight of the general direction of the interrupted love-affair between Anthelia and Mr Forester and of the arguments as to the nature of man which the latter regularly shares with Mr Fax. As a result, the reader is left adrift; from time to time, a curious episode may claim his attention, but he has no sense of firm intention or certain relevance. From Chapter XXV, and even more after Chapter XXX, <u>Melincourt</u> disintegrates into a loose gathering of brief adventures, most of them expanding upon, or in some way recapitulating, complaints or difficulties with which the earlier part of the novel had already been concerned. There seem to be two reasons for this. The first, Peacock's sudden decision to include comments on dilemmas just then immediately in the public eye, I have already mentioned. The second, I think, derives from the alterations of form that

Peacock is attempting in <u>Melincourt</u>. We have the
impression by this point in the novel that the
author's confidence has slackened; he feels a
nervous need to go over old territory, to check that
his opinions have been adequately communicated to
the reader: to repeat himself, in slightly different
terms and usually with less vigour and ingenuity.
When Peacock's conclusion comes, with the marriage
of the two lovers in Chapter XLII, almost all of the
impetus of the novel has been dissipated; the
complex mingling of themes achieved in the first two
volumes has fragmented long since, and even the
abduction of the heroine and the purpose of her
lover's search for her have not been sharply maintained in our interest.

It is by comparison with the lucid sufficiency
of a work like <u>Nightmare Abbey</u> that Peacock's method
seems so insecure in <u>Melincourt</u>. The mass of detail
is sometimes of dubious point and often of inexplic-
able arrangement; little is left alone, and the
expansiveness of the illustration diminishes the
tension and attractiveness of the principal incidents. Mr Forester, incapable of one word where ten
will do, is a prime offender. His loquacity is
ironized, yet at the same time rarely restrained; he
is unleashed repeatedly on readers already bemused
by the sheer quantity of material placed before them.
His introduction of Mr Fax is a model of redundancy
which has glazed one's eyes even by the second of
its interminable garnishes on its substance:

'"This is Mr. Fax," said Mr. Forester,
"the champion of calm reason, the indefatigable explorer of the cold clear springs
of knowledge, the bearer of the torch of
dispassionate truth, that gives more light
than warmth. He looks on the human world,
the world of mind, the conflict of interests,
the collision of feelings, the infinitely
diversified developements of energy and
intelligence, as a mathematician looks on
his diagrams, or a mechanist on his wheels
and pulleys, as if they were foreign to his
own nature, and were nothing more than
subjects of curious speculation"' (p.73).

The obvious danger is that the focus of the
novel will be lost amidst elaboration, and this in
fact frequently occurs--in the first two volumes as
well as the third. Since we are deprived of the assistance of a Fieldingesque command of the action,
masterfully linking together all the objects of its
scrutiny, we tend to be unsettled during much of

Melincourt. We wonder what has happened to Anthelia
or Lord Achthar, and why Mr Mystic should be given
such prominence so late in the action. The movement
of the story, after its finely-turned exposition,has
a jerky air, and points to an acute restlessness of
equilibrium in the book as a whole.

Peacock's staged, interpolating tales add to
this impression. In a number of cases, as with the
chapters given over to the life of Desmond, Peacock's
method adds statuesqueness to some exemplary circumstance which he wishes strongly to emphasize. But
Desmond's short, instructive autobiography is insert-
ed as Chapter XIII, while the book still retains some
sense of control and development; it is separate,and
deliberately so, and it works because its interrupt-
ion of Peacock's narrative is so pointed. Similar
effects are well managed in Peacock's other novels,
where they often provide trenchant dramatizations of
polemical notions more discursively presented at
earlier stages in the story. Melincourt, however,
inherently lacks the concentration and sureness of
its peers. Peacock comes increasingly to obtrude too
many of these tales onto an already uncertain structure, and to take too little care in fixing them convincingly within a general thematic framework. At
least half a dozen chapters are vulnerable to attack
on these grounds, and few have the excuse of wit or
charm to compensate for their clumsiness. In particular, Chapters XXVII and XXVIII, 'The Anti-Saccharine
Fête' and 'The Chess Dance', seem to me to be mere
empty interludes filling in time until the next turn
of the romantic plot can be contrived. 'The Chess
Dance' is the dullest episode in the book, over-ing-
enious in design and laborious in execution; and its
companion has little more in its favour. Chapter
XXXI, which paints a vigorous but long-winded picture of the obscurantist Moley Mystic, Esq., at his
fog-shrouded mansion of Cimmerian Lodge, is more
amusing and apropos. Yet its clever burlesque of
Mr Mystic, blinded by Kant and enfeebled by
solipsism, has no aptness to a position in the novel
between the brusque economic diatribe of 'The Paper-
Mill' and the Old English, rustic nostalgia of 'The
Deserted Mansion'. It is simply that all three
chapters are concerned with circumstances of which
Peacock disapproves and that his determination to
have his say is not subdued into any effort felicit-
ously to relate one to the other or any at all
integrally to the rest of the book. The most
awkward and worst-balanced of the incidents which
mostly make up the third volume of Melincourt is

Chapter XXXIX, 'Mainchance Villa'. Like much else
in Peacock's work, this chapter is given over to
condemnation of the forces of reaction; its
subject-matter is literary, and it gathers together
a rabble of venal, conservative hacks whom it establishes as the voice of the establishment and
bitterly denounces as supporters of the 'immortal
Gagging Bills' (p.405) just then under consideration. Like Chapter XXXI, the scenes at Mainchance
Villa respond to an immediate vexation. As one
might expect, they share the same faults: prolix
and strident, they expand hastily to meet the needs
of a situation not envisaged by their context, and
can pay no heed to the effect on Peacock's romantic
tendresses of the impetuous satirical pantomimes
they present. It is unsurprising, after the excitability and gratuitousness of incidents like these,
that Mr Forester's final acceptance by Anthelia
should seem so flat, and the supposed culmination of
the book therefore so downbeat.

Marilyn Butler has commented on the 'elegance
of shape'(12)of Peacock's narratives, their composed
'movement towards and away from a central pivotal
scene'. But she also admits in Melincourt the
intrusion of much subsidiary material and the repetition of many points that have already been made. I
think one cannot but agree with her complaints, as
one must agree with her praise. Melincourt is
potentially the richest, broadest-based and most
moving of all Peacock's novels. Its organization,
however, proves a task beyond the skills of its
creator.

In Headlong Hall, Peacock had little such
difficulty; it is his new desire to move towards
commitment which causes him problems. The spread of
topics in the book is extraordinarily wide. A
number of the prepossessions, such as the contrast
between outer show and inner worth, the relationship
between ideology and practice, infiltrate many of
the discussions and incidents in the novel, but
others are more particularly located in individual
sections. In my own copy of Melincourt a previous
owner has noted down the content of each of the
chapters, and has thus clarified the pointedness of
Peacock's handling of his themes. In all his books,
separate scenes address themselves to separate
topics, and at first glance Melincourt may seem no
different from its peers. The distinction, however,
lies not in surface procedure but in effect. In
Nightmare Abbey argument is constantly enlivened by

wit and fantasy; elucidation is assimilated to
amusement. Sometimes, this is true of Melincourt as
well. But in this novel we are more often aware of
dissertation than of comic bravura and Peacock
penseur takes over from the brilliant dandy of Headlong Hall.
     One result of this is that the status of the
author is decisively altered. The briskness and
acuity remain, but are put at the service of statement rather than of jokey, quick-paced buffoonery.
Peacock does not step forward officiously in propria
persona, but his voice has a pedagogic ring, and the
tone of his prose veers towards the solemn urgency
of a tract. Even in minor episodes one detects a
note of forcedness, of a viewpoint offered directly
for our assent. So, increasingly, Mr Fax and Sir
Telegraph Paxarett are excused from irony and are
given biting, short speeches whose evident aim is
the immediate conversion of the reader. Both speak
potently for the mingledness of reality, and the
presence of good and bad sides in every circumstance;
in addition, each also utters crisp apophthegms with
which we are obviously intended to agree, and which
often encapsulate truths basic to Peacock's intentions in the book. Sir Telegraph, for example,
supports marriage over celibacy ('What is life without love? A rose-bush in winter, all thorns, and no
flowers', p.75), while Mr Fax praises a similar,
Peacockian hopefulness as to the fundamental worth
of mankind ('Custom cannot kill the better feelings
of human nature: it merely lays them asleep',
p.360). Quite often, this new, adjudicatory role of
the novelist finds expression in overt complaint;
there are moments when Peacock signals his meaning
almost crudely. In most of his books, he is a
teasing, sophisticated conjuror; here, he
approaches the schoolmaster. So, when Mr Forester
is discussing the future of the world with the
cooler-headed Mr Fax, he suddenly bursts out into
reproof: 'The frantic love of money, which seems to
govern our contemporaries to a degree unprecedented
in the history of man, paralyses the energy of independence, darkens the light of reason, and blights
the blossoms of love' (p.428). In part, this is
ironized, like all of Mr Forester's high-flown
rhetoric in the novel. But it also matches the
anger and directness of comments on the corruption
of the times elsewhere in Melincourt. In too much
of this book there is a sense of telling, of
exhorting the reader to a particular opinion, rather
than of leaving things lucidly exposed but

unconcluded, as in <u>Nightmare Abbey</u>.

The tug between the desire to write an entertaining novel and the desire to accomplish some serious work of anatomy is sharply revealed when we come to consider the part played in <u>Melincourt</u> by quotation, especially quotation from the works of Lord Monboddo. All of Peacock's writing is dense with allusion to and citation from the literature of the past. Often this has only a localized significance, and provides witty barbs for after-dinner conversation. But it also forms a quiet commentary on the foreground of the fiction, which has usually to do with the dearth of centrality and purity in the society and art of the present day; it suggests the existence of higher standards; it subtly reprimands the contemporary scene by bringing to mind the greater achievements of Homer and Lucretius, or Chaucer and Milton. In some books, this technique is taken further, and a single writer or poem is used to give what Marilyn Butler has called 'imaginative presence'[13] to a principal theme. In <u>Melincourt</u>, this function is allotted to the Italian chivalric epics jointly read, and jointly taken as models, by Anthelia and Mr Forester. In <u>Melincourt</u>, however, there is another sort of quotation which does not occur to the same extent in any of Peacock's other books. This is the giving of long passages, excerpted generally from Monboddo, and often linked with the building up in the text of the character and habits of Sir Oran. In Chapter VI, 'Sir Oran Haut-ton', the footnotes extensively culled from current literature on the orang-outang loom almost as large as the material they are intended to illustrate. Given the great care with which the figure of Sir Oran is conceived and used, it seems unlikely that Peacock is simply being inattentive at this point. But his apparent obsession with Lord Monboddo, the remarkable late eighteenth-century Scottish lawyer, philosopher of language and critic of mankind, certainly requires explanation. Monboddo was a cultivated eccentric, bold in his questioning attitude towards the orthodoxies of his day. His theories of the relationship between man and the orang-outang have always unfairly laid him open to ridicule and have clouded over the brilliance of his enquiries into the development of man from ape-like ancestors and the growth of language from mere animal noises into a complex system of different parts of speech governed by intelligible rules. When one has encountered his extraordinary erudition, the freshness of so many of his perceptions and the

vast scale of his treatises <u>Of the Origin and Prog-</u>
<u>gress of Language</u> (1773-92) <u>and Antient Metaphysics</u>
<u>(1779-99), it is</u> difficult not to conclude, with his
biographer, that Monboddo was 'one of the best
thinkers of his time and place'(14). Equally, in
his forensic skill, his scepticism, his learned wit
and his interest in linguistic philosophy, he has
obvious affinities with Peacock. The problem arises
not when Peacock absorbs Monboddo's ideas and sets
them in fictive motion, as in the case of Sir Oran
or in the deteriorationist arguments which intersperse the novel. It is rather that the bulky
quotations from Monboddo's works exist in a very
uneasy relationship with the main body of Peacock's
writing. They are highly noticeable, but their
status is not easy to determine. The purpose of
footnotes is to provide support for statements that
are made in the text, and on one level Peacock's do
precisely that: we may use them to check up on
Monboddo, to gauge the substance that attaches to
Sir Oran and his various attributes. But if we
bring to <u>Melincourt</u> the same trusting views of
scholarship that may be appropriate to a well-researched edition of Shakespeare, we will soon lose our
way. For a start, common sense will tell us that
much of Monboddo's material is crazy, though quaint;
we know that it takes more to make a man than merely
adding speech to an ape. Also, when we read what
Peacock gives us of Monboddo's sources, we find that
his evidence is of the flimsiest kind: traveller's
tales, second-hand reports from across the globe,
the credulous flotsam of a lifetime of reading. So,
on the one hand, Peacock 'proves' his case for the
reception of Sir Oran as 'a specimen of the natural
and original man--a genuine fac simile of the philosophical Adam' (p.54); but on the other, characteristically, he undercuts any naive acceptance of the
standing of that proof. I think that the main
effect of these long citations is to tease the
reader, to make him uneasy as to the links between
fact and fiction, and to indicate the folly of
relying simple-mindedly on even the most reputable
of authorities. As usual, therefore, even though
Peacock admires Monboddo, he takes him with a pinch
of salt. That is salutory, and to be expected. But
Peacock's execution of his stratagem is imperfect;
evidently, since most critics have been merely bored
by the whole matter. The quotations, which must be
long, are too long (like so much else); the point
in their use is oblique; too many readers have felt
that their aim is to pass on information, that they

reduce parts of the book merely to reportage--and,in
the end, that our pleasure vanishes as our stock of
'knowledge' increases.
   The general tenor of Melincourt is not in doubt,
however. It is a novel about honesty and about
truth to basic human qualities, and as such it is
closely bound up with the central themes of Peacock's oeuvre. It confronts the great world of
power, fashion and politics, represented by Lord
Anophel Achthar, the Hon Mrs Pinmoney, and their
crew, and sets against it the intrinsic nobility of
Anthelia and Mr Forester, and particularly Sir Oran.
The predilection is for love, retirement, freedom
and sufficiency; 'civilization', in which nothing is
as it appears, is the enemy. The form of the novel,
indicating the superior merits of Anthelia, the
prize for its hero, twinning Mr Forester and Sir
Oran in their devotion to her, and then interposing
outside forces inimical to the satisfaction of their
love, amply demonstrates its intentions. Melincourt
is mainly composed of peregrinations, in the course
of which much of the country is covered, and human
behaviour is probed and often condemned. The electoral system, the maintenance of slavery so that the
polite may have sugar in their tea, the systematic
cheat of paper-money replacing gold, the follies of
luxury and excess, the patterns of marriage whereby
wealth alone, rather than suitability or inclination,
must decide one's partner, all are revealed for what
they are. 'The general diffusion of moral and
political truth' (p.421) is the aim of the reformers
in this book, and is embodied in practical terms in
the benevolence of which all the major characters,
even Mr Fax, are always capable, and in Anthelia's
search for her perfect knight. Although it is
bolstered by the sympathetic, complementary power of
love, and by the innate strength and good cheer of
ordinary people, this aim cannot fail to be difficult
of realization when, as Mr Forester says, 'Falsehood
is the great vice of the age' (p.427). Overall, in
Melincourt it is politics about which Peacock has
most to say, from the viewpoints both of institutions and of results for the populace at large; the
most powerful section of the novel is that which
evokes the injustice of rotten boroughs and draws
attention to the need for reform. But although
Peacock's attacks are violent, they are never simple-
minded. They offer evidence, cite parallels and
rehearse conflicting arguments as any academic analysis might do, though with an added spice of wit;
and most of Chapter IX, 'The Philosophy of Ballads',

in fact points out the extreme difficulty in the
modern age of defining either problems or solutions,
and thus reassures us of the full awareness of
dilemmas with which Peacock approaches this book.
   Many of the themes in Melincourt may be subsumed
into Peacock's deep, gloomy interest in the relations
between theory and practice, especially as these are
exposed in the conduct of public figures, politicians, clergymen, controversialists and the like. In
this respect at least Mr Forester is a model, for
although his excesses are mocked, he practises what
he preaches and, as he says, 'My reform commences at
home' (p.42). As in Peacock's other novels, the gap
between the way things really are, and the way we
might prefer them to be, provides comedy as well as
thoughtful insights into behaviour. One of the most
entertaining examples of this is when the meddling
Mr Fax, riding the hobby-horse of his Malthusian
theories of population growth, attempts to persuade a
cheerful rustic couple that they should not go ahead
with their marriage because of the unprovided children they may bring into the world as a result of it.
Peacock makes a telling contrast between the life-
denying system of 'General Reason' (p.365) by which
Mr Fax is motivated, and the resilient, natural
affection that binds the bridegroom, with his
'chubby-cheeks'(p.364), to his 'plain downright hon-
est-hearted old English girl',(p.371), Zukey. Mr
Fax's inquisitorial sternness is given short shrift
by comparison with the humorous colloquialism of
the lovers, and when bridegroom turns to bride with,
'the short and the long be this: I can't live without Zukey, nor Zukey without I' (p.371), we know for
sure that Peacock approves. The point is delight-
fully reinforced by the wit of the chapter's
conclusion, in which the unregenerate bridegroom, on
reaching the church, 'looked round over his shoulder
to Mr.Fax, and said with a very arch look, "My
dutiful sarvice to General Reason". And looking
round a second time before he entered the door,
added: "and Zukey's too"'(p.373).
   The two chapters given over to the tale of
Desmond are similar in purpose, but subtler in
manner and wider in reference. The tale is related
by Mr Fax, but in the first person. Desmond, a very
eighteenth-century man of goodwill, a student 'of
morals and of mind' (p.132), finding himself
destitute, moves to London where he tries to find
work writing for the periodical press. But he discovers everyone tainted and partial, and is forced to
pass on to the disagreeable job of tutor in the

family of Mr Dross, 'a tun of a man, with the soul
of a hazel-nut' (p.138), and his would-be fashionable
wife. After this, he makes a meagre living as a
lawyer's copyist, marries, and then accompanies the
lawyer into frugal exile in Westmoreland. There the
lawyer dies, and Desmond and his wife survive
'hardly' (p.146), but at least far from the chicanery
of the big city. In a continuation, Mr Fax and Mr
Forester discuss the case until they meet up unexpectedly with a transformed, carefree Mrs Desmond, who
takes them into a cottage of 'beautiful neatness'
(p.158) generously provided for them by Anthelia.
Once there, they note the family's general contentment, and are informed by Desmond of his determination to raise his children '"in a free, healthy, and
natural occupation"' (p.159) in the countryside.

The story is cunningly told to demonstrate the
viciousness of London life, the sounder pleasures of
rusticity, and the uselessness of conventional moral
precepts when one faces the necessity of earning
one's bread. The attack on the town, and on the
hypocrisy and money-mindedness that it fosters,is
forthright. As the well-meaning, honest young
Desmond fights his way in the world, he encounters
duplicity everywhere--literary and political corruption with Mr Vamp the editor, social corruption with
the Drosses, and selfishness with both. He takes on
the status of a lone champion of decency and truth,
single against 'the great feudal fortress of society'
(p.150). By the end of Chapter XIII, however, we
have seen what his staunchness has got him: poverty,
decrepitude, 'the utmost degree of misery and
destitution compatible with the preservation of life'
(p.128). Admiration here becomes duly tempered with
common sense; Desmond may be in Westmoreland, we
feel, but still lacks the pastoral satisfaction
which seems his proper reward. It takes Anthelia to
come along, out of the blue, before he and his
family can achieve the dependable competence which
has always been their aim. This seems a cool indication on Peacock's part of the need for utility as
well as altruism; high thinking may be praiseworthy,
he suggests, but it is not enough. The whole drift
of the tale of Desmond is towards a qualifying of
his virtue, an ironic exemplification that principle
alone will get one nowhere. 'The wheel of fortune
is like a water-wheel, and human beings are like the
waters it disturbs' (p.148); and it is only by
chance, by the intercession of a quasi-divine, kind-
hearted figure like Anthelia that one may escape
painful entanglement. Thus, as we see in the book

as a whole, though rural values may be preferable to urban ones, and virtue superior to vice, absolutes are not to be attained nor ideals completely realized in the everyday world. Anthelia herself emphasizes this point when she comments on the possible effects of 'mental improvement' (p.166) on a young woman: 'Even in its effect on herself, the ideal beauty which she studies will make her fastidious, too fastidious, perhaps, to the world of realities, and deprive her of the happiness that might be her portion, by fixing her imagination on chimaeras of unattainable excellence' (p.167).

Peacock's position is demonstrated with acerbity in his handling of fashionable life in Melincourt, whose intention is sharply to contrast the natural behaviour of Sir Oran, in particular, with the parody of it that passes muster in polite society. Peacock takes a sceptical view of civilization in which is implicated his instinctively pessimistic feelings about man's so-called progress from a barbaric past to a cultivated present. It is impossible, Peacock thinks, to separate civilization from society, or society from pretence; vested interests bind each irrevocably to the others, and consummate the linkage in the institutions of the modern state. As an alternative to this unhealthy, closed system, Peacock offers the suggestion of an easier, freer life which is remote from the pressures of the contemporary world. But in Melincourt this cheering alternative is shadowy and intermittent. The affection of Anthelia and Mr Forester, or the innate virtue of Sir Oran, is much less stressed than the calculation of the Hon Mrs Pinmoney or the villainy of Lord Achthar. The exposure of the beau monde begins early in the book with the arrival at Melincourt Castle of the matchmaking Mrs Pinmoney and her daughter Miss Danaretta Contantina, 'signifying ready money' (p.14), and shortly accompanied by the fortune-hunting Sir Telegraph. Peacock makes plain to us that the whole raison d'être of this elegant assembly is the acquisition, delighted possession and frivolous employment of wealth; and that in the pursuit of this goal it is prepared to sacrifice every quality which may genuinely give worth to our lives. The standards of this fashionable group are set against those of the 'romantic heretic' (p.22), Anthelia: on the one hand, riches and the chic nullity of a London drawing-room, on the other, the simplicity and integrity which best lead us towards fulfilment. Especially when discussion turns to 'that most commercial of all bargains,

marriage' (p.14), Peacock renders this choice between
cash and love with great vigour. When Anthelia tells
Mrs Pinmoney of her hopes of 'as true a knight-errant
in a brown coat in the nineteenth century, as in a
suit of golden armour in the days of Charlemagne'
(p.24), she is reproved with philistine savoir-faire:
'Well! well! my dear, when you have seen a little
more of the world, you will get rid of some of your
chivalrous whimsies'. Partly, this is just; but
partly, too, it points to the way in which 'the whole
sphere of fashion' (p.25) operates against the proper
aspirations of those who have rejected its hollow
absorption only in matters of status.
    The correlative of Peacock's attack on the
polite world is disparagement of the system which
supports and administers its hegemony. Of all his
books, Melincourt is the most reformist in tenor. It
seems to me to be unique among Peacock's works, for
it goes beyond the mere offering of festive consolation, and intends instead to effect change, to
promote active intervention as well as understanding.
In the other conversation novels, a similar political
complexion may be inferred from the discussions, but
rarely shows itself clearly on the surface; in the
romances, Peacock's thoroughgoing enquiry into the
rationale of the power of the state is cloaked by
the whimsical mediaevalism of the form he adopts.
Here, however, the focus of attention and the
proselytizing manner of the writing leave us in no
doubt as to the purpose for which the book was
devised. Often through the relentless voice of Mr
Forester, but also by Mr Fax and even Sir Telegraph,
Jacobin sentiments are regularly aired. Shelley
preferred Melincourt, in which he found 'more of the
true spirit, and an object less indefinite, than in
either "Headlong Hall" or Scythrop'(15). The 'true
spirit' is certainly that of political disaffection:
in a letter written during the composition of the
novel, Shelley characterized Peacock powerfully as
'an enemy to every shape of tyranny & superstitious
imposture'(16). Melincourt accordingly paints a bold,
discrediting picture of the political scene: the
upper classes use their money to buy them position,
which they then abuse for selfish ends, and the mob
connives greedily in a sham which ensures that the
country will be ruled by ambitious self-seekers
rather than by honest men. The irony is prolonged
and potent. However, although the three cardinal
'"points"' (p.289) for which Mr Forester speaks
('"the health, the morals, and the number of the
people"',) are quite disregarded by the state,

revolution is not encouraged. Unlike Shelley,
Peacock favoured gradual improvement over upheaval,
and in this work as in others he hopes, with little
real expectation of change, that man may sometime be
brought to his senses and that this will not entail
a recurrence of the bloodshed and destruction of
which the French Revolution had provided a recent,
vivid example.

These questions are most forcefully dramatized
in Chapters XXI and XXII, 'The City of Novote' and
'The Borough of Onevote'. In the first of these, a
group of characters including Sir Oran meets up with
Simon Sarcastic, his fellow candidate for a parliam-
entary seat at Onevote, in the neighbouring, popul-
ous but unenfranchised city of Novote. After dinner,
they congregate around the fire and a witty political
dialogue ensues, in the course of which Mr Sarcastic
expounds his system: 'I ascertain the practice of
those I talk to, and present it to them as from
myself, in the shape of theory: the consequence of
which is, that I am universally stigmatized as a
promulgator of rascally doctrines' (p.229). Mr
Forester takes issue with Mr Sarcastic's cynicism,
and puts forward his own more idealistic views:'The
progress of truth is slow, but its ultimate triumph
is secure; though its immediate effects may be
rendered almost imperceptible, by the power of habit
and interest' (pp.236-7). This chapter is finely
judged; it gives a basis in argument to the fracas
of the election itself, and also provides an interlude of calm before the frenzied activity that
follows it. Peacock gives a wonderfully fresh,
antipathetic picture of the Onevote election, a
matter of bribery, ale and large-scale deception, a
kind of Bartholomew Fair of the early nineteenth
century. Mr Sarcastic makes a profoundly ironic
speech of solicitation to Mr Christopher Corporate,
Onevote's single, large elector, and is duly elected,
together with Sir Oran. Preparations are made to
chair the triumphant new members of Parliament, but
Sir Oran is unwilling, and becomes violent when his
supporters use force to overcome his apparent
modesty; something within him repudiates the
charade in which he has been involved, and especially this final, humiliating attempt 'to violate the
freedom of the natural man' (p.249). Within
moments the scene has degenerated into a scrimmage,
and Mr Corporate's cottage is destroyed: 'the
ancient and honourable borough of Onevote was
reduced to ashes: but we have the satisfaction to
state that it was rebuilt a few days afterwards, at

the joint expense of its two representatives, and
His Grace the Duke of Rottenburgh' (p.251).

This episode has a richness and animation unequalled elsewhere in Melincourt; its crotcheteering cleverness, brisk pacing and high comedy mark it
off decisively from the more stolid material by which
it is surrounded. The irony of Mr Sarcastic, entertaining and beautifully maintained, exactly demonstrates the gulf between theory and practice from
which stems the central malaise in the nation's
political life. Mr Sarcastic himself, disenchanted
but energetic, is typical of the best of Peacock's
obsessives. He is a witty, sharp agent of the truth,
and is the source of much of the instructive vivacity
of the two chapters in which he appears. During the
election itself, we note a raised level of feeling
and much straightforward satire at the expense of
'persuasion in a tangible shape' (p.239). Mr
Sarcastic's address to his voter is splendidly handled and daringly uses the clichés of political declaration to expose the real linkage that exists between elected and electorate: 'The monied interest,
Mr.Corporate, for which you are as illustrious as
the sun at noon-day, is the great point of connexion
and sympathy between us: and no circumstances can
throw a wet blanket on the ardour of our reciprocal
esteem, while the fundamental feature of our mutual
interests presents itself to us in so tangible a
shape' (pp.242-3). It is in this speech, too, that
Peacock dextrously joins together his concern for
the proper use of wealth with his concern for the
well-being of the nation; elsewhere, we see both
harmed by the flood of paper money which has swept
through the country. In one sense, I think that his
distaste for paper money was simply a very busy bee
in Peacock's bonnet, and it recurs with such dogged-
ness that it seems hard to take it seriously. But
in Melincourt the dangers of paper money amount to
more than just a crotchet; a system which substit-
utes paper for gold, and empty promises for genuine
substance, sets an apt key-note for the book as a
whole, particularly in its political dimension, and
insidiously pervades scene after scene until it
reaches its climax in Chapter XXX, 'The Paper-Mill',
where Peacock gives us a brisk but also moving view
of the likely consequences of trusting to '"this
fatal bubble of paper-money"' (p.323) and not to
'"pretty golden guineas"' (p.322). Throughout the
episode of the Onevote election, our impression is
of wit intelligently directed at targets about which
the author feels deeply and into which he has

convincing insight: failed ideals, an air of the
ersatz and a gap between real and pretended motives
are common to them all. Even at the end, when Sir
Oran's intrinsic decency has revolted against the
corruption around him, Peacock's perspective does not
falter. Sir Oran may be able to destroy the immediate setting for his dishonour, but he cannot destroy the circumstances which brought it into being:
within days, Mr Corporate's cottage is rebuilt and
the injustice that it represents confirmed for the
lifetime of yet another parliament. Chapter XXIV,
which expounds the messages to be learned from the
Onevote election, strengthens this disillusion, for
it provokes Mr Forester into a powerful commentary
on the events he has recently witnessed, but offers
no hope of improvement beyond the bitter injunction,
'Read ancient books, the only source of permanent
happiness left in this degenerate world' (p.272).

Mayoux might have been talking explicitly of
Melincourt when he remarked on 'l'énorme part de
désillusion'(17) which one finds in Peacock's work.
The novel's general framework is deteriorationist;
it considers the relationship between natural and
civilized states and enquires whether or not some
residual virtue, some unlikely joining of theory and
practice, may not still be found in a latter-day
world. In the course of this scrutiny, it examines
two main areas of experience, the fashionable sphere
of the upper classes, and the political system by
which the country is governed. In both of these, it
finds wrong-doing, and discovers that each is entwi-
ned with the unhealthy love of money. Thus far, we
may see Melincourt as comprehensively pessimistic.
But there is another side to the book, represented
by Anthelia, Mr Forester and Sir Oran, and the purpose of this is to provide balance and cheerfulness
so that the work as a whole may amount thoughtfully
to 'une vision d'ensemble, dans laquelle l'espérance
et le rêve compensent les insuffisances du
présent'(18). However, it is in this compensation,
in the provision of romantic hopefulness, that
Melincourt seems to me to work least well.

I have paid great attention to the satirical
aspects of Melincourt since they are predominant in
its texture and give rise to some of its most successful scenes. But the novel is a romance as well
as a satire, and a knightly epigraph from Rousseau
alerts us to the context within which the love-affair
between Anthelia and Mr Forester is to be conducted.
The epics of the Italian poets whom both the lovers

read, and especially Tasso's Gerusalemme liberata,
form a link between them in which altruism and the
love of liberty are combined. Even in the first
chapter there is a predisposition towards romance in
the isolation and nobility of Anthelia, 'mistress ...
of a very ancient and venerable castle in one of the
wildest valleys in Westmoreland' (p.5) and dedicated
to the precept of 'Disinterested benevolence, the
mainspring of all that is really admirable in the
days of chivalry' (p.24). The world which she
inhabits is not everyday; it has the heightening
and amplitude of some old ballad of mediaeval lords
and ladies going about their pure and simple lives.
It is deliberately set off from the metropolis, and
Anthelia's aristocratic, urban guests are perceived
as intruders from a distinct and tainted nether
sphere. Only Anthelia, Mr Forester and Sir Oran
among the major characters are free of the values of
the beau monde, and are seen instead with the warmth
and largeness of a fairy-tale. Accompanying the
pervasive ironic urgency of Melincourt, and offering
a pointed alternative to its images of folly and
decline, we therefore have an element of fable which
gives a legendary, timeless grace to those chapters
in which it appears. Its tenor is almost Shakes-
pearean, and it reminds us of The Tempest both in
atmosphere and in particular situations. The
pastoralism of the novel, its fascination
not only with rural retreat but also with the grandeur and 'wildness' (p.9) of Nature's sights and
sounds, and with the concept of 'mountain liberty'
(p.10), harmonizes finely with the emotional suffu-
sion of these scenes.
     This is not merely a matter of the colouring of
a static circumstance. It involves struggle, a
degree of hardship and a final, long delayed reconciliation. The fair princess, Anthelia, living in
her remote fastness among the mountains, presses
upon her aspiring knight, Mr Forester, the task of
bearing a pennant of chivalry through the snares of
the modern world. Slowly he proves himself, in
spite of repeated setbacks, and successfully maintains the values of honour and unselfishness which
they share. In the end, somewhat ironized, especially by their conjunction with the flawlessly noble
Sir Oran, and having given a truer impression of the
irresolvable difficulties of life and of its resistance to the ideal, the two lovers are joined together, and Anthelia celebrates the victorious
conclusion of her desires: '"O Forester!" said
Anthelia, "you have realized all my wishes. I have

found in you the friend of the poor, the enthusiast
of truth, the disinterested cultivator of the rural
virtues, the active promoter of the cause of human
liberty"' (p.452). Although their quest has been
fruitful, and Mr Forester has fairly demonstrated
that a paladin 'in a brown coat' (p.24) can fight off
the harmful influences even of early nineteenth-
century English society, neither Anthelia nor her
knight-errant escapes unscathed. Both are mocked for
the excessive high-mindedness and impracticality of
some of their ideas, and our feeling in the last
chapter of the book is far from absolute. Hero and
heroine have supported something fine, and that is
good; but they have also paid little heed to the
necessarily mixed and imperfect nature of life, and
that is less good. It is hard to resist a sense
that Peacock's ultimate joke in Melincourt, and one
that he plays slyly on his characters as well as on
his readers, is that the novel's consummate knight-
at-arms, the embodiment of Anthelia's maidenly
dreams, is not a man at all but an orang-outang.

Peacock's design in the romantic sections of
the book, with the witty fantasy of their allegory
and their keen collation of rural virtue with
wordly vice, is splendid. But when one passes from
intention to achievement, one's feelings are rather
different. For Peacock miscalculates an essential
balance in his presentation of the chivalric side of
Melincourt. The vapid, long-winded Mr Forester is
given too robust a role for him to bear; Anthelia
and her concerns are absent too often from the
reader's attention; the angry panorama of the
contemporary world takes up too much space and is
overwhelmingly more forceful than the moments of
love and good nature which are supposed to provide
its antidote. The real charge of Peacock's plan is
skewed, therefore; instead of a harmonious counterpoint, there is a disturbing mixture of elements
whose exact purpose is not always easy to define.

This is even more of a problem because the
rituals of the music-room and dinner-table, which
assert the optimism of Peacock's views in his other
novels, are so muted in Melincourt. Characters sing
and dance as they did before, and there is a good
deal of eating and drinking, but the significance
has gone out of these activities. Instead of guaran-
teeing the comic side of Peacock's feelings about
mankind, they sink decoratively into the background.
Occasionally, when Sir Oran plays his flute, we see
music as an agent of concord, and the freshness of
Chapter XVI is certainly due more to its post-

prandial eulogies of wine and whisky than to its
intemperate complaints about 'bad books' (p.188) and
mankind's general decline. But, on the whole, with
this alteration there opens up a further fissure in
the close structure of the conversation novel.
Festive elements are subdued. The equilibrium between the joys of the flesh and of love, and the
amusing emptiness of crotcheteering, from which so
much invigoration is derived in Headlong Hall and
Nightmare Abbey, disintegrates in Melincourt. Tautness is lost, and the reassuring qualities of the
book are swamped by its censoriousness. What we are
left with is an admirable scheme, partially accomplished, but in the end unable effectively to play
off cheerful against gloomy matters as it seems to
wish.

Nevertheless, as I have indicated, there
remains a great deal to praise in this novel. The
gallery of characters is large and varied, and some
minor figures, like Mr Sarcastic, are as energetic
and acutely shaped as any in the rest of Peacock's
books. But there are two features of Peacock's
presentation of his characters in this novel which
also tell against its overall success. In the first
place, the quality of the talk is less diversified
and trenchant than in most of the other books;
instead of rapid dialogue, we are offered formal
speeches of a rather diffuse kind. In fact, almost
everyone in the novel speaks in the same way: the
conscious rhetoric, the Augustan moral abstraction
issue solemnly from all lips except Sir Oran's. The
careful differentiation of voices of Headlong Hall
is largely absent, though there are a number of
humorous rustics to enliven the stateliness. The
effect is of monotony, especially as the book is so
long and so much given over to the undistinguished
prolixity of Mr Forester; we feel as if the whole
dramatis personae has been reduced to a single
figure, and that we shall never escape from his
persevering garrulity. Secondly, the crotcheteering
in the novel is more prosaic than we might anticipate. No-one approaches the poetry of the Hon Mr
Listless in Nightmare Abbey or the ingenious obsessiveness of Mr Cranium in Headlong Hall; only the
explosive Mr Hippy, whose hypochondria points to the
age's solipsistic refusal to accept the truth about
itself, really can claim some degree of cousinship
with figures like the robotic philosophers, Mr Escot,
Mr Foster and Mr Jenkison, in that earlier book.
This is a diminution, but also offers leeway for

growth: at least two characters, Mr Fax and Sir
Telegraph, begin narrowly as crotcheteers and then
expand into full-blown creations as the novel proceeds. Structurally, their function is to accompany
Mr Forester, each representing a different kind of
excess, and each developing under pressure of circumstances into a more sympathetic character than his
first, circumscribed appearance would lead us to
expect. All three, in addition, are set against Sir
Oran, the figure whose actions speak louder than
words, and who reveals flaws in all who are compared
with him--so that if, from one perspective, the
greater realism of Mr Fax and Sir Telegraph reflects
on the dreamy altruism of Mr Forester, from another,
each of these men is shown to be lesser than the
mere ape to whom he condescends. When Mr Fax is
introduced, he seems nothing more than a parody of
the chill rationality which pays no heed to humanity
in its rigid application of scientific principles.
But as we see more of him, we recognize the value of
his clear thought, especially when this is attended
by small acts of kindness for which his system makes
no provision. Increasingly, we come to trust his
high common sense, especially by contrast with the
high romance of Mr Forester; it is hard for us not
to agree when he reproves his friend by complaining,
'You have formed to yourself, as you acknowledge, a
visionary model of female perfection, which has
rendered you utterly insensible to the real attractions of every woman you have seen' (p.115). In the
same way, Sir Telegraph appears on the scene as an
upper-class fashion-ridden booby, unthinkingly
attached to his elegant barouche, and concerned only
with the acquisition of a suitably dowered bride of
his own rank. Quite soon, however, Peacock enlarges
his role, and he relinquishes most of his early
empty-headedness to Lord Achthar, who incorporates it
into the reckless selfishness appropriate to an
aristocratic seducer. Sir Telegraph is then liberated into worldliness and acute judgement, both of
which qualities he sceptically exercises on Mr
Forester. He speaks sharply for the relativism of
man's values and manifests an unfailing good nature
of which one cannot help but approve. We have no
impression of malice or parti pris, therefore, when
he applies his cooler understanding to the exaggerations of Mr Forester's rhetoric and calmly asserts,
'You have made no allowance for the mixture of good
and evil, which I think the fairest state of the
case' (p.49). Overall, it seems to me, although one
may reasonably object to the less varied speech and

more humdrum crotcheteering in <u>Melincourt</u>, one could
not do other than praise the success of Peacock's
characterization of Mr Fax and Sir Telegraph.

The book's primary focus is on Anthelia. In her
castle, 'strongly guarded both by nature and art'
(p.7), Anthelia grows up under the joint influences
of poetry and the 'majestic forms and wild energies
of Nature' (p.9). She draws power from the craggy
landscape in which her castle is set and becomes a
'mountain-enthusiast' (p.16) and 'really romantic';
Peacock establishes links between the mountains,
liberty and chivalry and these together encourage
Anthelia's search for the ideal soul-mate who will,
like her, combine them all. The epic nature of
Anthelia's quest, and her fusion of the qualities of
independence, learning and love which Peacock most
admired in young women, give great emotional potency
to her presentation in the first chapter of the
novel:

> 'The murmur of the woods, the rush of the
> winds, and the tumultuous dashing of the
> torrents, were the first music of her
> childhood. A fearless wanderer among these
> romantic solitudes, the spirit of mountain
> liberty diffused itself through the whole
> tenour of her feelings, modelled the
> symmetry of her form, and illumed the
> expressive but feminine brilliancy of her
> features: and when she had attained the
> age at which the mind expands itself to the
> fascination of poetry, the muses of Italy
> became the chosen companions of her wander-
> ings, and nourished a naturally susceptible
> imagination by conjuring up the splendid
> visions of chivalry and enchantment in scenes
> so congenial to their development' (pp.9-10).

Thus early in the book, and with an evident access-
ion of feeling, Anthelia as heroine is laid before
us. <u>Melincourt</u> makes a plea for the liberation from
polite marital orthodoxies of a strong, cultivated
young girl, and demands that she should be able to
follow her own, truer impulses rather than the
dictates of the time-serving society around her.
Anthelia is indeed 'a romantic heretic from the ...
supremacy of fashion' (p.22), not least in her un-
abashed intellectuality. Also, like Susannah in
<u>Crotchet Castle</u> (1831), she is associated with the
delights of music and literature; she composes
'wild and impassioned' (p.442) stanzas during her
captivity at Alga Castle; and her reading is of the
'harmony' (p.164) and knightly virtue of the Italian

poets.

Anthelia is clearly a force of good in <u>Melin-court</u>, and an attractive, successful characteriz-ation: a figure whose significance is not over-stressed, and who brings zest and substance to each of her appearances in the novel. Her task is to find a man who will live up to her bookish ideals of noble behaviour, and at the same time, therefore, to reconcile the chivalric aspirations of the past with the more everyday business of a life in the present. But the difficult search on which she is engaged is too often concealed behind a screen of digressions, repetitions and addenda, and Anthelia herself is generally absent from view. She has her real effect only at the beginning and end of the novel, and when she discusses literature and freedom with Mr Forester in Chapter XV, and love in Chapter XX. For most of the rest of the time, our attention is engrossed by the restless movements of the plot and the long debates between Mr Forester, Mr Fax and Sir Telegr-aph. It is hard to see that this creates suspense or provokes mystery; irritation and a sense of thinness are more likely, I think, for Anthelia seems a needed counterbalance to the book's negativism. One feels that the whole work would have been improved if the romance surrounding Anthelia and the social satire associated with Mr Forester's wander-ings had been brought more into equilibrium, and Peacock's habitual dialectic between optimism and pessimism more vividly set in motion. As it is, Anthelia seems swamped by the contrary material which environs her, and unable to champion her cause with sufficient forcefulness.

Anthelia carries with her a weight of sympathy and approval; there can be no doubt that her principal function is a positive one. And yet, it seems to me, she is ironized as well. When she speaks, for instance, she is frequently infected by the condescending didacticism of her companions. So, when the otiose Mrs Pinmoney expresses surprise at her solitary way of life,'"Here is the best of company," said Anthelia smiling, and pointing to the shelves of the library' (p.19); in this circumst-ance, even by contrast with the empty chatter of her guest, Anthelia's self-consciously reproving tone of voice seems hard to take. Also, like her lover, she is prone to priggish ethical orations: both sexes, she is afraid, are too much influenced by the spirit of mercenary calculation--'The desire of competence is prudence; but the desire of more than competence is avarice: it is against the latter only that

moral censure should be directed: but I fear that
in ninety-nine cases out of an hundred in which the
course of true love is thwarted by considerations of
fortune, it will be found that avarice rather than
prudence is to be considered as the cause' (p.98).
Anthelia's sentiments in this speech are unexcept-
ionable, but their antithetical punctuation, setting
each phrase just too neatly against its neighbour,
undermines their acceptance at face value. An
important clue to this aspect of Anthelia's presentation is her comment on the dangers for a woman of
'fixing her imagination on chimaeras of unattainable
excellence' (p.167) and on the necessity, therefore,
that the ideal should cope with the real rather than
simply refusing to recognize its existence. Anthelia
may be a heroine, but her standards are untried and
she herself needs the test of experience almost as
much as does Mr Forester. It is characteristic of
Peacock that this testing, this deliberate conjunction of high notions and actuality, should produce
ambiguous results. For a start, Anthelia's Lake
District home suggests that absolutes may not be
attained on earth; it is a kind of paradise, but
like other paradises it must be left behind in the
search for growth and the proving of one's values.
The house itself, like Mr Forester's, combats any
perfectionist urge. It is a sensible accommodation
of old and new, and combines the Gothic charm of a
castle with the convenience of a country house:
'while one half of the edifice was fast improving
into a picturesque ruin, the other was as rapidly
degenerating, in its interior at least, into a
comfortable modern dwelling' (pp.8-9). Within the
building, the library in which Anthelia spends such
an unfashionable quantity of her time offers the
same message of fusion and eclecticism. This
library is a room where Greek and mediaeval styles
are finely blended, and where the pleasures of
literature may be enjoyed in conjunction with 'the
birds singing ... and the softened dash of the
torrent from the dingle below' (p.164). In the light
of these quiet exemplars of compromise and assimilation, Anthelia's firm stance and unrelenting standards acquire an air of excess, of stridency; they
seem slightly absurd, since they pay so little heed
to the real nature of the situation in which she
finds herself; we are invited to look askance and
to see in this a folly that she shares, like many
virtues, with Mr Forester.
    I have already indicated that the figures of
Anthelia and Sir Oran work very well in Melincourt,

but that Mr Forester often does not. He has an
important role as the novel's standard-bearer of
chivalry and social responsibility, though the other,
complementary side of his nature, his pomposity and
oddity, is regularly subject to the urbane qualification of Peacock's irony. It is certainly Peacock's
intention that we should see Mr Forester in a
favourable light as Anthelia's quixotic, latter-day
paladin, and a man well able to discriminate true
from false in the world around him. He speaks often
and grandly in condemnation of the follies of the
day, and consistently opposes the self-seeking which
encourage their growth; there may be something
risible, for instance, in the solemnity of his
attacks on the taking of sugar, but his censure of
such luxury, 'because its infallible tendency is to
enervate the few, and enslave the many' (p.263) cannot be lightly dismissed. Like Anthelia he is
associated with the better life of the countryside,
lives wholeheartedly by his principles, and therefore remains untainted by the vice with which, in
the course of his travels, he inevitably comes into
contact. His estate, a well-ordered Happy Valley in
which 'warm-hearted rustics' (p.285) pursue their
simple, natural occupations, establishes Peacock's
sense of both the possibilities and the limits of a
secluded existence: it is justly run, sufficient
and contented, but Mr Forester does not live there,
and must expose himself to danger and variety before
he can prove himself a fit partner for his would-be
bride. Peacock does not praise a fugitive and clois-
tered virtue; so the two lovers must both leave
their mountain retreats, places of beauty and purity,
but untested by refractory circumstances, and fend for
themselves amidst the more pressing dilemmas of
everyday.

As I have outlined it, Mr Forester's role in the
book seems to promise verve and interest. But in
practice he does not live up to expectations. His
status is uneasy, and he veers unnervingly between
absurd crotcheteering and the powerful, affecting
statement of major truths; we never know quite how
to take him, and the links that Peacock sets up
between the comic and the serious sides of his deteriorationism are not sure enough for the reader to
achieve any reliable perspective on his character.
The humour at his expense, shown in his insistence
that man has declined not just morally but also
physically by comparison with former times, peppers
scenes throughout the novel but then tails off when
he is called on to resume a less ironized function

as <u>Melincourt</u>'s prime mouthpiece of uprightness and
<u>benevolence.</u> Thus, his obsessiveness produces few
laughs; we are submerged by the unstoppable tide of
his talk. And that talk, though often clever,
virtuous, even witty, does not generate enough
variety and freshness to hold our attention for long.
Mr Forester as conversationalist concentrates many
faults and few virtues. His tone is strident; his
vocabulary is abstract; he repeats himself
endlessly, usually at least thrice, and allows no
topic to pass by without expansion and illustration;
his prefectorial air is constant. As with Mr Flosky
in <u>Nightmare Abbey</u>, he is too much; Peacock seems
<u>unable to control</u> him, and as our pleasure in his
speeches flags, so too does the effectiveness of his
part in the book's pattern of ideas.

Of course, Mr Foresteer is ironized, and one
might anticipate that this would give edge to his
character. Along with his many good qualities, he
is a prey to self-consciousness and extremism, and
Peacock does not allow these flaws to escape our
notice. Mr Forester talking impassionedly of
female education to Anthelia, or proposing to discover with her, in actuality, '"the realization of
the pictures of Spenser and Tasso!"' (p.282), undercuts the solemn pretentiousness of his own speeches,
and he condemns himself when he advocates that the
good should be pursued 'without regard to ...
previous habits, or the common practice of the world'
(p.50). Sometimes, this irony works to remind us of
the mundane realities to which Mr Forester pays too
little heed; but, often, it fails to restrain the
errors at which it is directed, and these continue
undeterred to offer themselves to the reader. It is
thus that Mr Forester, a distracting, irresolvable
mixture of hero and fool, the victim of a fatal uncertainty of focus, degenerates at last into a bore.

Sir Oran, fortunately speechless, quite out-
shines his mentor. If there were only one thing for
which <u>Melincourt</u> was to be remembered, it would have
to be <u>this noble</u> orang-outang, created baronet and
member of parliament and displayed to contrast with
the so-called civilization in which he finds his new
home. He draws together Peacock's long-standing
curiosity as to the problems of language acquisition
and blends with it a vital contemporary interest in
the fundamental qualities of mankind and the proper
status of apes and 'wild men'. As the notes make
plain, he is principally derived from the writings
of Lord Monboddo, but the primitivism of Rousseau
and the new concern of the Romantic poets for

characters of deep feeling, but inadequate speech,
must also have had some influence on his conception.
As Marilyn Butler says, he is 'a fine specimen of
Peacock's learned wit'(19), and appears on stage
with a full complement of esoteric references and
the disturbing air of combining scientific likeli-
hood and fantastic speculation in a single, thought-
provoking figure. It is not by accident that an
early reviewer in the British Critic detected in Sir
Oran 'the cloven foot of infidelity'(20); quite
apart from the sceptical light which he throws on
man's assumed moral superiority to the animal world,
he should also cause one to question the dividing
line between human being and ape, and thus to re-
assess the whole basis of the Christian religion,
with its allocation of soul to one side of this
barrier, but conveniently not to the other. That
such misgivings were current at this time, especially
in Shelley's circle, may be seen from Mary Shelley's
novel, Frankenstein, which was published only a year
after Melincourt and explores similar qualms about
the basic condition of man, though from a much more
tormented point of view.

Sir Oran is opportune not just for Peacock's
period, but for our own as well. He is a figure of
poetic grace and strangeness, in the line of Peacock's most compelling imaginative creations, and
arouses delight and wonderment whenever he appears;
it is not too much to say that he is present at most
of the best scenes in Melincourt, and that this is a
major factor in their success. In a book where too
much is explained, and garrulity seems the rule, the
silent Sir Oran provides a welcome relief; of all
the characters in the novel, only he reaches Peacock's highest level of fantasy, coherence and inner
conviction.

However, Sir Oran is not merely curious, forever
pulling up trees, ending fights or rescuing maidens
in distress; his place in the book's structure is an
important one. As Henkin says, in him 'Peacock
uncovers a scientifically established, ideally perfect man; a Noble Savage who, though (or rather,
because) unacquainted with the degenerate arts of
civilization, has all the instincts and puts into
practice all the precepts of true nobility'(21). In
all that he does, as well as in his drinking ('Sir
Oran testified, by a copious draught, that he found
much virtue in home-brewed ale', p.159) and his
soothing flute-playing, he demonstrates an innate
sense of rightness rarely to be found among his
companions. His prowess as knight-at-arms eclipses

Mr Forester's, for it is he who rescues Anthelia in
her three hours of need and who regularly provides
physical strength and sound judgement on behalf of
the forces of good. And when Mr Hippy describes him
admiringly as '"quite an Orlando Furioso"' (p.109),
it seems entirely appropriate that this model of
chivalry should be evoked in terms of the Italian
poetry which Anthelia loves. Sir Oran is paired with
Mr Forester and Anthelia at the same time that he
contrasts with most of the other characters. His
presence at Mr Forester's side is a source of irony
at the latter's expense, for one cannot help but
compare the silent usefulness of the ape with the
long-winded philosophizing of the man. His twinning
with Anthelia is that of kindred spirits, of beings
naturally good and pure, and seemingly destined for
one another by a visionary introduction amidst
surroundings of great beauty and in circumstances of
adventure. It is a mistake, therefore, to think
that Sir Oran is used only to make fun of Monboddo's
ideas, though that is one underlying function of his
character; rather, he offers a piercing, witty
comment on the modern world by demonstrating that
the most admirable human qualities may be embodied
not in a man but in an orang-outang. He is comic and
unlikely, but he is seriously employed to call up
doubts as to the vaunted superiority both of mankind
and of society. The irony is directed not at him
but at us; he is 'a personification of native
sincerity and true feeling'(22), whereas we, represented by the large cast of Melincourt, are governed
in general by nothing more praiseworthy than the
desire for wealth or rank. And I think certainly
the most sardonic of Peacock's innuendoes aimed at
the excessive idealists in the novel is his undeveloped hint that in fact a perfect knight may not be
found in nineteenth-century England, except in the
form of Sir Oran, and that if Anthelia's search were
prosecuted with determination she would thus end up
in the dependable embrace not of Mr Forester but of
his pet ape.
        The success of Peacock's characterization in
Melincourt is variable. In his presentation of Sir
Oran he is original and exciting in a way that recalls us to his triumphs in this genre; Anthelia is
one of the most affecting of his visions of womanly
power and independence; Mr Forester is too feeble
for the position he occupies in the book's pattern;
and the minor figures are mostly quite adequate to
their lesser functions. But overall, I think, it
seems hard to avoid a sense of some confusion, of

an imbalance in the handling of characters which comes from Peacock's similar imbalance in the rearrangement of the elements that go to make up this novel.

I hope I have shown that while there is much to censure in Melincourt, there is also much to admire. It is Peacock's longest book, and its unusually direct concern with contemporary abuses and pressedness of tone indicate the ambitiousness and urgency of the new direction in which he was pushing the form he had developed in Headlong Hall. At the same time, his attempt to juxtapose this with a chivalric allegory derived from the Italian poets points to a fresh confidence in the largeness of his talents. As a scheme combining immediacy of satire with eternal truths, and irony with romance, Melincourt is dazzling. But its intricate weaving of political and social satire with a contrasting, more hopeful thread of romance, all together organized around an examination of the possibilities of honourable life in circumstances of such corruption, is beyond Peacock's skill. As we approach the culminating marriage of Anthelia and Mr Forester, it is with little of the connectedness and inevitability we might expect. I take it that Peacock's intention is to prove that Anthelia's search may be ended, and that a hero may prove himself worthy of her hand, though that neither bride nor groom should escape some kind of irony, mainly on the grounds of exaggerated idealism. This is in fact what we have, but without the clarity or weight of emotion which would give conviction to such a completion of Peacock's plan. Instead, since the needed, romantic element of the novel has played so reduced a part in the action, and has depended so heavily on a character illconceived to give it support, it is difficult to feel strongly for the position the lovers are intended to vindicate; doubts then gather around the couple, and leave us in a more pessimistic frame of mind than was perhaps desired by the writer. Simply, in spite of its great virtues, Melincourt has not worked as an orderly whole. Marilyn Butler has called it 'a performance even more elegant and finished than Headlong Hall'(23); in conception, this is true; in execution, it cannot be.

CHAPTER III

NIGHTMARE ABBEY

Nightmare Abbey has been universally praised for its
vivacity and wit, and is the most popular of
Peacock's novels with the general reader. This
approval is undeniably justified. Nightmare Abbey
suffers from few of the errors of execution that mar
earlier books like Headlong Hall and Melincourt. It
has an air of confidence, and one of the many
delights that it offers is its virtuosic display of
Peacock's literary skills at their richest, most
precise and most trenchant. However, the brilliance
of its comedy and the crisp pointedness of its irony
should not mislead one into taking too singleminded
a view of this novel. It is a higher-pitched
companion-piece to Jane Austen's Northanger Abbey,
which appeared in the same year, 1818, and similarly
contrasts the inflamed imaginings of Romantic poets
and novelists with the more commonplace actualities
of upper-class life. But neither book contents itself with satirizing the obscurities of German metaphysics or the wildnesses of feeling of the Gothic
novel. Each also involves more complex and shifting
attitudes towards its subject. Peacock and Jane
Austen are not principally intent on a wholesale
condemnation of the major literary movement of the
time and of authors whose writings they evidently
enjoyed, in part at least. Instead, sympathy mingles
with censure; the simple vigour of pro and contra
mellows into a finer awareness of a reality in which
absolute positions may not be entertained. Consequently, the world presented in these books shifts
from the realm of satire into the freer realm of
comedy. They move off from mere keen commentary on
the follies of the day and into a fictional art whose
powerful joy in the creation of a Scythrop Glowry or
a Catherine Morland elevates characters and circumstances beyond the confines of the lampoon or the

skit.

However, <u>Nightmare Abbey</u> is clearly a work
which remains <u>in close engagement</u> with the cultural
problems of its period. Its intention is to provide
a sceptical diagnosis of Romantic malaise, a pungent
English gloss on Goethe's comment that '"the classic
[is] <u>healthy</u>, the romantic <u>sickly</u>"'(1). The novel
has a <u>carefully</u> focused <u>historical</u> appeal: it seems
less a fable than <u>Headlong Hall</u>, and more a comment
on actual events. <u>We have a teasing</u> impression that
revealing parallels can be drawn between figures in
the book and figures in the public eye. There is an
intriguing feeling that we are being offered witty,
perhaps libellous reports on some of the great men
of the day, with only the thinnest of disguises.
This excitement of the <u>qui vive</u>, of inside information sardonically made <u>available</u> to the outsider,
is not dissipated when we come to appreciate the
wideness of Peacock's scope in this book and the fact
that his method goes beyond the crude transposition
from life into literature that we find in a number
of Aldous Huxley's novels, or in W H Mallock's <u>The
New Republic</u> (1877). Books like <u>The New Republic</u>
<u>are parasitic</u> on the situations <u>from which they</u>
derive, and fade as those situations disappear into
history. But <u>Nightmare Abbey</u> achieves both immediate relevance <u>and longer-term</u> effect, and its
lasting comic fusion of materials drawn from life and
materials contrived by the imagination is rendered
with Peacock's greatest zest and cleverness.
<u>Nightmare Abbey</u> benefits from its position in
Peacock's <u>oeuvre</u>; of the novels he wrote before <u>The
Misfortunes of Elphin</u> (1829) it is certainly the
<u>best, and represents</u> the fruition of the form which
he had initiated with <u>Headlong Hall</u>. In particular,
the different elements <u>of Nightmare</u> Abbey are harmon-
iously fitted together and <u>the book leads</u> more incisively towards its conclusion than do any of its peers
except for <u>Gryll Grange</u>. The advance in skill and
judgement <u>that occurred</u> between <u>Melincourt</u> and <u>Night-
mare Abbey</u> was due to the rapid <u>maturing of</u> Peacock's
<u>talents</u>. This was a period of quick movement for
him, and of rare vitality: he never write so much
in such a short time again. The year 1818 alone saw
the publication not just of <u>Nightmare Abbey</u> but also
of his finest long poem, <u>Rhododaphne</u>. And both of
these works are sure of <u>their power</u> - suffering from
neither the anorexia of <u>Headlong Hall</u> nor the eleph-
antiasis of <u>Melincourt</u>.
<u>Nightmare Abbey</u> has youthful brio, but also the
air of <u>a fresh and individual</u> sensibility which has

come of age. This was the fullest time of Peacock's
life, when he was most intimately in touch with the
questioning, intellectual circle that had gathered
around his friend Shelley. New activities and
interests proliferated. There were love affairs,
boating trips on the Thames and a renewed impetus
given to his Greek studies by the enthusiasm of
Shelley and the barrister and littérateur, Thomas
Jefferson Hogg. Peacock's allowance from Shelley
allayed his earlier financial worries and paved the
way for the varied existence he now found open to
him. He grew increasingly confident of his abilities and adventurous in their use: Melincourt, for
example, was favourably reviewed, and commended by
Shelley ('Your "Melincourt" is exceedingly admired,
and I think much more so than any of your other
writings',(2). The circumstances in which Nightmare
Abbey itself was conceived can be gauged from the
letter to Shelley in which Peacock, talking of
excursions on the river and walks in the woods
amidst 'a continued series of cloudless sunshine and
delightful warm weather'(3), gives an impression of
buoyancy and ease.
        The influence of Shelley was crucial at this
stage of Peacock's career. There had been disagreements over Shelley's private life and his treatment
of his first wife, but the two men became more
intimate with the years. In March, 1817, Shelley
and his second wife, Mary Godwin, moved to Marlow,
where they were Peacock's near neighbours. The
households were on familiar terms, although Mary did
not forget that Peacock had given support to her
predecessor in Shelley's capricious affections.
Hogg, the poet and essayist Leigh Hunt, and Mary's
redoubtable father, William Godwin, were visitors;
there were rambles in Bisham Woods and outings to
Virginia Water and on the river. Above all, there
was talk. While Mary remained cool and complaining,
her husband and Peacock shared ambitions, tastes and
antipathies. The two men seem unlikely companions,
given the volatility of the one and the ironic reticence of the other. But they were both men of
ideas, in reaction against the orthodoxies of the
day; their perspectives were sometimes different,
but they had common interests in literature and
politics, and a shared sense of wrongdoing in the
world around them. One certain bond was their
rejection of religious faith and of the power of the
political establishment, their determined following
through of Jacobin and anti-authoritarian views which
had been stimulated during the French Revolution.

As important, however, were the fascinating areas of
their disagreement. Peacock was cooler, particularly
in his attitude towards contemporary poetry and the
effect of German novels and philosophical writings on
English culture; his friend responded fervently to
the latest trends and had even written two German-
influenced Gothic novels himself, as a young man.
Rich grounds for discussion are provided by this
array of strongly-held opinions, and one gathers from
the letters of these clever and disaffected confed-
erates a sense of a lively reciprocity which each
found invigorating. But their relationship was not
just a matter of mutual respect; there was also
warmth and sympathy, and in later life Peacock found
no other friend to whom he became so close. The
quality of Peacock's regard can be judged from his
'Memoirs of Percy Bysshe Shelley', which remains one
of the fairest appraisals of a poet notoriously
ridiculed and misunderstood. In his turn, Shelley,
similarly acute, sharply perceived the central
feature of Peacock's personality, not that he was of
a classical or satirical turn of mind, but rather
that he was antipathetic to tyranny and superstition.
    The deep understanding between Shelley and
Peacock leaves many traces on their works. During
the summer and autumn of 1817 both men were busy with
long poems, Laon and Cythna (later revised as The
Revolt of Islam) and Rhododaphne, and a good deal of
cross-fertilization seems to have taken place.
Shelley's poem has some resemblances in its conception and use of the Spenserian stanza to Peacock's
'Ahrimanes', and was revised by the novelist. Peck
suggests, per contra, that several lines in
Rhododaphne echo passages from Laon and Cythna, and
also finds reminiscences of Rhododaphne in Shelley's
later verse[4]. Each poem concerns itself with the
power of love to overcome the forces of disorder: in
Peacock, the rootlessness and transience with which
his poetry mainly deals, and in Shelley the oppressiveness of an unjust system of government.
Rhododaphne is a sensuous, musical verse-tale,
judiciously characterized by Mayoux as 'la fleur
unique, fort belle, à peine raide sur sa tige, de
l'hellénisme de Peacock'[5]. Shelley found it 'the
transfused essence of Lucian, Petronius and Apuleius'[6], and it is precisely to writers like these,
with their emphasis on the dictates of the heart and
the needs of the body, even amidst chaos, that the
poem is indebted. Its story resembles that of
Keats's 'Lamia' but is more neatly resolved.
Anthemion and Calliroë are pure young lovers, but

Anthemion is pursued by Rhododaphne,
'The magic maid of Thessaly'(7),
and tricked into acquiescence in the delights she
offers. But one day Uranian love, the passion for
the good which she has neglected and wronged, takes
revenge. Rhododaphne is destroyed, and Anthemion
resumes the simplicity and naturalness of his life
with Calliroë. As this summary indicates, the
conflict in the poem is between innocent love and
the excesses of a wild passion, and it is the former
which proves victorious. But it is a feeling of
vulnerability that the poem most movingly projects.
The links between Rhododaphne and Nightmare Abbey
are evident and interesting. Both are works of
weight, and search for palliation of the fears by
which all of Peacock's writing is more or less
shadowed. In each case, against a background of
anxiety and misguidedness we have a presentation of
love as the major positive force in our lives. In
its handling of this theme Rhododaphne is elegantly
nostalgic and dark in tone; Nightmare Abbey is
comically apropos and freshly stresses the power of
women to resist compulsion and to promote health.
When we look at Rhododaphne and Nightmare Abbey
together, we see that they form a diptych, each
examining different aspects of love but coming to
similar conclusions as to its overriding importance.
This is the great insight of the year 1818. Previously, the role of love had been significant but
not dominant in Peacock's fiction; in Nightmare
Abbey and its successors it becomes the surest path
to contentment.
    The intimacy between Shelley and Peacock at
this period extends beyond the sharing of ideas and
into particular textual detail. Shelley asks about
the progress of Nightmare Abbey, Peacock replies ('I
thought I had fully explained to you...',)(8), and
Shelley jokingly sends him 'a study for Night Mare
Abbey'(9) and suggests an apposite motto for the
book from Jonson's Every Man in his Humour(10).
Shelley's contribution to the novel is hard to over-
estimate. It is not simply that matter from his
personality has gone into creating the character of
Scythrop, or that the plot bears some resemblance to
events in which he was involved. Basically, these
are of minor concern. It is more to the point that
he rallied his friend's abilities and exposed his
work and notions to searching examination. It seems
to me that, before Nightmare Abbey, there is something undecided about most of Peacock's writing. The
comradeship of Shelley, especially during the summer

of 1817, the praise he gave even Peacock's poetry,
the fact that he took Nightmare Abbey seriously ('I
hope you have given the enemy no quarter. Remember,
it's a sacred war',)[11], all must have encouraged
Peacock in the amicable but discriminating way that
he needed. He recognised Shelley's genius; it was
the support of such a man, together with a new
ripeness in his own talents,which animated him to
produce a book like Nightmare Abbey, after false
starts in poetry and the drama, and with two
variously unsatisfactory novels already behind him.
Also, Nightmare Abbey was the last work that Peacock
wrote out of close personal contact with Shelley,
who left for Italy in 1818 and, although the two men
kept in touch by letter, remained there till his
death in 1822. There is a great difference in accom-
plishment between Nightmare Abbey and Peacock's next
book, Maid Marian, and there are many reasons for
this; but one of them must be that Shelley was
deeply connected with the first novel, and little
with the second.

One of the principal interests that Shelley and
Peacock had in common was in literature. Both men
were intensely bookish; constant literary reference
was an integral part of their experience. Their
letters are full of advice as to classical or modern
authors to be read or avoided, comments on the
poetry of the day and criticism of the cultural
scene. We have little information on Peacock's
reading during the time he was working on Nightmare
Abbey, which he probably began in the spring of 1818
and had finished by June 14[12]. We know that in
the summer he spent a good deal of the day out of
doors, on the river or in the woods, and that his
attention to books thus became 'as usual, at this
season, somewhat desultory'[13]. The novel itself
aptly bows to Rabelais and Samuel Butler, the two
masters of boisterous high comedy whose influence
pervades all Peacock's fiction. But the foreground
is occupied by parodies and reminiscences of the
Romantic poets, particularly of Coleridge, Byron,
Wordsworth and Southey, and disapproving asides on
Goethe and Kant, seen as types of German muddle-
headedness. The precise trigger to Peacock's unease
was the poetry of Byron: writing to Shelley he
says, 'I think it necessary to "make a stand"
against the "encroachments" of black bile. The
fourth canto of Childe Harold is really too bad. I
cannot consent to be auditor tantum of this systematic "poisoning" of the "mind" of the "reading
public"'[14]. Although Peacock is largely in

opposition, it is impossible to suppose that he
was not a careful, and sometimes appreciative,
student of the literature of his period. We might
nowadays disagree with his mockery of Goethe, his
dismissal of Kant and his refusal to come to terms
with Coleridge's prose, but the reality of his
concern cannot be doubted. Running through everything that he writes is a suspicion of fashion, a
desire that trivia should not distract attention
from true worth. In this book, therefore, we have
an impression not just of wit and a disengaged play
of mind, but also of genuine warning. Nightmare
Abbey is funny, but its problems are felt, and it is
this fine combination which makes the novel, within
its small compass, nevertheless 'many-sided and
complete'(15).

     From the beginning of Nightmare Abbey we are
aware of a new poise in the handling of effects.
The exposition spreads over Chapters I and II; it
is a prelude of a rather insistent kind, setting the
emotional tone of the book and indicating the
problems which will form its subject-matter. Chapter
I is full of dry wit--the Abbey is described as
being 'in a highly picturesque state of semi-dilapid-
ation' (p.1)--but is not quite comic. There is a
marked emphasis on atrophy, and a sense that the
springs of feeling have run dry. Chapter II adds to
this an undertone of apartness and hollowness, though
it recalls us to a less melancholy perspective by its
concluding reminder, in buoyant phrase, of 'the crazy
fabric of human nature' (p.18).
     Most of Peacock's books begin with sardonic
briskness; Nightmare Abbey is as clever and agile as
the others, but more disenchanted. The ghostliness
of the first few pages is partly ironic, and traves-
ties the gloomy excess of the Gothic novel, but it
also indicates the point of nullity at which most of
the characters have arrived. Like Mrs Glowry, who
'laid on external things the blame of her mind's
internal disorder, and thus became by degrees an
accomplished scold' (p.2), they may have a kind of
energy, but not one that is productive of life. It
is especially in love that things have gone wrong:
Mr Glowry's ill-advised marriage makes his house 'no
better than a spacious kennel, for every one in it
led the life of a dog' (p.3), and Scythrop's passion
for Miss Emily Girouette has a 'disastrous termination' (p.13). We feel that true emotion has lost
strength, and that vacancy and decline are the
result. On the other hand, the forces of waste and

folly are presented with alarming lushness and
animation: 'In the congenial solitude of Nightmare
Abbey, the distempered ideas of metaphysical romance
and romantic metaphysics had ample time and space to
germinate into a fertile crop of chimeras, which
rapidly shot up into vigorous and abundant vegetat-
ion' (p.14). This is elegant, but leaves a residue
of disquiet; we note again, in 'distempered', the
imagery of sickness which pervades the novel. Albeit
humorously, something is rotten in the county of
Lincolnshire; a real perturbation underlies the
brilliant surface of Nightmare Abbey. The matter is
displayed to us with unwonted candour when Scythrop,
'troubled with the passion for reforming the world'
(p.14), considers how society is to be improved:
'"Action," thus he soliloquised, "is the result of
opinion, and to new-model opinion would be to new-
model society"' (p.15). This may be so, and, talking
of Lucian and Voltaire, Peacock himself says that 'To
clear the ground of falsehood is to leave room for
the introduction of truth'(16). But in his fiction
advantageous action is almost never the result of
opinions; it comes instead from giving way to the
natural feelings inherent in us all. We should
therefore see the world of Nightmare Abbey, represented in the central figure of Scythrop, as one which
has lost a necessary link with soundness; fantasy
has taken over from common sense, and the morbidity
of the Glowries and their friends is the disagreeable
consequence.
    The first two chapters offer a highly-charged
evocation of these sombre circumstances, but are
enlivened by irony and by the presence of two
characters whose function is to remind us of a fundamental robustness in man's constitution. Diggory
Deathshead the footman, wholesomely equipped with 'a
round ruddy face, and a pair of laughing eyes'
(p.8), gives a hint of vigour amongst so much
impotence and ennui. His stay is short, but leaves
behind incontestable proof of fecundity: 'a flourishing colony of young Deathsheads to join chorus
with the owls, that had before been the exclusive
choristers of Nightmare Abbey'. Mr Hilary, Mr
Glowry's brother-in-law and 'a very cheerful and
elastic gentleman' (p.4), has an important minor
role as the voice of coolness in the book, but plays
an unemphatic part in this introductory section. It
would be a mistake to over-stress the Waste Land
aspects of the early chapters of Nightmare Abbey,
and I have suggested grounds why we should not do so.
Nevertheless, despite the controlled comedy of

Peacock's effects, there is an unavoidably disturbing
aura to his picture of a house where only malaise
flourishes and where health hardly shows itself at
all.

More than elsewhere in Peacock, imagery establishes the atmosphere and tone of Nightmare Abbey.
The novel's exposition draws heavily on metaphors
which derive from illness, from the notion of life
as a lottery and from a fear of dehumanization. In
particular, these metaphors are used of women, the
prime agents of sanity and truth in Peacock's books.
We begin with the monitory instance of Mrs Glowry,
who sacrifices love for material well-being and thus
provokes the 'wilful blight of her affections' (p.2)
and her own transformation into a shrewish automaton.
This prominent warning is given added point later in
the chapter, when Scythrop and his father are
comparing notes on the women they have known. Scythrop regrets their ill-judged education, '"which
studiously models them into mere musical dolls, to
be set out for sale in the great toy-shop of
society"' (p.6). Mr Glowry, sharing his son's views,
laments, '"I bought one myself, but it was confound-
edly out of tune"'. Partly, this is clever word-
play, and elicits a smile. But it also instills
unease, and alerts us to some of the human issues
which Peacock links to the more purely literary
framework of his satire.

By the time we have reached page 19 of the
Halliford edition and are commencing Chapter III,
the main lines of the book have been decisively
presented to us. The area of love is established as
the central concern of its story, and a proper
affection between man and woman is presented as the
aim of a good life; parallel to this, the writer
examines the extent to which the literary and philosophical interests of the major male figures, above
all of Scythrop, affect their relationships with
their companions and their achievement of the goal
of a loving marriage. Nightmare Abbey is, therefore,
anxious as well as amusing; behind its witty facade
there is an urgency new to Peacock--both more poignant than in Headlong Hall, and less strident than
in Melincourt.

Peacock's novels give us the sense that he
knows exactly what people are like, but does not
choose to write straightforwardly about them. It is
rare for us to be close to the consciousness of his
characters or for them to react or develop as we
expect from works within the mainstream of English

fiction. Nightmare Abbey, however, is a partial
exception to these generalizations. The intention
of the book is to bring the genuine into focus, and
the method employed is to set off the untidiness of
reality against the seductive neatness of speculative, impractical views of experience. Its vivacity
comes from recurrent clashes between the way things
are and the way crotcheteers would like them to be.
Scythrop is endlessly caught in this trap, at one
moment philosophically considering his schemes for
the regeneration of society, at another entranced by
Marionetta's resourceful coquetry. In different
guises, we find dilemmas like Scythrop's in all of
Peacock's novels. But nowhere else is our involvement so deep, and in no other book before Gryll
Grange do the characters impress themselves so
sympathetically on the reader.

So, when Marionetta dallies with the Hon Mr
Listless and Scythrop, helpless and bemused, begins
his volume of Dante in the middle, and turns over
'three or four pages at once--backwards as well as
forwards' (p.46), we are aware of having moved a
long way from the clever but exiguous dialectics of
Headlong Hall. This is accomplished social comedy,
with a sure grasp of mores and a richly dramatic
presentation of the main participants. Throughout
the novel, romantic entanglements are sustained by a
careful depiction of motive and response. Stella
impresses one first as a wild figure straight out of
Mrs Radcliffe (or Goethe), but soon adds to her
impetuosity a healthy ballast of sound judgement.
Marionetta, too, quickly develops from a cipher into
an entirely credible flirt, whose tactics Peacock
records with aplomb: 'Sometimes she would sit by
the piano, and listen with becoming attention to
Scythrop's pathetic remonstrances; but, in the most
impassioned part of his oratory, she would convert
all his ideas into a chaos, by striking up some
Rondo Allegro, and saying, "Is it not pretty"'
(p.34). As Mayoux says approvingly, this is 'souvent
de bon roman psychologique'[17]. More than elsewhere
in Peacock, such incidents are not at one remove from
observation, indicating only a general wisdom about
the human condition--they give us observation itself,
wry, acute and convincing, with an impression of
accuracy to the way people in fact behave. One
concomitant of this is that the characters, while
still exaggerated, are now more rounded than before;
another is that their problems, whether marital or
merely literary, become more substantial and more
moving than in most of Peacock's other works.

The main difference between the characters in
Headlong Hall and those in Nightmare Abbey lies in
the quality of their inner lives. In the earlier
book we have silhouettes, filled in with a certain
amount of detail, but still on the whole creatures of
a single obsession. Mr Toobad follows the same
pattern in Nightmare Abbey, but is an exception. His
companions are more fully depicted in terms of gesture, and are given a good deal of emotional elaboration. The incorrigible swaying movement of Scythrop's passion for both Marionetta and Stella, for
example, is registered with fineness and plausibility
as well as with irony. Even Mr Glowry, stridently
intruding upon the privacy of Scythrop's tower, gives
one a quite rich sense of personality, as he first
catches his son on the hop ('"You are a fox, Scyth-
orp; you are an exceedingly cunning fox, with that
demure visage of yours"', p.124), and then absolutely
refuses to be deterred by increasingly frantic and
highly comic excuses ('"It wo'n't do, Scythrop.
There is a girl concealed in this tower, and find her
I will"', p.127). Peacock has a subtle ear, and
turns to a nicety the old-fashioned bluffness of Mr
Glowry and the inventive dementia of his son. There
is a fresh interest here, not in automatisms of
thought and action, but in the recognizable workings
of the consciousness. Of course, there are limits
to this dimension of psychological realism, and we
become aware of them when we contrast Nightmare Abbey
with Northanger Abbey, whose adventurous, vital
heroine, Catherine Morland, is of a range and depth
entirely unequalled by Peacock.
    Nevertheless, the ambience of Nightmare Abbey
differs strikingly from that of its predecessors.
There, characters pursue vivid, parallel courses;
no-one influences anyone else, though no-one stops
trying. Here, especially in the figure of Scythrop,
we have entered into a world of cause and effect,
and clearly perceive the malign outcome in his private life of the heady imaginings to which he is
addicted. In this novel, people react to one
another; like Mr Glowry, they watch actions carefully and make deductions from what they see.
Often, as when Scythrop is scrutinizing Marionetta
and trying to understand her wiles, this leads to an
impasse; often, too, it produces comic misapprehen-
sion, as when Mr Glowry gives a premature consent to
his son's supposed engagement to Marionetta. This
does not impair our sense of there being a social
dimension to this book, perhaps ramshackle and
eccentric, but functioning. We are less conscious

than before of people's apartness; we see them
talking together, coming to terms with oddity and
inexplicability of conduct, and even quite credibly
falling in love. The fact that the plot of Nightmare Abbey operates firmly to connect the various
strands of the story is also of importance in this
respect. We have an impression of related concerns
and of characters who share pains and pleasures with
joint bonhomie: fathers worry about their rebell-
ious children, fashionable notions float perniciously
from person to person, and marriage is constantly in
the air. Peacock's novels have been compared to
debates or symposia, and these certainly provide the
models for Headlong Hall. Nightmare Abbey remains
disputatious, but also draws upon the tradition of
Congreve and Sheridan; its greatest delights are
its vivid theatrical scenes, humorously characterized
and sharply and rapidly staged, and securely grounded
in that recognition of communal living which is basic
to social comedy.

This alters the status of the crotchetters in
Nightmare Abbey. They are less able to confine
themselves within the sphere of their hobby-horses,
and perforce acquire fuller humanity. Here they are
part of the scene, and acquiesce in its affable camaraderie: even the Hon Mr Listless does not allow
his almost terminal languor to prevent him from
engaging in the cheerful diversions of a traditional
house-party. Only the ponderous Mr Flosky maintains
the relentlessness and abstraction of ancestors like
Mr Escot. The others are gregarious, like the Hon
Mr Listless, or poetic creations like Mr Asterias.
The attractiveness of these figures is not diminished
by the more realistic context in which they find
themselves. Peacock admires vitality and is fascinated by strangeness, and gives both their due. The
Hon Mr Listless and his indefatigable French valet,
Fatout, are treated with particular indulgence, and
move at a level of inspiration which is seldom
matched by crotcheteers in the other books. In one
scene, a game of billiards is proposed:
'THE HONOURABLE MR. LISTLESS.
Billiards! Really I should be very happy;
but, in my present exhausted state, the
exertion is too much for me. I do not
know when I have been equal to such an
effort. (He rang the bell for his valet.
Fatout entered.) Fatout! when did I play
at billiards last?
FATOUT.
De Fourteen December de last year, Monsieur.

(Fatout bowed and retired.)' (p.36).
This is dreamlike and Chaplinesque, and proceeds
with an insouciant appearance of logic, as if the
function of a phlegmatic valet were of course to
serve as a walking memory for his master. It has
the coolness and consistency of the best fantasy,
and its wit is unfailing.

Perhaps encouraged by its richer psychological
texture, critics have been prompted even more than
previously to make identifications between characters
in the novel (such as Mr Cypress and Scythrop) and
figures from real life (in this case, Byron and
Shelley). As I pointed out in my discussion of
Headlong Hall, to approach Peacock's books by this
route is to simplify his art. Certainly he borrows
details from the lives of his contemporaries: the
speeches of Mr Cypress, especially, are too dense
with Byronic references for the author of Childe
Harold not to have been specifically in Peacock's
mind when he was writing them. But Mr Cypress is
not merely a caricature of Byron, any more than
Scythrop is of Shelley. Both are fictional creations
which take some materials from life, some from literature and some from Peacock's imagination, and mix
them together, reorganizing, selecting and discarding
in accordance with the requirements of artistic
effectiveness and not of biographical truth. Thus
Mr Cypress is not Byron under a nom-de-plume; it is
rather that Byron has provided the impetus, and some
of the examples, for the development in Mr Cypress
of a crotcheteer who typifies a self-indulgent
Romantic melancholy which perversely turns its back
on the many instances of health and happiness in the
world. We should also note that Scythrop was not
formally associated with Shelley until long after
Nightmare Abbey was published, and that no mention
of the link occurs in Peacock's letters or in his
friend's. Shelley was hardly the most self-aware of
men, but he would surely have guessed that Scythrop
was meant as a bantering, critical version of himself, if this had been Peacock's chief aim. Instead,
he sent the novelist a warmly approving message in
which he describes Scythrop as 'a character admirably
conceived and executed'(18). There is further
evidence to dissuade us from accepting too tidy a
correlation between figures in the book and figures
from the outside world. Peacock distrusted biography
and felt that it usually amounted to nothing more
than 'the old village scandal on a larger scale'(19),
satisfying only a vulgar taste for 'gossip about
notorieties'(20). Quite apart from this, the whole

enterprise of writing someone else's life-history
seemed to him to be futile from the start, for, as
he says in his review of Moore's Letters and
Journals of Lord Byron, 'Few men are so ingenuous as
to enable their most intimate friends to distinguish
very accurately the artificial from the real in
their characters'(21). Peacock's own brief memoir
of Shelley he undertook reluctantly, when its subject
was long dead, and for the purpose of presenting
facts honestly and dispelling error, surmise and
malice that had accumulated around the poet. I think
that this evidence must give us pause before we
attempt any straightforward translation of Peacock's
characters into a satirical portrait-gallery of the
poets, philosophers and general intellectual riff-
raff of the day. Instead,while admitting that they
have ironic ties with the contemporary scene, we
should look to aesthetic rather than annalistic
qualities for an explanation of their genesis,
development and effect.

Peacock is always cavalier, in Nightmare Abbey
sometimes startlingly so, and at different moments
breathes life and power into almost every figure in
the novel, even into a circumscribed old crotcheteer
like Mr Toobad. Mr Toobad has little to do in most
of the book except to predict the coming of the devil
with great wrath, and we accept him amusedly as a
latter-day member of a class with which we became
familiar in Headlong Hall. But suddenly, during a
discussion of the health of society, he puts on
articulacy and interest, and speaks vigorously in
favour of the 'true men' (p.106) of the past as
against the 'false knaves' of the present. Then,
extinguished like a candle, he again subsides. However, although taken aback, we are not displeased;
for once, he has surprised us. This teases the
reader, but it also points to a sort of respectful-
ness on the part of the author. Characters may
indeed be bound up in their crotchets, but they are
given their chance and occasionally freed into a
wider world. It is as if, even in the most rigid,
something more flexible and various may shine
through. As Edmund Wilson says, Peacock is always
'on the human side'(22); he recommends judgement for
systems of thought, but tolerance for people; he
offers possibilities of animation from which no-one
is excluded.

In Peacock, ideology keeps us apart whereas the
senses bring us together. Prescriptive theories,
whether they deal with mermaids or with transcendental philosophy, are comically reduced, while favour

is extended to feelings of love and to the delights
of the dinner-table. Vociferous argument does not
end in consensus: the disputants are too tenacious
of their own views for agreement ever to seem
feasible. Instead, to soothe furrowed brows, Peacock celebrates an alternative and superior resolution in drink, good food and a catch sung perhaps
by Mr Hilary and the Rev Mr Larynx:
  'The bowl goes trim. The moon doth shine.
  And our ballast is old wine;
  And your ballast is old wine' (p.112).
Chapter XI, in which this cheerful song appears,
encapsulates Peacock's method of reasserting the
good fellowship which underlies the polemical
differences of his crotcheteers. In the early part
of the novel, he offers wine as a quiet counterpoint
to solipsism; in this chapter, Madeira comfortingly
frames the wide-ranging contentiousness of the
diners, accorded unanimous praise at the beginning
and enforcing a choric heartiness at the end.

The folly of most people in Nightmare Abbey is
that they too readily turn their backs on the simple
joys inherent in them all and most conducive to
happiness. They try to fit the world into pigeon-
holes of doctrine and hobby-horse, and of course it
reacts, intransigently upsetting their schemes,
preventing all of Scythrop's principles from being
put into practice. The crotcheteers are more than
just figures of fun; we may laugh at them but we
also laugh with them, as they struggle bravely and
absurdly to reduce the variety of experience to the
singleness of their obsession. We have no impression
of guilt: the work is too entertaining and the
crotcheteers too lively and innocent for that. Beneath all the misdirection here, and more powerfully
than in Headlong Hall or Melincourt, life wins
through, and we respond optimistically (though not
without shadows) to Peacock's trust in its sanity and
vitality.

The principal figure in Nightmare Abbey is
Scythrop; he is the nearest to a congenial hero
that we have so far encountered in Peacock's novels.
In fact, although education is not stressed, the book
is an authentic Bildungsroman, and thoughtfully follows the young Scythrop through early life and first
loves to a point of recognition vis-à-vis the world
and its ways. It offers us a witty inversion of
Goethe's The Sorrows of Young Werther, one in which
the hero does not use his pistol and survives instead to call for an invigorating bottle of Madeira.

We are never in any doubt as to where our attention
should be; from the start, even amidst such a
sprightly cast of characters, Scythrop is the pivot
of the action, and as the work proceeds the others
increasingly drop away and leave him at the centre
of our concern.

Scythrop is the most brilliant exemplar in
Peacock's books of the author's scepticism as to
schematized versions of existence which attempt to
dominate life's variousness rather than sensibly to
accommodate themselves to it. He is constantly
being presented with refractory personal problems,
especially amatory ones, which conflict with his
notions of how things ought to be. He has answers
for everything, based on speculative day-dreaming
rather than on observation, but encounters unexpected
difficulties as he tries confidently to put them into
effect. We see him entirely diverted by 'romances
and German tragedies' (p.14) and 'ponderous tomes of
transcendental philosophy' from the pragmatism with
which we ought to approach our encounters with our
fellow creatures. He is deluded into thinking that
reality can be neatly and systematically bound to a
regime of ideas, and comically perturbed when it
escapes its shackles. There are two main areas in
which Scythrop, to the detriment of his life, permits
himself to be ruled by the written word. In politics, with adolescent fervour, he devotes himself
to highflown notions of revolution which elevate
the principle of '"A few to think, and many to act"'
(p.15), and allots himself a grandiose position as
philosopher and iconoclast. In his relations with
others, in perfect complement, he applies the
exaggerated standards of passion and absoluteness he
has derived from his reading to the more mundane
circumstances of everyday. But preconceived notions
are routed by irresistible human impulses: life and
love, in the shape of the inconstant Marionetta,
simply refuse to be bound. 'Scythrop's romantic
dreams had indeed given him many pure anticipated
cognitions of combinations of beauty and intelligence, which, he had some misgivings, were not
exactly realised in his cousin Marionetta; but, in
spite of these misgivings, he soon became distract-
edly in love' (pp. 21-2). It is ironic how quickly,
and by what means, this destruction of Scythrop's
grand designs is achieved. It takes three days, and
involves nothing more esoteric than Marionetta's
feminine 'lures' (p.21).

Scythrop's tower is the symptom of his folly, a
bastion of retreat and separateness where wild ideas

can be indulged in solitude, safe from the cooler
perspectives and rough-and-tumble of society. It is
only in the security of this tower, and in the congenial company of the German-educated Stella, that
'deep schemes for a thorough repair of the crazy
fabric of human nature' (p.18) really have any credibility: as soon as they are exposed in the open
air, their absurdity becomes obvious.

From what I have said of Scythrop up to now, he
might seem a mere butt of Peacock's irony, a fool
who does not learn from his mistakes until the very
last moment (in fact, at least an hour after the very
last moment). But there is more to him than that.
He is not only Shelley, as I have said[23]; nor is
he only Werther, but turned head over heels; he is
also Candide. Like the protagonist of Voltaire's
story, Scythrop is the perpetual bright naïf; he is
mocked, but he generates sympathy as well. His in-
capacity, his resilience and his dogged determination
are presented with freshness and understanding; it
is hard not to admit a certain fellow-feeling for
him. As Shelley says, with his usual acumen, 'and
yet looking deeper into it, is not the misdirected
enthusiasm of Scythrop what J[esus] C[hrist] calls
the salt of the earth?'[24]. He is a likeable figure, because his situation has an edge of truth in
spite of its hyperbole, and he responds to it with a
fecklessness to which we may find humorous parallels
in our own experience. Thus, while we laugh at the
excesses and errors of Scythrop's behaviour, the
trappedness of his circumstances arouses compassion;
he is a character, not a marionette. The emotional
power of Nightmare Abbey would not be half so great
if we did not have this impression both that Scythrop is more than just an Aunt Sally and that the
dilemmas he faces are genuinely indicative of a
weakness in the real world.

If Scythrop's is the strongest characterization
in the book, then Flosky's is the weakest. His
function is straightforwardly to provide an extreme
and destructive instance of futile obscurantism on
the German model and of mental exertion divorced
from direct response and true feeling. There is
something twisted about him; his speech is meander-
ing, its syntax labyrinthine, its content impenetra-
bly absorbed and remote. It is not just perverse,
it is also null: 'Now the enthusiasm for abstract
truth is an exceedingly fine thing, as long as the
truth, which is the object of the enthusiasm, is so
completely abstract as to be altogether out of the
reach of the human faculties; and, in that sense, I

have myself an enthusiasm for truth, but in no other,
for the pleasure of metaphysical investigation lies
in the means, not in the end; and if the end could
be found, the pleasure of the means would cease'
(p.49). Flosky's long, congested orations, of which
this is a fair sample, burlesque the prolixity and
inanity that come when philosophy is cut off from
contact with ordinary life. This seems all very
suitable, and it certainly gives an easy target for
Peacock's xenophobic ironies at the expense of the
German manner. But Peacock does not avoid the cardinal danger in any parody of long-winded tedium;
that is to say, he simply reproduces it. There is
little fun in Flosky's endless monologues, which
imitate with all too perfect a fidelity the emptiness
of a transcendental dogma which has also transcended
sense. Throughout the book, Flosky is associated
with darkness; when he speaks, that darkness becomes
all too visible.
    Nor does one's dissatisfaction rest here. Some-
times, like the other crotcheteers, Flosky projects
a self-contained world which is pleasurable because
of its oddity and liveliness: 'There are two gates
through which ghosts find their way to the upper air:
fraud and self-delusion. In the latter case, a ghost
is a deceptio visûs, an ocular spectrum, an idea with
the force of a sensation. I have seen many ghosts
myself. I dare say there are few in this company who
have not seen a ghost' (p.116). This conveys precisely an impression of a confident, dogmatic personality, of someone who is fond of the sound of his own
voice and used to pronouncing ex cathedra, and with
the semblance of authority, on any subject under the
sun. It is typical of Peacock's handling of the
crotcheteers in his conversation novels. But sometimes this clever spinning of a personal obsession
into the secure, Uncle Toby-like cocoon of a hobby-
horse is disrupted. Then, irony and poise break
down, and are replaced by evident animus. Flosky
argues, for example, that 'It is very certain, and
much to be rejoiced at, that our literature is hag-
ridden' (p.50); he consistently celebrates the
morbid in preference to the healthy, the confused in
preference to the lucid. This offers a commentary on
Flosky's folly which relies on button-holing, almost
on statement, rather than on the subtle exacerbation
by which Peacock achieves his richest effects. In
addition, Peacock fails to inspire Flosky with the
comic zest which is so ample in his fellows. Partly,
this is inherent in the conception of a Teutonized
man of thought for whom life means words and not

deeds. Flosky is a figure of static introspection,
bereft of the enticing, physical vitality of his
peers which shows itself in the gestures,tics and
visual hallmarks that give them individuality; in
the end, his fellow-guests seem simply finer and more
appealing than he does.

One reason for Peacock's difficulties with
Flosky is that he irritates his creator excessively
and that this spills over into stridency of presentation. Another may well result from the close links
between Flosky, in the book, and Samuel Taylor
Coleridge, in the world outside. Flosky's speeches
are full of references to Coleridge's works both in
poetry and in prose: he talks of German metaphysics
and mediaeval ballads, alludes constantly to the Lay
Sermons and Biographia Literaria, and offers a tran-
sparent jibe at 'Kubla Khan' ('I composed five
hundred lines in my sleep', p.76). Mr Cypress, it
might be said, is coloured in the same way: Childe
Harold's Pilgrimage is omnipresent in his speeches.
But the difference is that Mr Cypress's appearance
is brief and that he is a figure of poetic vigour as
well as of boldly nuanced self-parody. Flosky
remains obstinately untransformed; he does not establish himself attractively like his companions, and
continues a mere rendition of Coleridge rather than
putting on fantasy and quickness as they do. As so
often, the note of personal animosity disrupts the
equilibrium of Peacock's writing. When he deals
directly with contemporary abuses, or contemporary
individuals about whom he feels strongly, the necessary veil of art, which permits him urbane accommodation, is pushed aside, and we are left with crudity
and condemnation.

We notice a striking improvement as we move from
Flosky to the Hon Mr Listless. He is a minor character, yet his symbolic power is unfailing. His ener-
vation provides a surreal comedy which never palls;
not just living but even laughing turn out to be an
'exertion' (p.38) and therefore 'too much' for him.
As an accumulation of negatives, a human being on the
verge of extinction, Mr Listless's consistency extends evocatively from his favoured position (recum-
bent) to his favoured conversational manner (indet-
erminate): 'My nerves, Miss O'Carroll, my nerves are
shattered. I have been advised to try Bath. Some of
the faculty recommend Cheltenham. I think of trying
both, as the seasons don't clash' (pp.36-7). Mr
Listless is the novel's prime warning as to the
danger of the forces of atrophy: his decay is so
far advanced that he is hardly alive at all. Yet the

impression he gives is certainly not negative. His
nullity is amusing and inventively exhibited, and he
is equipped with wit and a voice of recognisably
human timbre: '"There--loosen the lace of my stays a
little,"' he says to Fatout, '"for really this
plebeian practice of eating--Not too loose--consider
my shape"' (p.115). From time to time, he even
deviates into sense, and is duly moved to doubt when
Flosky attributes the decline of the modern world to
tea, late dinners and the French Revolution: as he
justifiably says, 'I cannot exactly see the connection of ideas' (p.48). But the most important thing
about Mr Listless is that, unlike Flosky, he functions as a salutary reminder, not a depressant.
    Mr Listless is inseparable from his valet,
Fatout; the two men complement one another perfectly. Mr Listless is agreeable but passive; Fatout is
associated with wine and love, and in one drunken
episode he regrets the absence of female company at
the Abbey until consoled by a brisk song '"About fair
maids, and about fair maids, and about my merry maids
all"' (p.64). In every circumstance each reflects
upon the other, Mr Listless all art, Fatout all
nature--the former monitory, the latter reassuring.
While Fatout is around, unselfconsciously pursuing
his life of pleasure, seeking respite from the un-
wholesome melancholy of his lodging, we are in no
danger of forgetting a basic healthiness with which
to contrast the surrounding malaise.
    Mr Asterias the ichthyologist surprisingly
equals Mr Listless in singularity and poetic energy.
He is misguided but also fascinatingly zealous, a
figure of genuine romance who mingles attractiveness
with absurdity: 'He had penetrated into the watery
den of the Sepia Octopus, disturbed the conjugal
happiness of that turtle-dove of the ocean, and come
off victorious in a sanguinary conflict. He had been
becalmed in the tropical seas, and had watched, in
eager expectation, though unhappily always in vain,
to see the colossal polypus rise from the water, and
entwine its enormous arms round the masts and the
rigging' (p.56). Mr Asterias has a fairy-tale air
about him; he is a visionary and a dreamer, and
like a dream he himself seems moving and alluring,
tangential to reality yet not irrelevant to life.
Thus, although we remain entirely aware of the extravagance of Mr Asterias's hopeless pursuit of non-
existent mermaids, and note its links with Peacock's
central critique of impracticality and obsessiveness,
we remember him principally as a source of delight.
    The crotcheteers in Nightmare Abbey are far

from being merely figures of fun; Peacock's
creative joy in their contrivance shines through
more powerfully than in any of the rest of his works,
and they arouse sympathy just as much as scepticism.
But there are also characters whose role is more
pointedly to uphold common sense against the morbidity of the Abbey. The most important of this group
is Marionetta, and it also includes Fatout and Mr
Hilary. All of them function normatively, though
with discretion; they show up the wrong paths taken
by others, but they offer neither models of conduct
nor formal adjudications of the rectitude or error
of their fellows. They encourage us as to a fundamental soundness, but not from a position of
strength. They are lone voices, and the comfort
they give us is nicely calculated not to seem inordinate. So, while it is little stressed, we properly
approve of Mr Hilary's lucid pragmatism and of the
calm and simple language in which he phrases his
acquiescence in the human condition: 'To reconcile
man as he is to the world as it is, to preserve and
improve all that is good, and destroy or alleviate
all that is evil, in physical and moral nature--have
been the hope and aim of the greatest teachers and
ornaments of our species. I will say, too, that the
highest wisdom and the highest genius have been invariably accompanied with cheerfulness' (p.109). As
the book proceeds, this functionary of 'sunshine and
music' (p.53) also establishes himself in parallel
as an apologist for 'the...solid wisdom of antiquity'
(p.105) in opposition to the 'Black Bile' (p.53) of
the Moderns. This pairing seems logical in terms
both of the thematic organization of the novel and of
Peacock's own admiration for the literature of Greece
and Rome. But it remains undeveloped; <u>Nightmare
Abbey</u> makes slight reference to the classics, and
they are never elaborated into a standard by which
contemporary literature might be exposed in all its
many deficiencies. Nor, indeed, does Mr Hilary speak
with convincing authorial weight. Although his rat-
ional viewpoint and firmness of appraisal are undeniably appealing, he is treated just like his peers,
and no different emphasis is allotted to his
speeches as compared with theirs. This is a matter
of Peacock's technique and of the mode of his
fiction: conflicting opinions clash together, and it
is from the circumstances of that clash, and not by
the use of a narrator or by firm indications of the
writer's own views, that our understanding of the
action is obtained. As Able says, in a book by
Peacock, 'all parties are justified, while none is

accredited'(25).

There are few women crotcheteers, and none after
<u>Headlong Hall</u>. Peacock's female characters serve as
a reproving gloss on their less clearheaded menfolk
and have an inherent grasp of actuality which is
generally missing from the opposite sex. Their prime
usefulness is that they inspire love and create havoc
with the rigid dictates of a hobby-horse, and thus
bring their admirers into closer touch with the world
as it really is.

Throughout <u>Nightmare Abbey</u>, Marionetta imports
liveliness and common sense into situations from
which they are unhelpfully absent. She has two main
virtues. Her nature is capricious, and this sets her
immediately at cross purposes with the susceptible
intellectuals whom she meets at the Abbey; they
seldom veer from the fixed path of their obsession,
whereas she exhibits 'all the diversities of an April
sky' (p.20). A part of this 'playfulness' (p.80) is
her complete lack of interest in bookish pursuits or
abstract ideas; her talents are in personal relationships, not in philosophical theorizing, and are
signalled in the musical turns with which she regularly animates and unifies the company. The second
of her merits is the straightforward acumen of her
response to those around her. Throughout her hair-
raising interview with Scythrop, when she bursts in
upon his 'reverie' (p.22), she reacts with a cool
self-possession which seems born of experience. '"For
heaven's sake," said she, "my dear Scythrop, what is
the matter?"' (p.23), and again, '"I prithee deliver
thyself like a man of this world"'. She bears within her the values of ordinary existence, and recalls
both Scythrop and ourselves to the truth of this
occasion by setting off her sang-froid against his
overwrought imaginings. Her role as an agent of
actuality seems confirmed by the unique constraint of
her position in the novel. She is the only character
who is dependent on others for her maintenance, and
the only one, therefore, who has acquired a less than
inflated view of the world and its freedoms. So,when
her aunt speaks to her, 'Marionetta listened in
silent submission, for she knew that her inheritance
was passive obedience' (p.30); it is little wonder,
given these unenviable circumstances, that she makes
the most of the prosperous young men who come her
way. Clearly, Marionetta is silly as well as sensible, and the triviality of her behaviour does not
escape Peacock's irony. But her main purpose, that
of running counter to the prevailing infirmity of
life at the Abbey, she fulfils with vivacity and

attractiveness.

In <u>Antic Hay</u>, Mr Gumbril Senior sourly notes,
'"<u>Experientia docet</u>--nothing falser, so far as most
of us are concerned, was ever said"'(26). In <u>Night-
mare Abbey</u>, if anyone proves him wrong, it is
Marionetta--with a little help from Stella, the
exciting radical who is her rival and complement,
and has a similar effect upon the vulnerable
Scythrop. The twinning of the two girls is elegantly
accomplished. Each is allotted one half of the
novel, and each represents a different, enticing
choice for the distracted lover who swings between
them. Marionetta is comedy, light-heartedness,
music and acceptance of the <u>status quo</u>; Stella is
tragedy, Teutonic seriousness, literature and rebellion. But underlying their diversity, Marionetta
and Stella share fundamental traits: they cause
tumult among men, they exercise an influence surprisingly stronger than their position in society might
suggest, and in the end they make the most important
decisions for themselves. Marionetta's power is to
act in accordance with orthodoxy, as a coquette, and
Stella's to act in opposition to it, as a freethinker,
but one motif is appropriate to both: '"<u>They alone
are subject to blind authority who have no reliance
on their own strength</u>"' (p.92). Together, the two
young women offer a forceful vindication of values
which Peacock upholds throughout his books: first,
they demonstrate the hidden and various capacities
of their sex; second, they point to the necessity
of freedom of choice in the major business of life,
that of marriage.

I have discussed the characters in <u>Nightmare
Abbey</u> in considerable detail. This is not only
because they are richer than in previous novels, and
repay a finer attention than before. It is also
because the whole book is grounded in personality,
and this had not been the case with the more ideological works which preceded it.

The organization of the novel reflects this
altered focus. There is an evolution from free-
flowing, disengaged dramatization towards carefully
judged, and often unironic, statement. A number of
the conversations are still rendered in theatrical
form, and there are superb dramatic set-pieces of
surprise and discovery, but on the whole we are more
aware of a context of story-telling and commentary
whose purpose is to offer us considered estimates of
the characters and their conduct. However, this
different direction in Peacock's writing should not

be over-stressed. Although it is more settled and definite than most of his novels, Nightmare Abbey remains characteristically Peacockian in essence. Even here the author gives us relative, not absolute perspectives, and if his position is more easily detectable than it was before, it still does not announce itself with directness.

The oppositions that lie at the heart of this book are insistently presented to the reader. It is not crudely asserted, but we are aware from the start of the novel of the battle that is being waged in Scythrop between false ideas and true feelings. Each side is keenly and lucidly defined. Contemporary literature, on the one hand, has joined with abstract philosophy and narrow intellectual obsession to produce a contagious disease which infects especially the cultivated intelligentsia and prevents it from reacting naturally to experience. Contending with this are the forces of sanity and optimism inherent in us all, even in crotcheteers, and embodied particularly in Marionetta and Mr Hilary. There is less reticence than in Headlong Hall, for the problem seems pressing, and cannot be allowed to linger in shadowy half-tones; each contest between crotcheteer and reality enlarges our impression of its prevalence and seriousness; a sense of struggle is always felt. This struggle surfaces most emphatically in the novel's scenes of comic error, but also rests implicit in almost every situation that Peacock creates. When Marionetta is teasing Scythrop, for example, there is a witty counterpoint between her superior emotional strength and command of tactics and his vacillating recourse not to experience, but to literature:

'"Let me alone," said Scythrop. Marionetta looked at him with a deprecating smile, and said, "You unjust, cross creature, you."-- "Let me alone," said Scythrop, but much less emphatically than at first, and by no means wishing to be taken at his word. Marionetta left him immediately, and returning to the harp, said, just loud enough for Scythrop to hear--"Did you ever read Dante, Mr. Listless? Scythrop is reading Dante, and is just now in Purgatory."--"And I," said the Honourable Mr. Listless, "am not reading Dante, and am just now in Paradise," bowing to Marionetta' (p.45). The neatness of this incident, and the tact which leaves its main point accessible but not laboured, are typical of Peacock's fine control of his resources in this book.

This is the first of Peacock's novels in which
plot is prominent, rather than merely providing
occasional pegs for comedy and a sketchy framework
for conversation. The story-line coherently draws
together the various elements of the book, and gains
substance from our greater sympathy for the characters with whom it is concerned. However, though
both are tales simultaneously of mystery and of moral
recognition, we should beware of thinking that Nightmare Abbey recounts Scythrop's adventures in the same
way that Northanger Abbey does Catherine Morland's.
The plot of Nightmare Abbey is better organized and
has a more rounded air, and a more satisfying conclusion, than in almost any of Peacock's other novels.
But its impetus and sense of development are not
strong. Generally, action in Peacock's fiction
moves by expansion and repetition rather than progressively. Even in Nightmare Abbey this is true.
The book would seem thin if it dealt only with
Scythrop and his paramours, and would reach its
climax, the exposure of Stella in Chapter XIII, with
too great a speed and too little emotional weight.
It needs the fresh blood of new arrivals at the Abbey
to arouse our curiosity and to retard the conclusion
of the narrative. Mr Cypress is introduced exactly
for these purposes; he is adventitious to the plot,
though not the tenor, of the novel, and appears by
chance in Chapter XI just as Mr Asterias had appeared before him in Chapter VII. Nightmare Abbey is
full of movement; the flurry first of arrivals and
then of departures ensures that we always have something brisk to hold our attention. Within the
chapters, too, Peacock offers surprise and variety,
with unexpected incidents as well as characters, and
constant changes in pace and format. This is just
as well, for although Scythrop's story is both diverting and instructive, a sense of actual changes in
his personality is hard to come by. Perhaps they
take place; they ought to take place, and we infer
that they do; but none of this is explained as it
is with Catherine Morland. Thus, without people
dropping in every now and again with engaging
suddeness, and a series of witty impasses deliberately contrived to prevent the story from reaching its
end in too disconcertingly brief a time, Nightmare
Abbey would appear almost as static as Headlong Hall.
However, the balance is skilfully judged, and the
gait jaunty enough for us to have no feeling of
stolidity; of all Peacock's books, Nightmare Abbey
is perhaps the nicest in its handling of incident and
the surest in its linking of character and action.

After Shelley read <u>Nightmare Abbey</u> he wrote to his friend: 'I know not how to praise sufficiently the lightness chastity and strength of the language of the whole. It perhaps exceeds all your works in this'[27]. As usual, Shelley's insight is exact; this is the first of Peacock's books to demonstrate a perfect command of his style and to make decisive use of its fineness and energy. This is its rare quality: it has poise, and can express minute distinctions, but it never loses vigour.

One of the most remarkable things about the language of <u>Nightmare Abbey</u> is its challenging sharpness of effect. This is principally derived from the undertones of misgiving and exhortation in the novel; the phrasing is as witty and vital as ever, but has an edge of concern. Even Mr Asterias can speak with eloquent vexation: "A gloomy brow and a tragical voice seem to have been of late the characteristics of fashionable manners: and a morbid, withering, deadly, antisocial sirocco, loaded with moral and political despair, breathes through all the groves and valleys of the modern Parnassus' (pp. 65-6). From time to time most of the characters make similar speeches in which direct condemnation of folly takes precedence over Peacock's usual obliqueness. In these cases, the author permits a kind of violence to rise to the surface of his writing, and it is hard to avoid being disturbed by its harshness; although the circumstances are qualified, their tartness remains in our minds; we are often encouraged to weightier considerations than we might expect.

Peacock's figurative language in this book is singular and thought-provoking. Images are more saliently placed and systematically used than before, and play an important role in the direction of our responses. I have already mentioned the imagery of disease which runs through the novel, giving a sense that the characters are literally infected, under attack from the twin viruses of misleading ideology and morbid fancy. A second cluster of images takes over the traditional opposition of light and dark and uses it to dramatize the conflict in which the characters are engaged. Our introduction to Flosky immediately evokes the ambience in which he looms throughout the novel: 'He called the sun an <u>ignis fatuus</u>; and exhorted all who would listen to his friendly voice ... to shelter themselves from its delusive radiance in the obscure haunt of Old Philosophy' (pp.10-11). Scythrop's darkness is more external and also more curable. His tower is a

place of shadow, and he takes his regular evening
seat contentedly 'with his back resting against the
ruined wall,--a thick canopy of ivy, with an owl in
it, over his head,--and the Sorrows of Werter in his
hand' (p.13). The darkness of Flosky and Scythrop,
which Peacock ironizes in the course of his attack
on the self-indulgent despondency of the Gothic, is
balanced by the light that flows from Marionetta.
On her first appearance she is linked with 'an April
sky' (p.20), and even when she is depressed 'her
playfulness had not so totally forsaken her, but
that it illuminated at intervals the gloom of Nightmare Abbey' (p.80). This playing off of light
against darkness has an almost poetic force; it
suggests to us that, although on one level the book
may be the comic life-history of a charming simple-
ton, on another it is the record of a struggle between life and death.

The brilliance of some of Peacock's similes in
Nightmare Abbey affects us with great intensity.
Under the influence of love, the Hon Mr Listless
seems 'to burst into sudden life, like the bud of
the evening primrose' (p.34), and when he offers to
get for Marionetta 'the very newest new book, that
every body reads' (p.40), he promises it will be
'fresh as a ripe green-gage in all the downiness of
its bloom' (p.41); Flosky talks of 'the fashionable
method of administering a mass of vice, under a thin
and unnatural covering of virtue, like a spider wrapt
in a bit of gold leaf, and administered as a wholesome pill' (p.52); for Mr Hilary, Flosky's advocacy
of mental power in modern literature is of the same
order of usefulness 'as the power of a hot-house
would be in forcing up a nettle to the size of an
elm' (p.53). These similes have an imaginative new-
ness whose authority is like that of a conceit; they
are surprising and make us think again; they raise
the emotional pitch of the prose. In general, they
impress us most by their concentrated sensuous
vividness. They are beautiful and disquieting, for
they lift us momentarily away from the life at the
Abbey and remind us of the vitality of the world
outside. These similes function in two main ways.
First, they offer mild admonitions on the harmfulness
of crotcheteering, since they establish the presence
of an attractive and health-giving realm which lies
open to the characters, but which most of them are
too blinded to enjoy. Second, they reassure the
reader of the continued existence of the delights of
Nature, and so prevent him from taking too exclusive
a view of the action: dangers may after all be

overcome, one feels, while greengages continue succulent and downy and the primrose produces its sudden
blossoms.

I have dwelt on the heightened quality of
Peacock's writing in Nightmare Abbey because this
distinguishes the novel from its predecessors and
contributes so much to the stronger grip that it has
on our feelings. Peacock has always been praised as
a stylist, and none of his works gives a finer display of the Mozartian grace and power of his prose
than does Nightmare Abbey. But the human context
that he creates in this book, and the urgency of the
problems that he deals with, raise it far beyond the
level of a mere exercise in literary craftsmanship.

The most evident of these problems has to do
with the value of modern literature and its function
in society. Peacock's concern is obvious not just in
his references to contemporary authors and parodies
of high Romantic folly but also in the more declara-
tory manner of the novel as a whole. This involves
changes in the techniques Peacock employed in his
earlier fiction, and these have already been discussed. But another significant difference is in the
use of the country-house setting. In Headlong Hall
it offered the characters freedom from constraint
and insulation from the unsympathetic standards of
everyday life. In Nightmare Abbey, however, there
are close links between the Abbey and the world outside. Characters come and go; journeys to London
are easily ventured. Nightmare Abbey is only
physically remote; its inhabitants seem well aware
of what is going on, and hold easy communication
with friends in the metropolis. Its use is less
alternative than before; it provides not so much a
pastoral retreat as a microcosm of fashionable
absurdity. Its value, therefore, is not that it is
distant and in some sense liberated, but that it
concentrates certain crucial dilemmas which were very
much at issue during this period.

Peacock's prose is always dense with phrases
from, and reminders of, other writers, and here
these seem especially pertinent. We find entire
sentences from Byron, Shelley, Coleridge and others
slipped into the text, along with ironic renderings
of some of their attitudes; we also find references
to a large, eclectic body of authors of the past,
ranging from Homer to Sheridan and including works
from the literatures of Rome, France, Spain and
Germany as well as those of Greece and England. At
times, we have the suspicion that this is cultivated

bric-à-brac, floating loose in Peacock's well-read
mind, and finding its way gratuitously onto the
pages of his book. At times, too, it is ostentat-
iously set off by inverted commas and impelled brusquely into the otherwise dextrous patterning of a
sentence. Although every tag in the novel adds colour to the bookishness of its perspective, Peacock
does lay himself open to the complaints I have just
been suggesting. However, more frequently his
allusiveness is pointed and nice. Occasionally he
plays games with the reader, as he does in all of his
works. So for Flosky, in Berkeleyan idiom, 'we may
very safely assert that the esse of happiness is
percipi. It exists as it is perceived' (p.68); and,
on the subject of love-talk, it is said that 'the
tender and volatile spirit of love often takes flight
on the pinions of some of the...winged words, which
are pressed into his service in despite of himself'
(p.84), in witty reference to the title of Horne
Tooke's best-known book(28). This is a characteristic tease, challenging the reader to solve a literary puzzle and to prove his quick wits. But many of
the other quotations have a more immediate bearing
on the themes of the novel. There is Mr Toobad, for
example, drawn to the Abbey by the report 'that a
mermaid had been seen "sleeking her soft alluring
locks" on the sea-coast of Lincolnshire' (p.57); or
Flosky, writing a ballad 'which is all mystery; it
is "such stuff as dreams are made of"' (p.76); or
Mr Hilary, remarking that 'We are most of us like
Don Quixote, to whom a windmill was a giant, and
Dulcinea a magnificent princess: all more or less
the dupes of our own imagination, though we do not
all go so far as to see ghosts, or to fancy ourselves
pipkins and teapots' (p.120). In each of these
instances some major writer of the past (respectively
Milton, Shakespeare and Cervantes) is placed in
apposition to some circumstance of the present;
usually this is oblique, though it becomes comically
straightforward in the third of the cases I have
cited. The effect is subtle. The classics, whether
of English or any other language, are not used as
bludgeons of the contemporary scene, nor are they
formally established as the models of excellence by
whose standard Peacock's own time will be judged.
Instead, past and present reflect on one another,and
encourage the reader quietly to consider the lasting
quality of Shakespeare, for example, by comparison
with the supposed ephemerality of Coleridge. Thus,
in this most originally devised work of literary
criticism, we are offered not only attacks on modern

writing which seems harmful, but also a stream of
hints as to an earlier writing which does not. As
usual, Peacock goes to great pains to subvert falsity
and instil doubt; when it comes to offering a com-
pensatory notion of the positive or the healthy, he
is more reticent. In Nightmare Abbey, we have an
exact impression of what is wrong in bad literature
but, apart from two speeches by Mr Hilary and the
inferences I have been describing, no equivalent
certainty as to what is right in good literature.
Partly, this is a matter of Peacock's constitution:
he responds more convincedly to disease than to
soundness. But partly, too, it is an index of his
fears, of his powerful conviction of the worthless-
ness of the cultural values of his age.

Peacock's primary focus is on the writing of his
contemporaries and its widespread destructive
influence. Epigraphs from Butler and Jonson set the
tone for a work which will deal with a whimsical,
self-indulgent literature cut off from its proper
roots in life. The first few pages establish, and
parody, the Gothic neurasthenia and impotence of the
Glowry household. Coleridge's 'Christabel', Kantian
metaphysics and 'the Sorrows of Werter' (p.13) are
explicitly mentioned, and the reader cannot fail to
note the Romantic and Teutonic tendencies of which
he must beware. Life and literature seem interdependent, comically and perniciously; if life goes
wrong for the habitual readers at the Abbey, then
literature must accept some of the blame. The basic
premiss of Nightmare Abbey is that the writing of the
day is derived from fancy about experience, rather
than from observation of it, and that this leads
people into unhealthy attempts to conduct their lives
as such writing dictates. Thus Peacock's aim is
therapeutic; as he expressed it in a letter to
Shelley, it is 'to bring to a sort of philosophical
focus a few of the morbidities of modern literature,
and to let in a little daylight on its atrabilarious
complexion'(29). The method is humorously to provoke
a free play of thought about the follies of the
characters as they struggle to come to terms with
the world within a narrow framework which they have
acquired only from books.

Although the scope of Nightmare Abbey is more
specifically literary than either before or after,
Peacock does not confine himself to books: his
interest is in integrity of feeling, and from novel
to novel he merely shifts the focus of his attention.
The situation here is the same as in Northanger
Abbey: Romantic excess provide the texture, and

much of the comedy, but our attention is firmly
drawn towards the moral consequences of such self-
indulgence at the same time that we laugh at its
absurdity. For both Peacock and Jane Austen, there
exists a level of complaint beyond the immediate, and
at this level each issues a warning to society of
the harmful results that follow from the usurpation
by the imagination of the position that ought to be
held by common sense. Unlike Jane Austen, Peacock
does not show us how this problem has developed,
except by his few brief comments on Scythrop's early
days; he begins in media res with the circumstance
already established and ripe for humorous expansion
and deflation. This gives an air of incident to the
book; both the general malaise, and its particular
example in the case of Scythrop, are carefully set
up for us, explored in tandem, and neatly encapsul-
ated between the image of Glowry père which begins
the novel and that of Glowry fils which ends it.
Nevertheless, even if there is not so convincing a
fullness of realization in Nightmare Abbey as in
Northanger Abbey, Peacock does share with Jane
Austen a disturbed consciousness of the social responsibilities of literature and its general implication for the way people lead their lives. In Nightmare Abbey, Peacock's moral questioning gains lucidity from the concentration of its attention and
force from the richer sense of personality through
which it is presented. Here we can have no doubts
as to the cautionary overtones of the work and the
dangers that attach to too naive an acceptance of a
literature which is founded only on dreams. As
always, Shelley grasped this at once, when he described the novel in medical terms which recognize its
remedial intent: 'Nightmare Abbey though no cure is
a palliative'(30).

I have already discussed some of the methods by
which thematic points are made, and crises provoked,
in Nightmare Abbey; as Kiely says, 'it is characteristic of Peacock to show that excesses of the mind
may be diminished, if not entirely dispelled, by
encounters with the commonplace'(31). Thus the
intemperance of much contemporary writing is heightened so that its innate foolishness becomes evident
to the reader; the conflicts that arise when such
writing is used as a model in the more humdrum
affairs of life are dramatized; and questions of
the worth and usefulness of literature are aired
both directly and by implication. Peacock's urbanity
is central; he refers everything to the standards of
a cool and modestly hopeful man of the world.

Whatever is cut off from the main stream of humanity,
and turns its back on sanity, he regards with understanding but also with disquiet. In all his novels,
it is life itself which wins, and although there are
doubts, man eventually proves himself resistant to
misguidance and celebrates his victory in the traditional heartiness of weddings and banquets.

In 'An Essay on Fashionable Literature' Peacock
comments that 'Works of mere amusement, that teach
nothing, may have an accidental and transient
success, but cannot of course have influence on their
own times, and will certainly not pass to poster-
ity'(32). Nightmare Abbey is Peacock's most amusing
book, but it also looks outwards, and presents its
carefully judged rendition of a problem which must
be heeded. It avoids triviality; it is pointed and
witty, but with the dandy's wit evoked by Ellen Moers
which 'has reference to a situation [and] triumphs
over an actual risk'(33).

The movement in Nightmare Abbey is from meretr-
icious Romanticism to a perception of man's positive
qualities. Although its comedy sometimes masks the
fact, the struggle in the novel is literally between
living and dying; it begins in a blighted garden
but ends, after numerous mishaps and false turnings,
with an optimistic bottle of Madeira. We feel that,
when Scythrop dissuades himself from suicide, the
forces of good sense have won a battle against 'the
darkness and misanthropy of modern literature'(34).
This is neither absolute nor conclusive, however.
It is a nicely turned gesture when Scythrop calls for
wine rather than a pistol; it assures us that sanity
has prevailed. But the world has not changed; Kant
and Childe Harold's Pilgrimage have not disappeared.
Although things have worked out well in this instance, nothing definitive has altered. If Scythrop
learns anything, we are left to infer what it may be;
there is no final answer presented to society on the
basis of his experiences. Instead, the dilemma and
the risk have been illuminated, quiet antidotes are
suggested, and Scythrop escapes thankfully from the
trap he has set himself. But it is with habitual
reticence that Peacock refuses to finish Nightmare
Abbey in either certainty or generality.

When the book was published, his friend Edward
DuBois wrote to Peacock to say that 'The Conclusion
of course displeased me...because it is flat, and
without that Castroneria or simplicité niaise which
would, under circumstances, have made a better wind
up'(35). This complaint seems to me mistaken as

well as presumptuous; however, Peacock did change
the ending of the novel for its republication in the
57th volume of Bentley's Standard Novels in 1837.
The revised version introduces Scythrop's final, un-
expiring call to Raven, '"Bring some Madeira"' (p.
146), and has been rightly praised for the new note
of wine-drinking cheerfulness with which it concludes
the work.

The entire latter part of the book is admirably
managed. The mass affiancing effected by Chapter
XIII is too much for most of the crotcheteers, and
they speed away from the Abbey leaving Scythrop at
the centre of our attention. Suspense builds up as,
hour after hour, Mr Glowry fails to appear with news
of a successful conquest of either Marionetta or
Stella. Scythrop's indecision is conveyed with
poignancy as well as wit: 'He watched...from ten
A.M. till Raven summoned him to dinner at five; when
he stationed Crow at the telescope, and descended to
his own funeral-feast. He left open the communicat-
ions between the tower and turret, and called aloud
at intervals to Crow,--"Crow, Crow, is any thing
coming?" Crow answered, "The wind blows, and the
wind-mills turn, but I see nothing coming;" and, at
every answer, Scythrop found the necessity of raising his spirits with a bumper' (pp.141-2). Although
this is funny, it is hard to withhold sympathy from
Scythrop's plight. But we note the prominence
freshly given to the pleasures of the table, and
sense that, after being shaken up and then left to
his own devices, he may prove less inclined to
morbidity than in the past. There is a growing
impression of Scythrop's residual attachment to
health and life: 'The next day was one of bright
sunshine: he sat on the terrace...and was not sorry,
when Raven announced dinner, to find himself alive'
(p.141). It is as if there were a conspiracy to
prevent him from killing himself. Raven offers due
Peacockian advice: '"There is a time for every thing
under the sun. You may as well dine first, and be
miserable afterwards"' (p.137). Marionetta and
Stella, with a last flourish of independent-minded-
ness and self-interest, are permanently lost to the
Hon Mr Listless and Flosky. Marionetta's new husb-
and has even helpfully assured her 'that people do
not kill themselves for love now-a-days,though it is
still the fashion to talk about it' (p.144). Mr
Glowry has a plethora of discouragements: for
example, incontrovertibly, '"there are yet maidens
in England"' (p.145), and besides '"the fatal time
is past"'. Scythrop listens meekly, and Madeira and

good sense--they are almost identical--win the day.
Thus the novel ends with life continuing and human
vitality dominant over darkness and fantasy.

Nightmare Abbey is the most accomplished of all
Peacock's books. In its overall perspectives, as in
the smallest details of its execution, it is
difficult to fault. It fuses comedy and satire in a
way that has often been attempted but rarely
achieved. It achieves a sure grip on the reader's
emotions, and, while it never ceases to be amusing,
it also vigorously explores a number of topics of
the greatest interest and importance both to Peacock
and his contemporaries and to ourselves. Artistically, I take this new power and pointedness to be a
result of the novel's richer human texture and more
compassionate view of its character's emotions and
circumstances by comparison with Peacock's previous
fiction, and the way in which it is carefully organized throughout. But beyond the brilliant success
of Nightmare Abbey as a work of art, a success which
Peacock did not equal until he wrote Gryll Grange at
the end of his life, there lies some other charm and
liveliness which seems to transcend the approving
categories I have so far employed. Speaking of the
qualities of Peacock's prose, I mentioned Mozart,
and the linkage has been often and appropriately
made; but perhaps this special virtue of Nightmare
Abbey is best expressed by Shelley, when he seeks in
A Defence of Poetry to distinguish the poetry from
the prose in literature: 'A story of particular
facts is as a mirror which obscures and distorts
that which should be beautiful: poetry is a mirror
which makes beautiful that which is distorted'(36).
There can be no doubt as to which of these
categories is the more suitable for Nightmare Abbey.

CHAPTER IV

MAID MARIAN

For the critic, especially the neat-minded critic,
Maid Marian is the most awkward of Peacock's novels.
It is different in mode from the three works which
preceded it, and offers the reader little that seems
distinctively characteristic of its author. Although
it is witty and ironic, and shares themes and attitudes with Peacock's earlier writings, its departure
from his usual manner remains striking. At first
glance, an easygoing romance like Maid Marian follows
on oddly from the intellectual vigour, the bizarrerie
and the sharpness of effect of Nightmare Abbey or
even Headlong Hall. This suggests that Peacock is
aiming for something new--a book which is less
fraught, perhaps, and more attentive to comic story-
telling than to the intricacies of polemical debate.
Such a change of direction arouses curiosity and
demands explanation, but it should not be allowed to
overwhelm our critical response to the novel itself.
Pleasing though it often is, Maid Marian represents
an excursion into a kind of fiction for which
Peacock's talents were little suited. It requires
qualities which are alien to his subtle and questioning intelligence; from the start we feel that the
form he has chosen is not quite appropriate to his
intentions. But there are reasons both in his
personal life and in the development of his writing
which go some way towards explaining why he should
have attempted something like Maid Marian.
     Headlong Hall issued energetically but rather
charily from a period of excitement and uncertainty;
Maid Marian comes from a time of consolidation. The
years of its composition--it was begun in the summer
of 1818, put aside after the autumn, and completed
in 1821--mark Peacock's establishment, and his acceptance of the pleasures and responsibilities of a
wife and a regular occupation. In January, 1819,

after an impeccable performance in examination, he
began work with the East India Company. This produced a steady income, and allowed him in 1820 to
marry a Welsh girl, Jane Gryffydh, with whom he had
last been in touch in 1812--a circumstance whose
sang-froid has astonished all later commentators, as
well it might. He still kept in touch with the
Shelleys, but was no longer subject to the stir and
iconoclasm of daily contact with them. His wife, his
friends and his distinguished colleagues at India
House provided less frantic companionship. We feel
that Peacock is settling down, and has accepted new
roles as bureaucrat and family-man that seem remote
from the rebelliousness of Melincourt. He even began
to contribute clever and well-argued articles to the
Reviews, starting brilliantly with 'The Four Ages of
Poetry' in 1820. Everything seems to point to peace
rather than turmoil, and a quieter and more composed
frame of mind than that which gave rise to most of
Peacock's earlier writing.

The novels which preceded Maid Marian built upon
the format which was first devised for Headlong Hall.
Melincourt largely followed this model, but attempted
to enrich its texture by including more narrative and
a higher charge of sentiment, and greatly enlarging
its perspectives. Nightmare Abbey marked a return to
the purity of Peacock's first book, and the accompli-
shment of its promise. The excellence of this work
has about it an air of finality; we feel that the
mode which it employs has been developed to its
highest state of organization. It therefore seems
that, by about 1818, Peacock had reached a position
of maturity, and had pushed to its limits the special
kind of fiction of which he was the originator.
These circumstances point to change: indeed, they
predicate either change or stagnation. The potential
seriousness of Peacock's problem, and the context in
which he searches for its solution, can be gauged
from the two essays in literary criticism which he
wrote at this time. The first, which dates from 1818
but remained unpublished, is 'An Essay on Fashionable
Literature'. It is a restrained, carefully worded
attack on frivolous and transient values in literature, and shows up the irresponsibility of books which
intend only to entertain. The second, 'The Four Ages
of Poetry', makes its impact by irony and éclat
rather than by cool exposition. But its bravura has
a serious purpose, and it tries, like its predecessor, to determine a proper role for the author when
the age in which he lives seems so antipathetic both
to 'the empire of thought'[1] and 'the empire of

facts'[2]. Each of these articles condemns writing
whose only aim is comfortably to pass a few hours of
leisure; equally, each points to writing which
combines pleasure with the due consideration of
matters of importance. Peacock clearly felt that his
conversation novels satisfied these criteria, and it
is plain that the form that was to follow them would
have to do the same.

The form that Peacock chooses is the romance.
Its advantages are several. It offers a world of
activity and emotional warmth which runs counter to
the stasis and high-pitched argumentation of Headlong
Hall and its peers; it implies a freer and more
optimistic view of the human condition than had
previously been possible, and permits an easier life
to the affirmative elements which no Peacock novel is
without; and it embodies, or may embody, ironies
directed against the busy emptiness of the world outside its confines. This assembly of attractions must
have seemed irresistible to Peacock. Maid Marian was
begun during a genial, indolent summer, a time of
contentment passed in the agreeable company of works
of comedy and fancy, with excursions on the river
which often lasted the whole afternoon. Peacock said
himself, 'I do not find this brilliant summer very
favourable to intellectual exertion. The mere pleasure of existence in the open air is too absorbing for
the energies of active thought'[3]. Even Peacock's
reading, of which we have a bare record in his diary,
was more lighthearted than usual. Melincourt, for
example, draws material from a wide variety of learned
sources, including the six large volumes of Lord
Monboddo's Of the Origin and Progress of Language,
whose concern with linguistic philosophy is elaborated in a fantastic display of erudition involving
the major languages of Europe, but also Chinese,
Huron and Algonkin. Behind Maid Marian lurks nothing
more demanding than old ballads (read on August 4, 12
and 13), The Merry Wives of Windsor (read on September 8), Don Quixote (read from July 13-16), and a
great deal of the leisurely mythologizing of Nonnus
and Statius[4]. Peacock also read Adam Smith's
pioneering economic analysis, The Wealth of Nations,
during this summer, and it has left its quiet mark
on Maid Marian. In addition, stories of Robin Hood
and his merry men were familiar to everyone from the
ballads, and enjoyed a revival of interest in the
Romantic period owing to the researches of the antiquarian Joseph Ritson, to whose work Peacock is much
indebted. The appeal of these tales of forest life
is demonstrated by Scott, who kept a finger on the

pulse of the time and published his own treatment of the topic as Ivanhoe, a darker, more substantial book than Peacock's, in 1819.

This evidence seems to define Maid Marian as the outcome both of Peacock's literary impasse and of his less troubled feelings about the world. Its genesis was enthusiastic; in his diary, which is remarkably spare and unemotional, Peacock talks of it with excitement: 'Could not read or write for scheming my romance. Rivers castles forests abbies monks maids kings and banditti dancing before me like a masked ball'[5]. The novel itself amply fulfils the expectations of vigorous movement, gallantry and comic animation which are aroused by these comments. But the legend of Maid Marian provides an ironist like Peacock with materials for more than just a 'comic Romance'[6]; his intention is to combine lively storytelling with 'oblique satire on all the oppressions that are done under the sun'[7]. It is here that the book's problems begin. It makes new demands in the handling of plot and the evocation of atmosphere, and Peacock seems unable to meet them. Even from the work as it stands we can see that the form of Maid Marian was deeply attractive to Peacock, and gives freedom to elements of his sensibility which have a more restricted scope in the conversation novels. But we have to wait for seven more years, until the publication of The Misfortunes of Elphin, before he learns to manage this form with ease.

Throughout the first chapter of the book, and even in the first sentence, we feel that something is amiss. Peacock usually begins his novels by setting the tone of what is to come and acclimatizing his readers to the surprises that are in store for them. But in Maid Marian the writing is so clumsy that it is hard to know how we are supposed to react. Peacock's uncertainty of voice is evident from the start in the awkwardness of his rhythms and the preciosity of his tone: '"The abbot, in his alb arrayed," stood at the altar in the abbey-chapel of Rubygill, with all his plump, sleek, rosy friars, in goodly lines disposed, to solemnise the nuptials of the beautiful Matilda Fitzwalter, daughter of the Baron of Arlingford, with the noble Robert Fitz-Ooth, Earl of Locksely and Huntingdon' (p.1). The next sentence is more assured: 'The abbey of Rubygill stood in a picturesque valley, at a little distance from the western boundary of Sherwood forest, in a spot which seemed adapted by nature to be the retreat of monastic mortification, being on the banks of a fine trout-stream, and in the midst of woodland coverts, abounding with excellent game'. The phrasing here is exact and has the ironic pointedness that we expect from Peacock. But then we descend to a jarring flatness: 'The bride, with her father and attendant maidens, entered the chapel; but the earl had not arrived. The baron was amazed, and the bridemaidens were disconcerted' (pp.1-2). After this the paragraph becomes more fragmented in manner, and even more difficult to assess. Matilda, for example, looking out for the earl, is the first to catch sight of 'the glitter of snowy plumes, and the light of polished spears' (p.2). The baron notices how 'the foaming steeds swept up to the gate like a whirlwind'. These read like chivalric clichés, but their context gives us no dependable clue as to Peacock's intention: it may be that we should see them ironically, or that we should admire their splendour--it is impossible to decide. And the paragraph ends limply, with the feeble repetition of "the organ was in full peal, and the choristers were in full voice".

Although his command seems insecure in this introductory section of Maid Marian, Peacock succeeds at least in indicating a low opinion of the clergy and a sense that this unluckily delayed marriage will be of some importance in the latter part of the book. Nevertheless, there is a striking contrast with the exposition of Headlong Hall, where the complex task of setting up the conditions that are to govern Peacock's new kind of novel is accomplished with wit and economy. In Maid Marian there is a disquieting lack of confidence. The poised rhetorical dexterity which is the mark of Peacock's writing is replaced by ungainly, often faltering effects. We are frequently rather baffled, feeling that some point is being made, but unsure as to what it may be. With most authors it would be unfair to pick out a single paragraph as I have done here, and to diagnose its flaws as indicative of a larger-scale malaise. But Peacock is usually vigilant to the highest degree: every word, every cadence is judged; there are whole books where the writing does not slip. Against such a background, Maid Marian's first chapter seems extraordinarily lax.

The roots of Peacock's dilemma lie in the alteration of mode that he attempts as between the conversation novels and Maid Marian. The achievement of his first three books is that they permit both comedy and irony, within the framework of a holiday

from everyday reality, but that they do not seem
escapist: their concerns are coherent, and their
wit anything but trivial. When one looks at these
works, and especially at the too profuse and varied
canvas of Melincourt, one infers that Peacock's need
is for a controlled and limited compass--that powerful, direct emotions will be too much for him. In
these novels his feelings are most affecting when
they are presented guardedly, through a screen of
verbal juggling put up by the crotcheteers, and in a
tone of non-committal sympathy. But Maid Marian
calls for ease and openness: it grows from a tale
with well-defined outlines and demanding vigorous
incident, sharply-etched characters and a straightforward moral point. One of the reasons why Peacock
chose this tale rather than any other is that he
responded wholeheartedly to these demands. However,
he finds the translation of material from Ritson's
Robin Hood (1795) into a book by Thomas Love Peacock
to be altogether more refractory than he supposed.
He is constrained by the expectations of his public
into providing a variety of episodes for which his
literary skills are inappropriate, and developing a
plot-line in which he has little interest. He is
forced to speak overtly of the joyful life of the
forest, the pleasures of freedom and companionship
and the sway of love. He is deprived of the
judicious safeguards which allow him balance and
authority within the nicely adjusted framework of
his earlier novels.
     There are two principal areas in which Peacock's
difficulties show themselves. The first is the conjunction of irony and romance which he is forced to
attempt throughout the work; the second is the
extent and kind of the story-telling which Maid
Marian obliges him to develop.
     For Peacock, the charm of the legends of Robin
Hood seems to have been that they provide subdued
opportunities for political comment and that they
involve a rich evocation of the delights of Old
England. The figure of Robin Hood, the noble outlaw
who robs the rich and gives to the poor, bears an
intrinsically democratic message to which Peacock
must have felt sympathetic. His companions, Friar
Tuck the renegade cleric, and Maid Marian the aristocrat freed from the burdens of her class and her sex,
are similarly tailor-made for the expression of anti-
ecclesiastical and egalitarian views. The pastoral
existence that these characters lead in Sherwood
Forest offers wide scope for admiring descriptions of
the beauties of Nature and the liberties that may be

enjoyed in the absence of the so-called rule of law.
Clearly, these elements are interdependent. But
Peacock is uneasy in his balancing of one with the
other; he cannot quite decide whether points should
be left implicit in his narrative or should be dramatized with some emphasis, as they are in the conversation novels. A number of episodes are briskly told
but are understated in thematic terms. Incidents
such as the rescue of a young girl from her rich old
bridegroom are entirely consistent with Peacock's
general purpose in Maid Marian but add nothing to its
development; they are almost self-contained short
stories, and belong in a simplified fictional world
where action is more stressed than implication. At
the same time, Peacock is unwilling to leave things
consistently at this populist level. He wishes to
adapt the material he has inherited, to give it a
subtler and more particular aim, and he does this by
obtruding ironies addressed at the follies of his
own day and by spelling out, sometimes at length,
the ideological position he intends to convey. Thus,
for part of the book we have adventures which are to
be valued largely for their excitement and energy;
but we also have more static interludes such as the
drawing up of 'the laws of their forest society'
(p.110) in Chapter XII, the object of which seems to
be to bring to the surface a group of ideas which
has already been suggested in the course of the
action. The fineness of Headlong Hall and its peers
comes from their playing off of a brilliant satirical
foreground against a background that is romantic and
celebratory but also muted. In Maid Marian, where
this arrangement is inverted, Peacock becomes nervous
as to his success in communicating what he wants to
say. Hence, the infelicitous mixture of embodiment
and explication about which I have been complaining.
     One result of this is that Peacock's irony
comes to seem random and even decorative rather than
a basic condition of the work. It is mostly directed
at the clergy, who are endlessly tagged as 'ghostly',
but there is little force to its operation. It does
not maintain the kind of tantalizing perspective
that we find in most of the other novels, even in
The Misfortunes of Elphin, and does not justify
Peacock's claim that Maid Marian was to contain
satire on 'all the oppressions that are done under
the sun'(8). The writing is sometimes so indetermin-
ate that it is hard to decide whether irony is intended or it is simply that the fastidious Peacock is
lapsing into triteness. When we read, for instance,
that 'Many moons had waxed and waned, when on the

afternoon of a lovely summer day a lusty broad-boned knight was riding through the forest of Sherwood' (p.162), we may feel uneasy as to the tone of the prose, and suspect that Peacock is poking fun at the conventional properties of the literature of gallantry, but we cannot be sure either from the sentence itself, or from its context, that we are to interpret it in this way. A greater problem is caused by the parallels that are drawn between the twelfth century and Peacock's own time. These are much less frequent than in The Misfortunes of Elphin, but their abruptness invariably damages the congruity of the passages in which they appear. Occasionally they refer to persistent foibles such as Peacock's disapproval of paper money, but they may also be of more general application: 'Some of the women screamed, but none of them fainted; for fainting was not so much the fashion in those days, when the ladies breakfasted on brawn and ale at sunrise, as in our more refined age of green tea and muffins at noon' (p.5). This comparison is witty, but it links up with no overall relation of past and present. We do not feel the England of Peacock's time looming in thought-provoking tandem with the freedom and chivalry of the mediaeval period. The impact of local ironies like these is transient and slight: the present comes off worse than the past, but we are all eager to believe in happier lives elsewhere, and Peacock is no exception. Comments of this sort seem to me, therefore, to be both ineffective from the point of view of satire, and harmful to our enjoyment of Peacock's writing. Their crassness contrasts greatly with the quiet forcefulness of his presentation of Maid Marian and of some aspects of the forest life, where he is content to suggest the differences between old and new, but not to thrust them so particularly at the reader.

It appears from his conversation novels that Peacock is largely indifferent to plotting, though individual episodes may be skilfully done and we always have the impression of variety and liveliness of movement. But Maid Marian and The Misfortunes of Elphin derive from tales of daring, not from the more immobile circumstances of a debate. Whatever his thematic interests, Peacock cannot escape the necessity of constructing stories, arranging action in a meaningful way and contriving a plot whose influence will extend over all the elements of his book. In the later novel, this is well done; in the earlier it is not. After the first few chapters, it fails to generate any real sense of cumulative

effect; we feel even more strongly than in the rest
of Peacock that chapters could easily be separated
out to form stories in their own right. The whole
of Chapter XV, for example, is virtually an independent adventure, told rapidly and well, rather in the
style of Scott, but adding little to our sense of
the book's general concerns. Incidents like these
at least have advantages of animation and incisiveness, but the mess in which they leave the novel is
considerable. Loose ends abound: the character of
Sir Ralph, suddenly become surplus to requirements,
is brusquely dismissed--'Di lui la nostra istoria
più non parla' (p.146); Friar Tuck is brought back
willy-nilly, at a late point, to sing a pleasant
song and reveal an unsuspected mistress; Sir
William of the Lee, previously unmentioned, springs
surprisingly into action on p.174 in order to
identify King Richard to the astonished foresters.
In addition, since the major figures in this book
are so much more active than their predecessors, and
spend a good deal of their time in flight or pursuit,
or in fighting, Peacock is constantly trapped into
telling us what they have been up to since their last
appearance in the narrative: they do not conveniently sit still, like the crotcheteers of Headlong
Hall and its fellows. Peacock is clearly uninteres-
ted in this aspect of his novel, and merely catalo-
gues his information in a way that is rushed and
featureless: 'Sir Ralph, on reaching the abbey,
drew his followers together, and led them to Locksley
Castle, which he found in the possession of his
lieutenant; whom he again left there with a sufficient force to hold it in safe keeping in the king's
name, and proceeded to London to report the results
of his enterprise' (p.47). Writing like this, which
is not uncommon in Maid Marian, is destitute of the
kind of satisfaction that we rightly expect from
fiction. It has the chill economy of a bureaucratic
report, and we would not be taken aback to be told
that it came from the files of Peacock's work for
the East India Company. As the book progresses,
prosaic statement of this sort becomes increasingly
the staple of Peacock's manner: moments of liveliness, such as the siege of Arlingford Castle, are set
amidst a mass of material which the author has made
little attempt to enliven or to dramatize.
    The results of Peacock's deficiencies in story-
telling are seen with particular acuteness in the
mid-section of Maid Marian and in its conclusion.
After a shaky start, the novel's exposition in
Chapters I-IV proceeds with firmness. We are

introduced to the powerful figure of Marian around
whom the book will revolve and to the three men (her
father, Robin and Sir Ralph) who are most under her
sway; a contrast is established between the freedom
and naturalness of the life of the forest and the
oppressiveness of the law; interest is shown in the
clergy, in hunting and in notions of marriage. But
the difficulty is that Peacock has no idea where to
go next: once he has set up the circumstances of
his novel, he can contrive no crisp narrative to draw
out their implications and conduct things to a conclusion. Books like Headlong Hall rely little on their
plot; their aim is instead to condition the reader
to a puzzling, dialectical world which will challenge
his expectations and startle him out of his complacency. Maid Marian, however, makes demands which
Peacock cannot meet. From Chapter V onwards, tension
is lowered and our concentration flags; no real
impetus leads us from scene to scene, individually
pleasing though these may be. The dispersal of the
characters and their various wanderings are necessary
for no aesthetic reason, but instead because Peacock
finds he must fill in the time somehow before he can
write a thankful finis to the whole unexpectedly
troublesome venture. These peregrinations we perceive to come from incompetence, therefore, and not
from design. It seems certain that Peacock himself
was aware of the difficulties he faces here. Maid
Marian is the only one of his novels which was not
written continuously; it was started in 1818 but
soon interrupted, and the last three chapters were
unceremoniously appended in 1821. These chapters
roughly and sometimes confusedly deal with topics
and relationships ushered in during the first part
of the book, but achieve neither convincingness nor
resolution. On the last page of all, congested with
material for an entire series of subsequent volumes,
we feel the true extent of Peacock's failure to
devise a story-line appropriate to his intentions for
this novel.
     In Diderot's Jacques le fataliste, with both
naiveté and sophistication, the narrator muses,'Qu'il
est facile de faire des contes!'(9). I think that
Peacock's experience in Maid Marian of attempting a
subtle joining of irony and romance, and within a
framework of chivalric enterprise, indicates the true
riskiness of such an apparently simple affair. Although he manages a shapely handling of action in
The Misfortunes of Elphin and Gryll Grange, story-
telling is not Peacock's forte, and in a book where
it is dominant he cannot fully achieve the taut

balance which is the hallmark of his art.

When we come to look at the patterning of
events in Maid Marian, we find a thoroughgoing vindication of these remarks. However, even in a work
of such uncertain development, it is possible to
discern the vague outlines of what was evidently to
be an exciting experiment for its author.
The first four chapters of the novel neatly
expound its major themes and establish both the
roles of the central characters and their relationships vis-à-vis one another. A main part of
Peacock's intention seems to be to prepare for the
entry of Marian, at this point still unregenerate as
'Matilda Fitzwalter, daughter of the Baron of
Arlingford' (p.1). Initially, she appears boldly at
her interrupted wedding to Robin; then she is
richly celebrated by the men who surround her, even
her peremptory, hot-tempered old father; when she
comes before the reader as the embodiment of a life
of vitality and naturalness, 'in a dress of forest
green, with a small quiver by her side, and a bow
and arrow in her hand' (p.33), she strikes a new
note of female strength, and is revealed as the most
important figure in the book. This introduction,
with its direction of our sympathy towards Marian
and her rightful partner, Robin, '"companions from
the cradle"' (p.23), and its sharp elaboration of
notions of outlawry, clerical hypocrisy and true
feeling, admirably sets up the circumstances to be
followed through in the remainder of the novel.
Chapter IV is invigorated by the presence of Marian
and regains the sprightly repartee of Peacock's
earlier books:
    '"Well, father," added Matilda, "I must go
    to the woods."
    "Must you?" said the baron; "I say you must
    not."
    "But I am going," said Matilda.
    "But I will have up the drawbridge," said
    the baron.
    "But I will swim the moat," said Matilda.
    "But I will secure the gates," said the
    baron.
    "But I will leap from the battlement," said
    Matilda.
    "But I will lock you in an upper chamber,"
    said the baron.
    "But I will shred the tapestry," said
    Matilda, "and let myself down."
    "But I will lock you in a turret," said the

baron, "where you shall only see light
through a loophole."
"But through that loophole," said Matilda,
"Will I take my flight, like a young eagle
from its aerie; and, father, while I go
out freely, I will return willingly: but
if once I slip out through a loop-hole----"'
(pp.37-8).

Not only is this a most effective dramatization of
the essential point of this, as of all of Peacock's
novels; it is also so wittily staged that one cannot
wonder that <u>Maid Marian</u> caught the roving theatrical
eye of the impresario J R Planché, who adapted it
into a successful opera which was played at Covent
Garden. Although Planché found the book 'too slight
to form the entire framework of a three-act
opera'[10], and included material from other sources,
the conviviality and lyricism of his work are clearly
derived from Peacock. And in fact in the first
section of the novel, with its engaging mediaeval
cast, entertaining incidents and candid manipulation
of the reader's responses, not to mention its charming songs and occasional boisterous comedy, we find
all the requirements for popular art not only in
Peacock's time but in our own as well.

It is after this exposition that <u>Maid Marian</u>'s
difficulties really begin. We sense an immediate
hiatus, partly signalled by the resurgence of
complaints about paper money ('by which one promise
to pay is satisfactorily paid with another promise
to pay, and that again with another in infinite
series', p.49), before Sir Ralph, newly assailed by
'The eyes of the fair huntress of Arlingford' (p.48),
can be trundled into adventure. Accordingly, his
search for Robin, whom he correctly perceives as his
competitor, 'brought him one evening into a beautiful sylvan valley, where he found a number of young
women weaving garlands of flowers, and singing over
their pleasant occupation' (pp.49-50). He talks to
them and is invited to the Gamwell feast, with its
Maypole 'hidden in boughs and garlands; and a
multitude of round-faced bumpkins and cherry-cheeked
lasses...dancing around it, to the quadruple melody
of Scrapesqueak, Whistlerap, Trumtwang and Muggle-
drone' (p.54). This episode reminds us that one of
Peacock's own favourite activities in old age was to
'keep up these old English customs'[11]. We think
of ballads or fairy-tales; there is a sense of
release from previous worldly tensions; one of the
girls says, '"we shall dance with flowers, and in
flowers, and on flowers, and we shall be all

flowers"' (p.51). The feast begins in sunniness and
comedy, continues with the triumph of Robin and
Marian, valued guests of the Gamwells, and concludes
satisfyingly in the discomfiture of the sheriff of
Nottingham and of Sir Ralph. What we notice here is
the contrast between the opposing groups: on the
one hand, the real comradeship that binds together
the celebrating country-folk and their friends the
foresters; on the other, the merely formal together-
ness of Sir Ralph and the upholders of established
order. This contrast is reinforced by the story of
the abbot of Doubleflask which the sheriff tells Sir
Ralph. It concerns a presumptuous abbot, expensively
entertained by the foresters, who hunts down Robin in
revenge to an old woman's cottage, in which he captures what he imagines to be the outlaw. In fact,
Robin has slipped away, and the abbot is left humil-
iatingly with 'an old woman in a green doublet and
breeches' (p.61) who rails loudly that 'she knew a
true man from a false thief, and a free forester
from a greedy abbot' (p.62). All of this is assured
and pleasingly done, and reflects on some of Peacock's principal themes in the book. Yet we respond
to it not so much as part of an evolving story but
as a story in its own right. It does not build on
what went before, and it does not lead into what
comes next: Chapter VII returns us to the domestic
buffoonery of Friar Tuck (still labouring manfully
as brother Michael of Rubygill Abbey), Marian, and
the unsuspecting baron 'cutting his way valorously
through a rampart of cold provision' (p.68).

From this point on, for another three chapters,
we are aware of a subsidence of interest and excitement. The rescue of young Gamwell is described, and
a good deal of historical material supplied. Evidently, Peacock is biding his time until another
major escapade can perhaps give a stronger, or at
any rate a different, impetus to his narrative.

The excuse for this escapade is provided by
Prince John, who visits Arlingford and is, like
everyone, 'grievously smitten by the charms of the
lovely Matilda' (p.88). He supposes that the
dignity of his royal favour will be overwhelming to
'the daughter of a simple baron' (p.89) and 'is
graciously pleased to fall into an exceeding passion'
when it is rejected. He musters his men and marches
on Arlingford Castle. The seige of Arlingford
mingles comedy with adventure, and presents us with
excellent examples of Peacock's skills in the description of action:
          'On one side, the crimson light quivered

by its own agitation on the waveless
moat, and on the bastions and buttresses
of the castle, and their shadows lay in
massy blackness on the illuminated walls:
on the other, it shone upon the woods,
streaming far within among the open trunks,
or resting on the closer foliage. The circ-
umference of darkness bounded the scene on
all sides: and in the centre raged the war;
shields, helmets and bucklers gleaming and
glittering as they rang and clashed against
each other; plumes confusedly tossing in
the crimson light, and the massy light and
shade that fell on the faces of the combat-
ants, giving additional energy to their
ferocious expression' (p.92).

This is writing of intelligence, care and distinction, at least as good as anything achieved by Scott
in his well-known account of the seige of Torquil-
stone in Ivanhoe. Surely, though, it is too consciously arranged, too composed; it has the polish
that comes from a cool exclusion of the unnecessary,
but this polish works to Peacock's disadvantage in
situations like these. The local colour of 'bastions
and buttresses' seems contrived; the alliteration of
'gleaming and glittering' is merely mechanical. Our
overall impression is of an incident which is handled
with complete competence, but which has not fired the
author's imagination. I think that this is too often
the impression that is left by the passages of combat
in Maid Marian; that they have every quality of
sufficiency, but lack the idiosyncratic freshness of
Peacock's prose at its best.

The seige of Arlingford ends with the burning
of the castle and the flight of its inhabitants into
the woods. Thus at last Marian succeeds in joining
Robin's band, which seems completed and authorized
by her presence as '"queen of the forest"' (p.103).
It is at this moment that Peacock chooses abruptly to
alter the manner of his narration, and to introduce
two chapters of static exposition. In the first of
these, the characters are pastorally renamed and the
principles of a life spent '"in the high court of
Nature"' (p.100) and of chastity are affirmed. In
the second, the constitution of the Sherwood outlaws
is tabulated by Little John, a young man is forcibly
invited to dinner, and Friar Tuck sings a jolly anti-
clerical song. The purpose of these chapters is to
elucidate the implications of Peacock's story and to
give a definitive (though sometimes ironic) statement
of its meaning. It seems to me that this purpose is

123

crude, since the main features of the leafy world
inhabited by Robin and his merry men have already
been demonstrated in action, and that what it
attempts sits uneasily with Peacock's procedures in
the rest of the book.

After this interlude of explication the novel
grows increasingly fragmentary, and it becomes
obvious that Peacock is simply waiting until some
possibility of ending things will present itself.
So he assembles a group of nicely done but obviously
time-passing brief adventures: the young man is
properly united with his betrothed, and her elderly
lover left 'rubbing his gouty foot, and uttering
doleful lamentations for the gold and jewels with
which he had so unwittingly adorned and dowered the
bride' (p.128); the baron, Robin and Marian, making
for safety, are sheltered by friendly cottagers and
vigorously fend off a last effort by Sir Ralph to
take them captive; in Chapter XVI, added by Peacock
in 1821, like the material that comes after it, Robin
and Marian, having left the baron in good hands,
conceal their true identity and trick Friar Tuck
into a fight with staves, and then discover to his
embarrassment--'"never till this moment did I see a
blushing friar"' (p.158), says Robin--that he has
been keeping a mistress, in defiance of their code.
These adventures are entertaining and give us
further, lively instances of the merits of Robin and
Marian and of the well-deserved esteem in which they
are held, especially by the oppressed and disadvant-
aged. But it is hard to feel that they give us anything new, or that they are in any way essential to
the development of Peacock's story. Instead, they
occupy an agreeable four chapters and thirty-seven
pages, flesh out the major characters, and duly
retard the very convenient return of King Richard
with which the book will end.

The concluding section of the novel is frankly
incompetent. As we are told, 'Robin and Marian
dwelt and reigned in the forest, ranging the glades
and the greenwoods from the matins of the lark to
the vespers of the nightingale, and administering
natural justice according to Robin's ideas of
rectifying the inequalities of human condition' (p.
160), and we might think this a satisfyingly idyllic
resolution of the conflicts with which the book is
concerned. But the legend of Robin Hood seems to
demand some larger sense of the restoration of
'natural justice', and this has usually been found
in the resumption by Richard of his sequestered
kingdom. Accordingly, Richard himself becomes the

last of the wandering knights to be detained, banqu-
eted and laid in fee by the foresters. This involves Peacock in awkward changes of tack which he is unable to conceal from the reader. For one thing, the
simultaneous presence of the lawful king of England,
Richard Coeur-de-Lion, and the surrogate outlaw king,
Robin Hood, obliges Peacock to fudge some of the distinctions between legal (but illegitimate) and illeg-
al (but legitimate) that he has been establishing
throughout the novel. For another, the return of
Richard brings with it the repossession by Robin of
his earldom and his inevitable adieu to the woodland
realm with which he has become so sympathetically id-
entified. There seems no solution to these difficulties, and Peacock makes little attempt to find one.
Instead, he rushes ahead--on a single page--to the
death of Richard and the usurpation of John, and a
second flight into Sherwood by Robin, Marian and
'Their old and tried adherents' (p.178). I think it
is impossible to make convincing sense of the contradictory indications which Peacock gives his readers
in this part of Maid Marian; all that one can say
with certainty is that he seems determined to end the
novel on a note of festivity and in circumstances of
'sylvan liberty' (p.178), and that he does this by
fiat rather than by the natural evolution of his
story-telling.

Although this résumé of the action of Maid Mar-
ion has emphasized deficiencies rather than excellences, it also indicates some of the advantages that
accrue to Peacock's new mode in the book. In a curious way, having moved off from the mainstream of
fiction in Headlong Hall, Peacock moves back towards
it in Maid Marian. He divests his writing of much of
its paradox, its complexity and its obliqueness, and
leaves himself with the more emotive ingredients of
romance. Peacock's conversation novels are comedies
of a taxing and intellectual kind; they make considerable demands on a reader's attention. By comparison, Maid Marian offers the less formidable delights
of a familiar, good-humoured story amply endowed with
adventure, song and situations which arouse an untroubled sympathy; it is not by chance that the only
one of Peacock's books to be adapted for popular presentation should be this one.
With few exceptions, therefore, Maid Marian provides moral certainties and accepted truths. As the
novel proceeds, we find ourselves in a position of
unexpected impregnability. There is no devious balancing of pro and contra: once we have grasped the

ironic transposition of legitimate and illegitimate
on which the book is based, we know precisely who is
good and who is not, and also what our feelings should be. Our position is determined: pleasures of identification and admiration which were denied us in
the earlier novels assume surprising prominence. From
her first appearance we know that Marian is the
book's heroine and that she is to be approved; everyone is attracted to her, and there is no irony or re-
serve about the response that she generates. In the
same way, our relationship with Robin Hood, Little
John and the others is uncomplicated: we are to like
some of them because they are 'true' and to dislike
the rest, who are 'false'.

This has immediate consequences for the social
circumstances of the novel. Its ambience is sociable
and easygoing; truths are quickly recognized, the
good are vindicated, a sense of community develops.
We feel ourselves very far from the vulnerable camaraderie of Peacock's earlier writing. There are few
problems of communication, for the characters are
participants in the same world, and have the same
general views; they are undisturbed by crotcheteering obsessions, but come together as readily as their
predecessors did in drinking canary, eating good
meals and singing cheerful songs. So, even when Mar-
ion quarrels with her father, there is a deep affini-
ty which colours their disagreement, and we are more
aware of their closeness than of their apartness.

The less anxious tenor of Peacock's writing in
Maid Marian permits a more frankly celebratory evocation of the freer existence led by the outlaws in
Sherwood Forest, and also encourages fuller characterization than we usually find in the conversation
novels.

The pastoralism of Maid Marian is cleverly double in its aim. Peacock's books always contain admiring descriptions of the beauties of Nature, and
always establish a quiet opposition between 'the
country', source of health and lucidity of vision,and
'the town', source of fashionable misguidance. In
Maid Marian Peacock presents the world of the foresters with particular emotional force, and with an
aura of approval from which there are few detract-
ions. Following on from the ballads and folk-tales
which were his basic material, he gives a warm and
lively account of Robin Hood, Maid Marian and their
followers, and of the exciting, remunerative lives
that they lead. He talks of the charm of his forest
setting, the sun shining brilliantly 'on the full

green foliage' (p.162), the deer surrendering themselves to umble pie and '"the love of the fern and the
foxglove"' (p.23) providing an instinctive affection
to bind man and woodland together. It seems plain
that he intends a major impression made by his novel
to be that of the festive delights of the outlaws in
the forest.

But a number of the radical dissatisfactions of
Peacock's own times, and voiced by his contemporaries, also loom near the surface of his writing. The
stories which Peacock is using have an intrinsic political message, and he makes the most of its sardonic
reversal of the values of an unjust society. His
Robin Hood is like other Robin Hoods in standing up
for the poor against the exactions of the rich, and
in representing the forces of decency in a world
where their growth has been unfairly curtailed. But
Peacock is eclectic: he selects the question of law
as being central to his book, and plays elaborate,
ironic games with the gap that he perceives between
the notion of the law in principle (involving desiderata of justice, even-handedness and legitimacy) and
the fact of the law in practice (involving inescapable
realities of despotism, partiality and the misapprop-
riation of authority). Thus he emphasizes the condition of strife to which the land is reduced by the
absence of its rightful ruler, and the consequent
facility with which petty tyrants betray every one of
the criteria by which the law ought to operate. Against these tyrants, who are supported at least by a
facsimile of legality, Peacock places the outlaws in
every respect their superiors: cast out from society, dispossessed, hunted, and yet living out meritor-
ious lives in terms of a natural justice in tune with
the best instincts of the people. The main figures
in this opposition are Robin and Marian, '"twin plan-
ts of the forest, and...identified with its growth"'
(p.23). They exist beyond a world of statutes and
charters, but in their superficially criminal environment, where robbery is a daily matter of course,they
still uphold the honest qualities of an authentic
process of law. This gives scope for the witty subversion of a large grouping of 'lawful' self-seekers,
and the elevation in turn of the pastoral context and
more democratic ethos of the foresters.

However, Peacock does not leave his handling of
the situation only at this agreeable level of directness and simplicity. He contrives a further pattern
of ironies which is directed not at the sheriff and
his gang, but at Robin and his merry men. This
pattern is made clear to us in Chapter XI, which is

incongruously placed but contains some of the most
intelligent writing in the whole novel. The action
centres on the re-baptism of Matilda as Marian, and
the setting out of the conditions of life in the
forest as a preparation for the mocking '"articles
of Legitimacy"' (p.110) in Chapter XII. Its core
lies in the long speech of Father Michael of Rubygill Abbey, now transformed into the familiar Friar
Tuck. What he says is carefully organized on the
basis of images of the flora and fauna of the woods,
and the naturalness of the activities of the foresters. By an elegant and thought-provoking irony,
pastoral elements are consistently given a colouring
of the outer world from which they seem a refuge.
Friar Tuck talks of their living '"in the high court
of Nature, and in the midst of her own nobility"'
(p.100); their '"goodly grove"' is described as a
'"palace"'; the songbirds are '"unhired minstrels
and musicians"'; Robin is '"king...both by dignity
of birth and by virtue of his standing army"'. The
sights and sounds of the woodlands are used for more
than merely sentimental or visual appeal in this
passage. We feel that the life of the forest is
rich and pleasing, but not devoid of harshness:
beautiful wild flowers may carpet the earth, but the
deer are there to be hunted and eaten--'"Is it not
written that the fat ribs of the herd shall be fed
upon by the mighty in the land?"' (p.101). Equally,
the figurative language reminds us that Robin's outlaw kingdom amounts in its structure only to an
extension of the kingdom he has left behind. It
forces us to recognize the sway of authority even in
the least trammelled of societies. Thus, although
life in Sherwood under Robin Hood is preferable to
the exactions of the sheriff of Nottingham, Peacock
indicates that, in the end, all rulers are brothers
under the skin. For example, Robin is compared with
William of Normandy, and it is seen that both men
fought for their claims and raised contributions by
force, and differ simply in that '"William took from
the poor and gave to the rich, and Robin takes from
the rich and gives to the poor: and therein is
Robin illegitimate; though in all else he is true
prince"'.

One element of the pastoralism of Maid Marian
which is handled with less assurance is the presentation of the book's virgin-heroine. Marian is the
most animated character in the novel, and her presence invariably brings a higher emotional level to
Peacock's prose. Our formal introduction to her in
Chapter IV immediately removes her to a different

sphere from that inhabited even by her partner,
Robin, and his band. She comes before her father,
brother Michael and Sir Ralph in a dress of forest
green, with the bow and arrows of her favourite
sport in her hand. We see her as a fresh goddess of
the forest and as the prime agent of its virtues;
everyone else seems shadowy by comparison. This is
because she alone is entirely at one with Nature, and
can therefore never be contained: 'Her black eyes
sparkled like sunbeams on a river: a clear, deep,
liquid radiance, the reflection of ethereal fire,--
tempered, not subdued, in the medium of its living
and gentle mirror' (p.33). The apotheosis of Marian
which Peacock achieves here is one of the most emotionally charged scenes in the book. I have praised
his evocation of her as an Artemis appearing lightly
for the hunt, and it is a fine piece of writing. But
a problem is caused by Marian's virginity. Of
course, this is traditional, and it would be hard to
reconcile an Artemis, a Diana, a chaste huntress,
with the notion of sexual love. Yet Marian is a
creature of the senses, spry, physical, fond of
active pursuits; sexuality seems the natural concomitant to her character. Like all of Peacock's
young women, she has little in common with the pale
waifs of much early nineteenth-century fiction. A
part of her aura is sexual: it is hard not to feel
that something like passion is the strong force that
binds her and Robin together. The novel copes with
none of this. The contradiction of imposing virginity upon a girl whose nature seems quite opposed to
it is simply left standing, and is even compounded
as the book proceeds by its growing emphasis on the
chastity which has been instituted as one of the
principles of life in the forest.

Maid Marian shows what Peacock can do in the
way of robust and effective characterization, especially when this is encouraged by traditions of popular affection. The presentation of Marian and
Robin is crucial to the book, and richly achieved.
But even minor figures are lively; a bishop, briefly
introduced, is nicely caught: '"Oh! by my fay," said
the music-loving bishop, "here comes a harper in the
nick of time, and now I care not how long they
tarry"', and then promises, '"I will fill thee with
sack; I will make thee a walking butt of sack, if
thou wilt delight my ears with thy melodies"' (p.
124).
Marian is first described in detail by Friar
Tuck, who leaves us with the impression of a

nonpareil:
  '"She is the all in all," said brother
  Michael, "gentle as a ring-dove, yet
  high-soaring as a falcon: humble below
  her deserving, yet deserving beyond the
  estimate of panegyric: an exact economist
  in all superfluity, yet a most bountiful
  dispenser in all liberality: the chief
  regulator of her household, the fairest
  pillar of her hall, and the sweetest
  blossom of her bower: having, in all
  opposite proposings, sense to understand,
  judgement to weigh, discretion to choose,
  firmness to undertake, diligence to conduct,
  perseverance to accomplish, and resolution
  to maintain. For obedience to her husband,
  that is not to be tried till she has one:
  for faith in her confessor, she has as much
  as the law prescribes: for embroidery an
  Arachne: for music a Siren: and for
  pickling and preserving, did not one of her
  jars of sugared apricots give you your last
  surfeit at Arlingford Castle?"' (pp.10-11).
Though this is rapt, it does not cloy; comedy
tempers its exaltation. Marian's sweetness is associated with strength, and is initially expressed in a
fine image drawn from Nature. From the start, we
are led to see in her the embodiment and reconcilat-
ion of all of the various, opposing elements in the
novel: she is the harmonious centre around which all
else revolves. In particular, she transcends the
barriers of sex and fully represents, for the first
time, Peacock's noble vision of the life that is
open to women once they have freed themselves from
the burdens of submissiveness and unthinking domest-
icity. So Marian pickles and embroiders and breaks
hearts, as we expect of any herione worthy the name,
but also commands, argues and fights as well as any
man--better in fact. Like Rosalind in As You Like
It, therefore, she combines the positive qualities
of both men and women: a girl quite able to fend
for herself, even against the famous skills in sword-
play of King Richard himself, but at the same time as
affectionate a partner as any knight could wish for.
It seems to me that Marian is the prime example of
Peacock's singularly modern views of womanhood. In
his other books, the main female characters are
intelligent and independent-minded; they hold themselves proud, and in all respects show themselves the
equals of their lovers. But it is only here that he
follows through the implications of these

circumstances, and deliberately sets out to create a
figure whom we must judge in its own terms and not
by reference to our normal standards of sexual appropriateness.

Although the novel is littered with instances
of Marian's beauty and of its effect on the men
around her, this is not the most striking aspect of
her character. Linked with her omnicompetence is
her genuine power of body and spirit. She is
usually dramatized in the context of the world of
Nature: everything about her indicates vigour and
activity. When we are introduced to her in person
we are told that her hair is 'curled like wandering
clusters of dark ripe grapes under the edge of her
round bonnet' (p.33) and that the plume of feathers
above this bonnet has 'an almost horizontal inclination, that seemed the habitual effect of rapid
motion against the wind'. Her gentleness is '"the
gentleness of the summer wind, which, however
lightly it wave the tuft of the pine, carries with
it the intimation of a power, that, if roused to its
extremity, could make it bend to the dust"' (p.21).
This intrinsic energy shows itself physically in
her prowess with the bow, and psychologically in the
control she can exert on even the staunchest of her
adversaries. Her father, the valiant beef-eating
baron, sadly admits to this fact: '"Matilda is my
daughter; but she has me in leading-strings, that
is the truth of it"' (p.43). One result of Marian's
all-embracing strength is that she cannot be subdued,
and that her love may be obtained as a gift but not
by compulsion--an axiom which is appreciated by Sir
Ralph and Prince John only after repeated attempts
to conquer her will.

Robin is by no means so substantial a character
as Marian. His role is a supporting one, and he is
presented with none of the emotional heightening
which gives her such prominence. We are made aware
of his rectitude and we quickly see that he stands
for a better kind of justice than the law which has
deprived him of his lands and title (and all because
of his harmless but persistent fondness for the
chase). He is the genial outlaw of tradition, and
his heart is in the right place; as Marian says, he
is '"a brave man, and a true man, and a generous man,
and a young man, and a handsome man; aye, and an
honest man too"' (p.35). We acknowledge him as someone who has broken free from an unjust system and who
lives in happy autonomy, supporting himself from the
forest's plenty and by egalitarian theft. Our introduction to him, at his brusquely curtailed wedding to

Marian, stresses his strength and free-will, but also
associates him with a love that comes from within,
and is not dependent on the social cachet conferred
by riches or suitability of family; he asks Marian
whether she has given her love to him as '"Earl of
Huntingdon"' (p.4) or as '"Robert Fitz-Ooth, the son
of his mother"': '"Neither to the earl nor his
earldom," answered Matilda firmly, "but to Robert
Fitz-Ooth and his love"' (p.5). It is Robin's
genuineness and warmth which lends force to the
ironic presentation of Robin Hood the outlaw as Robin
Hood, king of the forest. Although, as I have pointed out, Peacock undermines our acceptance of Robin's
new monarchy by linking him with more orthodox rulers
such as William of Normandy and Richard the Lionhart,
there remains an element of approval in this charade.
For, if Robin holds sway, at least he does so by
'"the free choice of his people"' (p.100) as well as
by force of arms. Thus, flawed though his position
may be, Robin rules by natural authority and not
merely by imposing himself upon his subjects.
    Of the lesser characters in the book, the most
interesting is Friar Tuck. Together with the baron,
he is Maid Marian's principal exemplar of the festive eating and drinking which Peacock always connects
with notions of a good life. His special fondness is
for canary,which he recommends as a panacea for all
ills. In addition, he is the only one of the foresters to keep a mistress, though her appearance in
the novel is both late and ghostly. Evidently, Friar
Tuck is being used to remind us of the pleasures of
the flesh and to celebrate their satisfaction; with
conspicuous irony, Peacock chooses an ecclesiastic
to point to the hypocritical supposed abstinence of
the church, which runs counter to nature and is be-
trayed with regularity (but in secrecy) by clergymen
less honest and ebullient than Friar Tuck. It is
fitting that this paragon of fleshly delights should
also be the singer of many of the good-natured songs
in the novel, since his function is to awaken from
torpor the joys which lie latent in all of us, and
to point out the folly of his clerical brethren who
conceal their love of such creature comforts 'under
the semblance of a sanctified exterior' (p.45).

    My comments on the characters of Maid Marian,
and especially on the heroine herself, have generally
concerned themselves with the freedoms these figures
enjoy, and their resistance to the impingement of
the law upon their affairs. The groundwork of the
book, as of most of Peacock's writing, derives from

the contrast he draws between man in a natural state,
which is to say, free, and man in society, which is
to say, constrained. In Maid Marian Peacock refines
upon this contrast by choosing to concentrate on the
notion of law, or regulation, as being particularly
harmful to the life of love and liberty which he
values so highly. His attack is neatly organized:
we see three aspects of the problem, all smoothly
dramatized by the Robin Hood story. First, there is
the legal system as a whole and its large-scale
corruption in practice; second, there are the roles
which the world forces upon both men and women, and
the restriction which may result; third, there is
the clergy, who provide an excellent example of virtually everything about which Peacock is most disapproving.

In this novel we often feel that Peacock is
pressing us to see his characters not in terms of
their names or titles, but as they are, individuals
whose liveliness cannot be bounded by the sharp
confines of the stereotype. Thus we sympathize with
Friar Tuck, who breaks every rule of friarly behaviour, not despite, but because of, his irregularit-
ies. In the same way Robin is labelled 'outlaw', but
in fact maintains a more honest way of life than
those who have expelled him from society. The best
example of all is Marian, whom Peacock presents as a
figure who has not allowed herself to be governed by
limited notions of the qualities that are appropriate
to womanhood. We see her as a girl who has escaped
constraint, and can therefore reveal the unexpected
extent of her capacities. But it is not merely the
established associations of a word like 'woman' that
Peacock is questioning in Maid Marian; a whole range
of titles is similarly scrutinized. We come to see
even a word like 'father', much less 'baron' or
'earl', as a designation which places the person to
whom it is applied and consequently restricts his or
her proper freedom of action. Robin was an aristocrat in name when he lived as Earl of Huntingdon;
but he is a truer aristocrat as plain Robin Hood, the
outlaw of Sherwood Forest. We are also made aware of
the dangers of a sort of caricature, as when the
baron, a rather thin figure as he blusters about
emphatically being a'father'--which involves locking
his daughter up--becomes more sympathetic as he and
Marian develop into companions instead of playing
the roles of bully and (unsuccessfully) bullied. The
clearest and most moving exposition of this theme
occurs in Chapter XI, when the foresters cast off
the names which were imposed upon them in the

outside world, and elect instead to define themselves
in terms more suitable to their real condition: '"May
I never again have roof but the blue sky, nor canopy
but the green leaves, nor barrier but the forest-
bounds"' (p.104), says Marian, '"I am no longer lady
Matilda Fitzwater, of Arlingford Castle, but plain
Maid Marian, of Sherwood Forest"' (pp.104-5).

Just as choice is approvingly opposed to coerc-
ion in Maid Marian, so the secular is approvingly
opposed to the ecclesiastical. Except in so far as
they are human beings, Peacock in his earlier books
has no time for men of the church as such: he may
regard Dr Gaster, for example, with a tolerant eye,
but it is as a bon viveur, not as a clergyman. In
general, in this novel, monks, friars and abbots are
shown as greedy hypocrites who are either in league
with the authorities or, in the case of the bishop of
Nottingham, actually are the authorities themselves.
Their lives are spent in avid eating and drinking
which they have to conceal from those around them,
since it is not in accordance with their vows, and in
imposing unnatural ordinances upon others. There is
irony in the adjective 'ghostly' which is--too often
--applied to them: they are both spiritual in the
sense that we expect, and yet not genuinely so, and
also immaterial, having no substance or human force.
The contrast between the parasitism and self-seeking
of a clerical life, and above all its hypocrisy, and
the moral resolve, honesty and practical helpfulness
of the foresters needs no further discussion. But
the point is especially well made in Maid Marian by
the use of Friar Tuck, the jester and good fellow who
upsets preconceptions even of the chastity of the
clergy, and comically demonstrates the triumph of
humanity and its needs over the limitations of a set
role: only in Rabelais do we meet other friars who
are so little friarly and who please us so much.

Friar Tuck's well-hidden inamorata is provided
by the irreligious Peacock in order to remind us of
the power of love, as well as that of canary and
venison, in our lives. From the first chapter,
where wordly considerations prevent Robin's marriage
to Marian, but not their declaration of the affection that unites them, love is felt as a potent force
which is antipathetic to petty social regulation.
Peacock several times attacks arranged matches which
have nothing to do with personal preference and take
place only for financial advantage. Our impression,
which we have throughout Peacock's work, is that a
love which is freely given can provide the deepest
satisfaction of which man is capable. Despite the

awkward emphasis on Robin's cult of the Virgin Mary
and the chastity of Maid Marian, there is nothing
abstract or merely spiritual about the way love is
presented in this book; it has a vigorous human
dimension which adds warmth in particular to the
characters of Robin and Marian.

The relationship between this ideal of love and
the larger themes of the novel, especially its
rejection of authority imposed from outside, is
evident; indeed, it is a relationship which runs
throughout Peacock's fiction and provides one of its
strongest positive elements. Almost every incident
in Maid Marian in some way dramatizes Peacock's
disapproval of established and peremptory power and
preference for the happiness which a release from
external impositions can produce. The correlative of
this is a profound disquiet at the way in which
societies are organized, and an enduring suspicion
as to the implications of the word 'civilization'.
Peacock's sympathies lie all on the side of a radic-
alism which is drawn almost towards anarchy, and
which sees hope more in the festive pleasures of the
individual or small group than in the possibility of
some larger-scale regeneration of the world. He
goes out of his way here not only to indicate the sad
continuity of dominion as between Robin and his
brother potentates, but also to forbid the reader
any too easy acclamation of the mediaeval past at the
expense of a gloomier present--slyly, he introduces
deliberate anachronisms (the canary drunk by Friar
Tuck, the cavaliers supposedly active on the field of
Hastings) which force us to perceive the tales of
Robin Hood for what they are: genial legend and not
authentic history. Equally, the bitter wit of his
definition of the social order ('the preservation of
the privileges of the few who happened to have any,
at the expense of the swinish multitude who happened
to have none, except that of working and being shot
at for the benefit of their betters', p.84), though
applied immediately to 'our more enlightened times',
certainly applies with the same force to most of the
circumstances he is depicting in Maid Marian.

These sceptical notions are given liveliness for
the reader in Peacock's portrayal of the law and its
support as the villains and of Robin, the so-called
outlaw, as the hero. At the beginning of the novel,
Sir Ralph neatly expounds this paradox, which is
then cleverly elaborated in successive episodes.
Robin, he says, has acted foolishly in continuing
with his hunting '"in defiance of all authority"'
(p.8) and '"in denial of all law"', '"and has thus

made himself the declared enemy of church and state,
and all for being too fond of venison"'. With the
greatest pointedness, this connects church and state
as twin pillars of established power, and indicates
their modus operandi as the legal system. At once
we perceive Peacock's main complaint about this
situation: that if the law is in the hands of a
small group rather than of the people as a whole, it
cannot be other than partial and unfair in its
effects. Set against the corruptness of this authority is the individualism and integrity of Robin,
symbolized in his dedication to the chase. In Maid
Marian, hunting seems more than merely an appropriate
activity for the foresters, supplying them with sport
as well as food; it also represents the traditional
rights and healthy pursuits of native woodlanders,
here greedily curtailed by the demands of '"the
king's mandates"' (idem). Peacock's playing off of
these opposing factions informs most of the action
of the book, with more or less proficiency, and
reaches its apogee in the sustained parody of the
notions of 'laws' and of legitimacy in Chapter XII.
There are three primary elements to Little John's
'stentorophonic' (p.110) enumeration of the principles of the forest society in this chapter. Firstly,
in brisk inversion of the edicts which govern most
kingdoms, the precepts which regulate the woodland
realm of Robin and Marian amount to the granting of
free-will to all; their purpose, as Little John
unashamedly says, is '"To keep what we have, and to
catch what we can"' (p.111). Their laws, therefore,
acknowledge the true basis of self-interest on which
societies are organized, and make a mockery of the
pretentious articles of legitimacy by which this
fact is usually screened from view. Peacock's
attack is directed here against both the free-booting
impulses that underlie most behaviour (in Robin's
world as much as in Prince John's) and the hypocrisy
which seeks to cover this up by a tangle of laws
apparently promising justice to all. Secondly, it
builds upon the sardonic parallel which Friar Tuck
establishes in Chapter XI between 'king' Robin and
all other kings, and follows this though in further
qualification of the superiority and separateness of
life in Sherwood. But, thirdly, it maintains a fine
balance in its illumination of the positive and
negative aspects of Robin's forest community. Perhaps the forms of this community do indeed mimic
those of the tyrannical régimes to which it seems an
alternative, but with this difference--that the
'"forest law"' (p.107), in spite of its deficiencies,

remains closer to '"the law of nature"' (p.126) than
that which operates beyond the limits of Sherwood.
So in the end, in this chapter as in the novel as a
whole, our impression of Robin and his merry men is
coloured by doubt but remains celebratory rather
than disapproving. Peacock is too intelligent to
believe in never-never lands of perfect freedom and
ease, but in Maid Marian he gives us a forest world
which unites many of the qualities he liked with few
of those he disliked.

This aspect of the book is handled with firmness
and conviction, but its conclusion, in the return of
Richard to his rightful position, goes badly awry. I
have already discussed this matter, and would like
only to reaffirm the problem here. The use of
Richard is little prepared for, and sits uneasily
with the careful discriminations which I have just
been interpreting; I think it is called forth by our
expectations of the Robin Hood legend, and not by the
particular needs of Peacock's story. I also think
that it leaves the reader with an unfortunate sense
of Peacock's clumsiness, not borne out by his handling of other incidents in the course of the novel.

Maid Marian is a work about which most readers
have had reservations, and I have pointed out the
good reasons why this should be so. It uses a form
which is intrinsically difficult of realization and
in which Peacock shows himself far from comfortable.
His grasp of this form greatly improves in The Misfortunes of Elphin, but in Maid Marian he proves
harmfully indecisive in his organization of the
romance and satirical sides of his story. In addition, he is forced into a kind of plotting for which
he has little talent and in which he can arouse
little interest. Against these flaws, of course,
one can set compensations. Madden exaggerates when
he talks of the book's 'immense gaiety'(12), but it
is often pleasing; it gives moving substance to the
pastoral undertones of Peacock's previous novels; it
has a wealth of agreeable characterizations which
are nicely accommodated to its thematic concerns; it
includes many entertaining and thought-provoking
episodes of a more popular, accessible sort than before. But in the end I think it is hard to avoid a
sense of failure in Maid Marian, a feeling that it
is a book in which a considerable artist, whose
skills and intelligence are frequently evident, is
trying his hand at a form for which he was temperamentally unsuited and in which it is impossible for
his intentions to be fully achieved in practice.

CHAPTER V

THE MISFORTUNES OF ELPHIN

The second of Peacock's mediaeval romances, The Misfortunes of Elphin, has always been more popular than his first. Some early approval has an obvious parti pris--'the author has succeeded in rendering these valuable records of antiquity highly acceptable, not only to natives of the principality, but to the public in general'[1]--but is confirmed by the favourable notices which appeared in other periodicals. The Literary Gazette sums up the praise which the novel received on its publication by describing it wholeheartedly as 'one of the most amusing volumes which we have perused for a long, long time'[2]. Although The Misfortunes of Elphin is different from the books for which Peacock is best known and which we find indicative of his qualities as a writer, its appeal has not faded. The fineness of its prose moved even the reticent editors of Peacock's works to praise the 'perfection of dry restraint'[3] which they considered it to attain, and when he was translating two of Peacock's novels into French it was The Misfortunes of Elphin that Jean-Jacques Mayoux chose to complement his other, more evident choice of Nightmare Abbey. From the start, the book's decisiveness and concentration have been admired, and it also has a much fuller sense of romance than before: the Westminster Review remarks perceptively that, 'Absolutely speaking, it is neither romance nor satire, although apparently professing to be the one, and being really deeply imbued with the spirit of the other'[4]. In fact, The Misfortunes of Elphin is suffused by richer emotions than any of Peacock's previous works, and very skilfully manages the difficult celebration of these emotions against a background of both immediate and longer-term political ironies.
     This is a far cry from the dissatisfaction that

has been felt with Maid Marian. But the circumstances of Peacock's life do not appear to have altered
very much between 1822 and 1829, and if the form of
the novels is alike, one may reasonably ask why The
Misfortunes of Elphin should succeed whereas Maid
Marian does not. It is partly that the earlier book
was precipitate, and counted on a greater degree of
adroitness than Peacock could sustain. It is also
that Peacock's organization of his materials has
changed. Maid Marian is insecure in its balancing
of romantic and satirical elements; in The Misfortunes of Elphin, pastoral and legendary qualities
whose power is dissipated in its companion cast a
unifying light over the major concerns of the novel.
   Peacock's working towards some effective means
of manifesting the troubled vein of romantic sentiment which runs through his works was compelling.
The years which separate Maid Marian from The Misfortunes of Elphin are a measure of the strength of
this impulse. Much more than before, these were
years of security and domestication and of growing
success in business. Peacock's agreeable house at
Lower Halliford, to which he moved in 1822, provided
him with a rural retreat outside the bustle of
London, a place of refuge from whose safety a less
harassed view of the world might be possible. His
family life at this time seems to have been contented: the household was quite well off, he had the
support of his mother, his wife proved sympathetic,
and four children were born. It is hard not to feel
that Jane Gryffydh gave impetus to Peacock's presentation of the vigour and Celtic beauty of Angharad
and her daughter Melanghel in The Misfortunes of
Elphin, or that his pleasure in her company contributed to the novel's affirmation of the joys of love.
The only personal cloud upon the couple's happiness
was the sudden death in 1826 of their daughter
Margaret, then not quite three years old, which
pained Peacock deeply and sowed the seeds of his
wife's invalidism. However, she was still able to
encourage his interest in Welsh antiquities and to
teach him the language, thus giving a basis of
scholarly understanding to his taste for the gnomic
boldness of old Welsh literature. Peacock's life
must have been rounded and full: weekdays were spent
at India House, among some of the best minds of his
period, weekends in relaxed enjoyment of family concerns and country matters at Lower Halliford.
Address and energy characterize the works which he
produced between Maid Marian and The Misfortunes of
Elphin. There were trenchant articles contributed

to the Reviews, especially a well-known assault on Moore's The Epicurean, and sharp satirical poems written in 1825-6 but not published, in the form of Paper Money Lyrics, until much later. Even for a writer as wayward and eclectic as Peacock, however, they amount to a meagre production for such a long period. Above all, they are not of a highly imaginative kind. Of course, Peacock was certainly busy: his advancement in the East India Company was rapid, and there was a consequent increase in his responsibilities. He was also devoted to his children, and we can assume that a good part of his free time would be spent with them, or in relishing the society of his wife and mother. In addition, he was executor of Shelley's estate, and after the poet's death in 1822 devoted much effort to the unravelling of his complicated affairs. But these occupations still do not quite account for the gap between the first and second of Peacock's mediaeval books. It seems to me that a principal explanation for this gap is simply that Peacock needed a breathing-space: there is much in Maid Marian which is better handled in the later novel. I think that the years between 1822 and 1829 were a period of moral and emotional growth for Peacock, a period during which he acquired, perhaps mainly from his own experience, a less impeded relationship with romantic joys than had been possible in his early works.

So, in this fifth novel, Peacock maturely takes stock of the links in his writing between satire and romance. In previous books, except for Maid Marian, criticism had predominated; The Misfortunes of Elphin is an attempt to moderate this criticism and to bring nearer the surface the optimism which underlies its disquiet.

In Maid Marian there is an awkwardness which Peacock seems incapable of resolving; in the Misfortunes of Elphin everything has an air of precise articulation. The description of the Great Plain of Gwaelod and its privileged port of Gwythno at once guarantees us a sharp and quizzical perspective:

'This port, we may believe if we please, had not been unknown to the Phoenicians and Carthaginians, when they visited the island for metal, accommodating the inhabitants, in return, with luxuries which they would not otherwise have dreamed of, and which they could very well have done without; of course, in arranging the exchange of what they denominated equivalents,

imposing on their simplicity, and taking
advantage of their ignorance, according
to the approved practice of civilised
nations; which they called imparting
the blessings of Phoenician and Carth-
aginian light' (p.2).

On the one hand, this first chapter seems to offer
us a straightforward enumeration of the circumstances of the story: we are efficiently informed as
to its setting and period, and are given a glimpse
of King Gwythno and his amenable subjects. But on
the other hand, the tone of the writing cautions us
cooly against acquiescence. We are reminded by
Peacock that 'we may believe if we please', and it
is with subtle sleight of hand that the first paragraph moves from its lulling introduction ('In the
beginning of the sixth century, when Uther Pendragon
...', p.[1]) to the jokey surmise of its conclusion
('imparting the blessings of Phoenician and Carthag-
inian light', p.2). This is Peacock's usual, clever
procedure. Plain exposition, preferably supported
by historical or literary reference, prepares the
reader for a narrative which will have no ulterior
design on his feelings. In practice, what follows
cunningly mingles fact with fiction, observation
with cynical interpretation. The reader is left
anything but easy; his expectations are constantly,
if amusingly, undermined; Peacock's ironic independence of mind is everywhere evident. It is a game
he cannot resist, this almost imperceptible swaying
from statement to supposition, and it is with deliberate teasingness that he draws along his polite
and innocent readers, at first unaware that they are
being fooled.

This undertone of testing is essential to the
success of Peacock's best work. The writing is keen
and bright; each sentence impresses one with its
economy and exactitude. Gwythno, for example, warned
to 'beware of the oppression of Gwenhidwy' (p.4;5),
settles in a palace built just where the river
Mawddach enters the fertile plain of Gwaelod. 'Here,
among green woods and sparkling waters, he lived in
festal munificence, and expended his revenue in
encouraging agriculture, by consuming a large quantity of produce'. This has wit, and the sprightli-
ness which set an unmistakable mark on Peacock's
most accomplished prose. It is a matter of clarity
of shape and neat rhetorical pointing. The details
are pared down and firmly marshalled, and there is
no slackness in the relationship of parts: the
punctuation silhouettes each unit of sense, while

the expectant rhythm ensures a measured flow of meaning. Yet the intellectual control, the appearance of
order, frequently resolve themselves into laughter.
As in the conversation novels, we detect a stealthy
impulse to poke fun at the act of writing itself as
well as at the hypocrisies of circumstance: in this
book, too, Peacock's scepticism and wariness extend
to his own art as much as to the folly that is its
subject.

It would be wrong to give gloomy weight to this
complexity of tone: above all, Peacock is a comic
writer, and in The Misfortunes of Elphin it is good
humour which is paramount. Our primary response is
to the vigour of Peacock's story-telling, the romantic charm of his settings and characters and the
sophisticated wit of his manner; by and large,
shadowy undertones remain exactly that. Peacock's
irony is a question of discrimination rather than of
denunciation: it brings out the true motives which
lurk beneath conventional behaviour. So Teithrin ap
Tathral, the book's single conscientious official,
and Elphin, while visiting Seithenyn to warn him of
the consequences of his neglect of the embankment,
'found his highness, and his highness's household,
convincing themselves and each other with wine and
wassail, of the excellence of their system of virtual
superintendence' (p.10). This is funny, and places
the situation crisply before us, but implies no
bitter condemnation. The comedy of illogic, which
appears at its best in the interview between Teithrin, Elphin and Seithenyn, has a similar blend of
acuity, tolerance and high spirits. The concerned
visitors complain that the embankment has become
rotten, but Seithenyn simply draws a smokescreen of
rhetoric over the problem: '"But I say, the parts
that are rotten give elasticity to those that are
sound: they give them elasticity, elasticity, elasticity"' (p.16). The verve and inventiveness of
Seithenyn's speeches do not conceal the insecure
foundations of their argument, but Peacock's purpose
is not only to reprove. As Kiely says, 'there is
little sense of moral outrage or despair'(6). We
are amused by the verbal acrobatics, our delight in
the characters is confirmed, we perceive exactly how
things stand; but we are left with no crudely moral-
istic residue. Peacock's trust in the basic sturd-
iness of human nature is amply sufficient in The
Misfortunes of Elphin to provide a remedy for uncertainties which, in the twentieth literature, have
given rise to a whole literature of perplexity. In

some of Peacock's early novels the hopefulness is
fragile, and his poetry is clouded by threats of
mutability and necessitarianism. This book is fairy-
tale, however: its form encourages cheerfulness.
Seithenyn is the novel's presiding genius, and best
expresses its mood in his hearty injunction: '"But
all is one. Cupbearer, fill"' (p.17). Thus,
although Peacock perceives the folly of most of man's
efforts, and acknowledges the resultant collapse of
many of the orthodoxies and most of the institutions
by which his life is buttressed, we have no sense of
desolation. Instead, in The Misfortunes of Elphin,
there is a romantic liberation, an advance towards
joys which may provide much-needed assistance as one
faces up to the busy nothingness of an existence in
the big world.

   There is no attempt to persuade the reader that
he is enjoying anything other than an agreeable, but
not unmoving or irrelevant, fiction. The Misfortunes
of Elphin is a work of deliberate artifice, and has
only tenuous links with actuality. The virtues that
it praises are universal,as one expects from a romance, and are not immediately related to a particular
era. The special relevance of the book to the England of 1829 is either slight or oblique. The satirical asides on Peacock's own period are intermittent
and often poorly handled; the wider political dimension of the work is rich and considered, and though
it grows from the context of the late 1820's its
recommendations are of the most general kind. The
same is true of the elements which Peacock opposes
to the absurdities of the beau monde: they are
assuredly not to be found in the drawing-rooms of
London's official classes or even in the suburban
placidity of Lower Halliford; despite the fact that
they exist potentially in everyone, they can blossom
fully only in the sunny easiness of some Old England
or Old Wales of the imagination. The novel turns
away from the intimate local reference of most of its
predecessors, and chooses instead to elaborate a
number of their broader concerns within the quiet
context of an idyll. As in the best pastoral, this
is not a mere avoidance of difficulties: conflict
is as significant as celebration. After the bursting
of the embankment and the great flood, life does not
instantly become perfect at Elphin's salmon-weir on
the Mawddach; there are adventures and trials to be
undergone before culmination, in the marriage of
Taliesin and Melanghel, will be possible. The book is
therefore less anxious, but not bland; it mingles
seriousness with play in a manner which is uniquely

Peacock's.

The Misfortunes of Elphin, with its stories
from Welsh antiquity and the times of King Arthur
and his knights, offers Peacock great leeway for
freeing himself from the pessimism which close engagement with the follies of his own day usually induced in him. As a corollary, more positive emotion
may be given its head. There is a faith in fundamental human goodness, above all when this is liberated from the constraint imposed by society and
established authority. Love is viewed with powerful
approval, and is seen as the central source of satisfaction in a good life. Landscape, particularly
the splendid valleys and mountains of Wales, is
enjoyed as something natural and invigorating, and
fortunately beyond the reach of civilization. In
addition, as in all of Peacock's writing, a deep
comfort is derived from the pleasures of the flesh:
from boisterous eating and drinking, and the songs
which often accompany them.

The most telling outlets for romantic sentiment
in the novel are the songs. There are more of them
in this book, fourteen in all, variously original to
the poet, or translated or adapted from the Welsh,
and their function is more important than before.
The range is considerable, from the rhapsody of the
bard's 'The Song of the Four Winds', based on the
Englynion of Llwyarch Hên, through the reflective
intimacy of 'The Consolation of Elphin' to the high
comedy and rhythmic insouciance of 'The War Song of
Dinas Vawr':

'The mountain sheep are sweeter,
But the valley sheep are fatter;
We therefore deemed it meeter
To carry off the latter' (p.89).

This is the best song in Peacock, and highlights the
attractive swing and confidence of the verse in his
novels. But the songs and poems are rarely only
decorative: they contribute largely to the local
colour of the book, and from time to time also take
on dramatic or thematic pointedness. Their Welshness
is central, particularly in the poetry and strangeness they derive from their models in ancient Celtic
verse:

'The summer night was still and bright,
The summer moon was large and clear,
The frail bark, on the springtide's height,
Was floated into Elphin's weir.
The baby in his arms he raised:
His lovely spouse stood by, and gazed,
And, blessing it with gentle vow,

Cried "TALIESIN!" "Radiant brow!"' (p.143).
They sometimes attain a note of genuine passion or
of the heroic:
    'Close the portals; pile the hearth;
    Strike the harp; the feast pursue;
    Brim the horns: fire, music, mirth,
    Mead and love, are winter's due.
    Spring to purple conflict calls
    Swords that shine on winter's walls' (p.136).
These feelings are better suited to poetry than to
prose. In the main body of The Misfortunes of
Elphin there is always the threat of a sardonic
smile, but their poetic form insulates the songs
from their prose context and safeguards them from
the witty questioning which otherwise conditions
almost every aspect of the book.

However, it must be plain from some of the
songs I have quoted that while their use in the
novel is well considered, one may have doubts as to
their merits as poetry. The epigraph to the first
chapter is from Gray's 'The Bard', which is a work
of real sublimity and emotional power. But Peacock
writes too often in a style of mannerly loftiness
which is characteristic of the lesser poetic lights
of his period. His taste for argumentative antithesis and an orderly arrangement of effects can
have disastrous results on verse which intends to
convey a sense of the grandeur and richness of the
past and of far-off places:
    'Gloyad, nymph with tresses bright,
    Teeth of pearl, and eyes of light,
    Guards these gifts of Ceidio's son,
    Gwendol, the lamented one,
    Him, whose keen-edged sword no more
    Flashes 'mid the battles roar' (p.137).
Nevertheless, their content often saves Peacock's
songs from falling prey to the prim discipline of
his poetic sensibility: their fascinated evocation
of Welsh history and landscape seems able to compensate even for quite glaring errors of taste.

One of the aims in which The Misfortunes of
Elphin best succeeds is in deriving capital from the
curiosity and charm of remote times and settings.
With some irony, and a cool awareness of the folly
of taking simple views of any circumstance, Peacock
is clearly part of the mediaeval revival of his
period. So in this book attractiveness clings to
every element of Welsh life: the passion of its
ancient poetry, the beauty of its women, the soundness of its civilization, the allure of its legends;
above all, the majesty of its scenery: 'Around,

before, and above [Angharad and Taliesin], rose
mountain beyond mountain, soaring above the leafless
forests, to lose their heads in mist; beneath them
lay the silent river; and along the opening of its
narrow valley, they looked to the not-distant sea'
(p.71). Although the point is not explicitly made,
Wales seems valued not only for itself but also because it is the antithesis of the fasionable triviality of the modern world. The reminders of its
particular culture are omnipresent: most of the
chapters begin with quotations from the triads, and
references to Welsh lore are dense in the body of
the writing. There is a notable satisfaction in re-
counting Welsh stories and quoting from famous Welsh
poems; at times, Peacock the pedant makes his appearance, surprising us with the fruits of his researches: '"The sigh of Gwythno Garanhir when the
breakers ploughed up his land" is the substance of a
proverbial distich, which may still be heard on the
coast of Merioneth and Cardigan, to express the
sense of an overwhelming calamity' (p.42).
     Another area of powerful feeling in the book,
though it is the opposite of sunny, arises from
notions of collapse and destruction. Especially
during the storm, the breaching of the embankment
and the flooding of the plain of Gwaelod, we could
almost imagine ourselves to be back in the menaced
world of Peacock's early poetry. In this part of
the novel he writes engrossedly about scenes of
catastrophe to which there are no parallels in his
other books. Nothing is allowed to distract our
attention from the force of the wind, the collapse
of Seithenyn's castle before the buffetings of the
waves, the irresistible violence of the water as it
pours over a peaceful, fertile land. It is an episode of apocalypse, and reminds us more of the
Romantic poets than of the witty sphere which Peacock's writing normally occupies:
     'There was another pause of deep silence.
     The noise of the sea was louder, and the
     gusts pealed like thunder through the
     apertures. Amidst the fallen and sleeping
     revellers, the confused and littered hall,
     the low and wavering torches, Angharad,
     lovely always, shone with single and sur-
     passing loveliness. The gust died away
     in murmurs, and swelled again into thunder,
     and died away in murmurs again; and, as it
     died away, mixed with the murmurs of the
     ocean, a voice, that seemed one of the many
     voices of the wind, pronounced the ominous

words, "Beware of the oppression of
Gwenhidwy"' (p.23).
I think one may detect a slight irony in the ghostly
warning which concludes this paragraph, but for me
these few sentences reach a kind of elevation which
is deeply felt and true. They give us circumstances
of calamity, vigorously imagined, and presented with
a directness which seems intended only to intensify
their effect. There is something buried in Peacock
which, at a time of revolution such as this is, links
him with his contemporaries in their response to
disaster. The point of the introductory section of
the book is to indicate the dangers of Seithenyn's
genial but negligent conservatism, which leads inescapably to the extinction of his world and of the
values it embodied. This we might reasonably expect
from a radical like Peacock, convinced of the political corruption of his period. But what we might not
expect is the zest of the prose: Peacock appears to
revel in the prospect of things being swept away, of
the end of an old era and the healthier beginnings
of a new one. Nowhere else in his works do we have
such a sense of his longing for change, for life to
be easier and more fulfilling than was possible within the embrace of the society of his day.

But for Peacock there is usually a limitation to
moments such as these. He certainly permits an open
expression of alternatives to the ills he sees around
him, and more rarely may also speak frankly to some
appealing notion or other. However, except in Gryll
Grange, this is sporadic. Momentarily it is indulged, and then irony intrudes; there are repeated
movements down from a high pitch of sentiment. One
paragraph which well exemplifies this movement
starts with: 'A long pause of deep silence ensued,
during which [Teithrin, Elphin and Angharad] heard
the intermitting peals of the wind, and the increasing sound of the rising sea, swelling progressively
into wilder and more menacing tumult, till, with one
terrific impulse, the whole violence of the equinoc-
tial tempest seemed to burst upon the shore' (p.25),
continues with a comparison between the destructive-
ness which is shared by great storms and great
heroes, and ends in the feeble comedy of the bard
incongruously transported by awen[7] and joining his
song with 'the uproar of the elements'. This seems
partly a matter of deliberation, and partly a result
of the author's temperament. Peacock's intention in
The Misfortunes of Elphin is to mingle romance and
irony, and to give the first of these a greater
influence than it enjoys in his previous novels.

This calls for a difficult accommodation of contary
impulses, and there are times when the quality of
Peacock's expression seems incompatible with the
demands of the situation. For instance, when the
tower of her father's castle falls, Angharad is one
of the first at risk, and amidst an exciting scene
of ruin and shrieking the wind rushes in and tosses
her 'light white drapery and long black tresses'
(p.27). This paralleling of adjectives and crude
alliteration does not consciously aim at bathos, if
we are to judge from the context and from the attitude towards Angharad throughout the novel; rather,
it is a failure of tact. A case like this alerts us
to the restricted range of Peacock's sensibility.
The obverse of his brilliance and command is prosai-
cness of imagination. Sometimes, in the fastidious
amalgamation of disparate ingredients which is required by The Misfortunes of Elphin, we note the
successful fusion of political satire with a framework of romance. This is especially true in the
evocation of Elphin's pastoral idyll after the flood.
But sometimes we also note that Peacock's sureness
may desert him when his concern is to do justice to
some grand moment which calls for commitment rather
than for scepticism. Timothy Webb has a point when
he writes that, for Peacock, 'a slightly tipsy house
party constituted the Bacchic; the real savagery,
the wildness, and the emotional excesses of the
Dionysiac were excluded from the comfortable
precincts of his sensibility'[8].

Evidently, it is possible to have feelings
which are deep but not Dionysiac. Nevertheless, it
seems to me that the problem Peacock has set himself
in The Misfortunes of Elphin is a formidable one.
He wishes to combine overall ironies directed at the
governance of states and particular, local ironies
referring to his own time, with celebration of a
life of unpoliticized retirement. The first of
these is strikingly well done; the second is crass;
the third has its weaknesses, but offers a richer
texture of romantic pleasure than in any Peacock
novel up to this date.

There are pastoral undertones to all of Peacock's books, and nowhere are they stronger than in
The Misfortunes of Elphin. In this work Peacock is
able freely to explore the contrasts between public
and private spheres, between social hypocrisy and
genuine fellowship, which form the basis of much of
his writing. The circumstances are propitious: the
legendary subject-matter, the placing of the story

in the far past, the emphasis on the power of Nature
and the joys of rustic seclusion, all encourage a
sharper sense of the pastoral than in a novel like
Headlong Hall. Thus, privacy and independence of
constraint are consistently set against the oppressiveness of the big world: a peaceful existence in
natural surroundings is everywhere preferred to a
life wasted among the power struggles of a court.

The entry into the pastoralism of the book is
done with verve. The first few chapters dwell on
the fragility and decrepitude that complement the
apparent stability of Gwythno's reign, and vividly
chronicle the disaster which brings it to a close.
They mark a decisive end, after which change, and a
fresh beginning, are inevitable. The early part of
the novel is lively and there is a good deal of
action, some of it of a most energetic kind.
Chapter V signals a movement towards serenity: 'An
amphitheatre of rocky mountains enclosed a pastoral
valley. The meadows gave pasture to a few cows;
and the flowers of the mountain-heath yielded store
of honey to the bees of many hives, which were
tended by Angharad and her handmaids' (p.44). The
turmoil of life at court is rejected in favour of a
sensible making do with lesser resources: 'Elphin
was the first Briton who caught fish on a large
scale, and salted them for other purposes than home
consumption' (p.45). The change of feeling as
between the time before and the time after the del-
uge is striking. One almost thinks of the waters as
cleansing, since they sweep away so much that is
corrupt and replace it with an existence spent satisfyingly under the aegis of Nature.

The main characteristics of the pastoral world
are the joys it confers and the moderation of its
endeavours. People are easy with one another, and
loving relationships can develop more straightforwardly than they could at court. The weir itself is
economically designed, and captures only salmon:
'The smaller fish passed freely up and down the
river through the interstices of the piles'. Venison
is replaced by wild goat. The impression is of idyll
and adequacy. Although Elphin is a prince and
Gwythno a king, and the local people 'still acknow-
ledged their royalty, and paid them tribute in corn',
these attributes are not emphasized. Gwythno willingly deserts his palace for Elphin's mere 'dwelling'
(p.44) beside the weir, and it is with irony that we
are told of the contempt of the vainglorious King
Maelgon for the fish-catching Elphin.

However, The Misfortunes of Elphin is not

anodyne; its pastoral elements are tested like everything else. This is mainly done through the agency of Taliesin as he makes his way from court to court and adventure to adventure, until wrongs are righted and he can at last celebrate his marriage to Melanghel. His mettle is tried above all by his dealings with kings, mainly with Maelgon and Melvas, but he always emerges triumphant: though there is conflict, he is always surer and nobler than his adversaries. We are pointedly made aware of the contrast between Taliesin's natural strength and the hollowness and bluster of those who are pitted against him: one of the book's central themes concerns the difference between the real power of the individual and the merely factitious quality of 'might' which passes for power in the outside world.

The first proving of Elphin and his community comes in Chapter VII, 'The Huntings of Maelgon'. Their tranquillity is harshly interrupted by a hunting party led by Maelgon; Angharad and Melanghel find refuge in a cavern, Taliesin is 'absent on the borders of his favourite lake' (p.64) but Elphin is carried off by the invaders. The scene is highly charged. The hunters are preceded by a 'growing tumult', and wild goats and a stag flee before them; Maelgon's men are described as an 'avalanche' (p.65) which 'came thundering down on the track of the flying prey'; they make 'fearful havoc' among Elphin's winter stores; after their depredations, his home is seen as a 'plundered sanctuary'. The battle between might and right is incisively presented to us: on the one side, brash aggression, on the other, thrift, retirement and harmony. As the well-paced story proceeds and this battle is more fully expressed, the direction of Peacock's sympathies becomes even clearer: by the end of the novel we can be in no doubt at all as to his wholehearted approval of the virtues of Elphin and his family, or of the important role that these virtues play in the general scheme of The Misfortunes of Elphin.

Peacock's relish for Welsh legend, landscape and antiquities certainly imparts enthusiasm to the texture of his book. But there is a disadvantage to couleur locale, and it is one which he does not always avoid. Sometimes the fiction turns awkwardly into fact, and we feel ourselves to be reading not a novel but a garrulous and button-holing guide-book. There is some conflict in The Misfortunes of Elphin between the demands of telling a good story and an impulse towards tabulating information which may

form the background of the novel, but is too profuse
not to be distracting. In Chapter VI, for instance,
we are told a great deal about the Druids, and this
seems to contribute little towards the development
of the book as a whole: 'The Derwydd, or Druid,
wore a robe of white. The Ovydd, or Ovate, was of
the class of initiation, and wore a robe of green.
The Awenyddion, or disciples, the candidates for
admission into the Bardic order, wore a variegated
dress of the three colours and were passed through
a very severe moral and intellectual probation'
(p.61). Although one may suspect irony in the latter
part of this quotation, in general it lies flatly
on the page, calling to mind nothing more interesting
than a blunt article on 'Druidism' from some earnest
nineteenth-century encyclopaedia. In passages like
this, Peacock's learning lies heavily on him, and
his desire to do justice to the considerable body of
Welsh esoterica he has at his disposal overcomes his
usually fine sense of the fictional needs of individual episodes. These passages are not often long,
but there are a good many of them, and even when
they are relieved by wit and common sense they are
inescapably dull. Occasionally, too, this scholarly
burden on some parts of the novel is puzzling as
well as tedious. We feel that the triads especially
must have a more important role than that of
providing quaint epigraphs and mise-en-scène. But if
this is so, I am unable to discover what it may be.
Some of this material does valuably contribute
towards heightening and giving substance to the
book; but much seems dragged in because of its
attractiveness to the writer and not for any disc-
ernible artistic purpose. Of course, Peacock's
earlier romance is light-weight, and it might be put
forward in rebuttal of my criticisms that in The
Misfortunes of Elphin he has become aware of the
problem, and is taking care that his new novel will
be more firmly grounded than its predecessor. In
principle, and much to the book's advantage, this is
correct. Yet one's objection to the stolidity and
gratuitousness of some of the information presented
here is not so easily disposed of, and seems to me
to be the consequence of a genuine error of judgement
on Peacock's part.
      In fact the superior substance of this book is
due not only to its lavishness of Celtic detail, but
even more to the greater breadth of experience which
it accommodates. Narrowness of outlook, and an
eclecticism verging on eccentricity, are constant
dangers to a writer like Peacock. But although it is

oblique, and humorously segregated from the everyday, this novel has a feeling of perceptiveness about it. It has withdrawn from close engagement with the outside world but it has a sense of Peacock's having made forays, and experienced it deeply sometime. Imported into the mediaevalism and make-believe are insights-- often piercing insights-- gained from living among men, and observing them with disenchanted clarity. These insights have a force which we cannot help but recognize: 'The condition of the head, in a composite as in a simple body, affects the entire organization to the extremity of the tail, excepting that, as the tail in the figurative body usually receives the largest share in the distribution of punishment, and the smallest in the distribution of reward, it has the stronger stimulus to ward off evil, and the smaller supply of means to indulge in diversion' (p.5). That is amusing, but also Coriolanian: as a comment on life, its accuracy is undeniable. Behind Peacock's fiction, fanciful though it is, lurks a firm grasp of the way things happen. There is no expectation of change, and the novels are composed as entertaining, sardonic consolationes rather than as immediate exhortations to a better life. There is seldom any jarring to this: Peacock's views are not highlighted pedagogically as points to note, except when he feels pressured into direct comment on the errors of his time. Instead, a nice mingling of imagination and observation operates in The Misfortunes of Elphin to give us the sense of an understanding gained in the world which supports, and gives weight and credibility, to romance.

The attractiveness of The Misfortunes of Elphin is enhanced by the insouciance and diversity of its story-telling. Of all Peacock's books its plot is the most sprightly: there is real command in the spacing and contrasting of episodes, the organizing of suspense and the economy and poise of individual scenes. What Peacock is principally after in The Misfortunes of Elphin is liveliness; he wants the reader to be constantly entertained by brisk turns and strange developments. The book is much less dense with thematic material than the conversation novels; there are few long discussions, and from the start the impact of atmosphere and event is greater than in any of the rest of Peacock's works.

We see this best on one occasion when we ourselves are fooled by the writer. In most books we feel we know more about what is going on than any of the characters, and have a pleasingly unassailable grasp of the action. But in Chapter X, 'The Disappointment of Rhûn', we are tricked by Peacock's playing on exactly this complacency. Rhûn has been sent by his father Maelgon to capture Angharad, but has found only Taliesin and Teithrin at home. He fails to persuade them to tell him where Angharad is hidden, or to find her himself, and determines to lie in wait. He and his 'bard of all work' (p.84) see Taliesin leave his dwelling and move towards a cataract, behind which they notice the opening of a cave. Taliesin sings and Melanghel reciprocates, and he then moves towards the waterfall. Rhûn and his companion follow Taliesin into the cave but find it deserted. 'While thus engaged, they heard a rushing sound, and a crash on the rocks, as of some ponderous body' (p.86). A large rock has been rolled over the mouth of the cave; they hear the triumphant voice of Teithrin, saying, '"Foxes! you have been seen through, and you are fairly trapped"' (p.87). This is a neat dramatic reversal, for the reader as well as for Rhûn: we have been as innocent as he is of the joke about to be played on him. But our confidence in the novel is not sapped by this sudden twist. The scene is handled with dexterity, and we are bound to be amused by it. It contributes little to the book's ideological purposes; it is an agreeable tale, wittily told, and has the additional charm that it startles the reader out of any lazy inclination he may have simply to sit back comfortably and allow Peacock's humour to wash over him.

Episodes such as this one impress us with their freshness and variety. Also, though not invariably, each chapter seems different from its predecessor: the content and format change all the time, administering new, slight upsets to our expectations of settledness. The examples are numerous. Chapter XII is largely given over to donnish musings and the description of Caer Lleon and the court of King Arthur; Chapter XIII returns to the main thread of the action, contains the clever conversation of the abbot and Taliesin, and reintroduces Seithenyn; Chapter XIV is mostly in dramatic form, and presents a sharp verbal sparring-match between the abbot and Melvas on the subject of might and right. These pointed alternations do not result in confusion. Instead, we have an agile movement from topic to topic and technique to technique which especially distinguishes The Misfortunes of Elphin among Peacock's works.

Also, while he is as sensitive as ever to the gap between real and pretended motives, and the gulf

that separates individual liberty and satisfaction
from the impositions of life in society, Peacock's
irony is reduced in this novel. Often it lies almost
undetectably in the prose, and has to be broadly
assumed from the context of the chapter rather than
immediately or certainly grasped. At other times, it
is subsumed into comedy and loses much of its qualifying force. When we read that, 'Prince Rhûn being
safe in schistous bastile, Taliesin commenced his
journey to the court of King Arthur' (p.88),the
effect is merely jokey, reminding us of the games
with words to which all readers of Peacock must become accustomed. Another favourite technique is the
wide-eyed description of some happening or person in
terms surprisingly other than those we would normally
use. Thus, 'Maelgon waxed wroth. Elphin, in a point
which much concerned him, held a belief of his own,
different from that which his superiors in worldly
power required him to hold. Therefore Maelgon acted
as the possessors of worldly power usually act in
similar cases: he locked Elphin up within four stone
walls, with an initimation that he should keep him
there till he pronounced a more orthodox opinion on
the question in dispute' (p.69). The wit of this
passage rests on the irony of the words 'intimation'
and 'orthodox', but the tone is playful and the
undermining of the notion of authority, which we find
everywhere in Peacock, is subsidiary to the fun of
the writing.

Fun is in fact a central criterion in The Misfortunes of Elphin. Themes and episodes are picked
up for a moment, cleverly set in motion and then
dropped in favour of something new. The harmony of
the atmosphere and the vigour of the narration
prevent incidents from appearing gratuitous, and at
the individual level there are consistent certainties, but on the surface our principal sense is of
vivacity and movement. This is a book which operates
in bursts, but where we have no overall impression of
disorientation. Even the suspensiveness which we
always feel in Peacock produces a less clouded expec-
tancy here than in earlier books. Events are left
unfinished over several chapters, encouraging our
curiosity, before being nicely explained. 'Beware of
the oppression of Gwenhidwy' (p.4), for example,
sounds a threatening but faintly comic note throughout the introductory part of the novel, before its
prophecy is violently fulfilled in the great storm
which brings about the dispossession of most of
Gwythno's kingdom.

In The Misfortunes of Elphin Peacock constantly

teases the reader by playing cunning verbal tricks
or leaving things up in the air. Even at the conclusion we are teased: we imagine we may be moving
towards a grand resolution as the final chapter
approaches, but what we get instead is something
humorously downbeat-- the last, cautionary flourish
of a book in which skilful story-telling is entertainingly paired with the provision of constant small
shocks to our unthinking acquiescence in the <u>status
quo</u>.

Characterization in <u>The Misfortunes of Elphin</u>
is energetic and substantial. In the conversation
novels we are often aware of speakers rather than of
personalities, except for the women, but here there
is a rounded humanity and a liveliness which is more
than merely intellectual even to quite minor figures.
The richest characterization in the book is that
of Seithenyn, the jovial, incompetent guardian of
Gwythno's embankment. He emanates a freedom which is
untroubled and easygoing and does as he chooses no
matter what the circumstances may be. He is completely resistant to authority or duty, and has an important thematic role to play, but there is nothing
unduly purposive about him: his vitality is paramount. He is an image of man's irreducibility, and
even in retreat remains unconquerably 'a portly and
somewhat elderly personage, of an aspect that would
have been venerable, if it had been less rubicund
and Bacchic, who continued plying his potations with
undiminished energy, while the heroes of the festival
dropped round him, like the leaves of autumn' (p.91).
However, Seithenyn's function is not simple. He
is sprightly, unconstrained and pleasure-loving, but
his blinkered conservatism and ineptitude in the face
of change (at the time of the flood he can only wave
his sword uselessly and demand to be led to the
enemy) are evident targets for Peacock's irony. It
is in the earlier part of <u>The Misfortunes of Elphin</u>
that his qualities are shown to be harmful: we feel
that his winning, disorderly vigour does not quite
compensate for his irresponsibility. But what we
feel after the flood is that although he is culpable,
he has also encouraged the end of a corrupt old
regime and the growth in its place of something finer
and more natural. And in this new world, no longer
dangerously ennobled, Seithenyn becomes a more purely
agreeable figure than he ever was before. He is a
kind of minor deity: even his faults are productive
of good in the end.Like a god, too, he seems indestr-
uctible and omnipresent,and surprisingly resumes his

sway in Chapter X, when we have thought him long
dead. It is hard not to conclude that he represents
pleasures which Peacock believes to be intrinsic to
a good life and of which he approves. Certainly
Seithenyn is the main agent in the novel of the wine-
drinking and beef-eating that Peacock usually places
appreciatively in opposition to crotcheteering debate, and for that reason alone we should take indulgent note of his festivity and intransigence. Also,
in spite of his initial blemishes, Seithenyn always
seems attractively human: warmth of feeling invariably attends his appearances in the book. Although
he is used to ironize a reactionary position which
Peacock heartily disliked, our overall impression
cannot, therefore, be a negative one: it is in large
measure due to him that The Misfortunes of Elphin is
so vivid and its thematic intentions so engagingly
subsumed into comedy.

Seithenyn is a Welsh Silenus, a tutelary spirit
of an amiable and approachable type. Taliesin, by
comparison, is daring and heroic, and set apart by
his special gifts and the mystery of his birth. His
quality is poetic, almost supernatural; he has about
him a rarefied aura of magical power. In the hall of
Maelgon he commands immediate notice: 'Taliesin
stood on the floor, with his harp, in the midst of
the assembly, and, without introduction or preface,
struck a few chords, that, as if by magic, suspended
all other sounds,and fixed the attention of all in
silent expectation' (p.74). From his first appearance he is extraordinary, a child of 'surpassing
beauty' (p.47) who arrives from nowhere, seems linked
with fruitfulness and prosperity, and writes to
Elphin:

'When hostile steps around thee tread,
A spell of power my voice shall wield,
That, more than arms with slaughter red,
Shall be thy refuge and thy shield' (p.48).
Taliesin is in some ways the central character of
The Misfortunes of Elphin, though the novel does not
bear his name. Particularly when he is set against
Maelgon's hypocritical, false bards, he is seen as
an index of truth, honesty and natural behaviour. As
he passes through the book, a testing takes place,
and his merits are displayed and tried. We see them
everywhere victorious, offering a vindication of the
romantic strengths represented by those who cluster
contentedly around Elphin in the aftermath of disaster.

The figure of Taliesin is rendered with some
fineness, though its outline is clear. In the minor

characters there is a neater, more limited sense of
roles to be played; they are fresh, but their function is soon drawn to our attention. One of the best
calculated characterizations is that of Melvas, which
is succinct, but nicely filled out and perfectly sufficient for its purpose. He is plainly seen from the
beginning: 'He took what he wanted wherever he could
find it, by the most direct process, and without any
false pretence' (p.125). His career wittily illus-
trates the abuses of authority; it indicates that
when a man is put in a superior position, and given
unlimited power, his feelings begin to produce injustice rather than justice. So in Melvas, who is
restrained by no affection or respect for others, but
only by greater might than his own, individualism becomes selfishness. The point is not hammered home,
and Melvas himself remains an appealing figure as
well as an efficient vehicle for some of the novel's
thematic concerns.

    As usual in Peacock's work, systems and instit-
utions are attacked, but people are treated with sly
indulgence. We have no strong sense that Seithenyn
is blamed for causing the flood, or that the various
kings whom Taliesin meets on his travels can really
help the oppressions carried out in their names. A
brisk parade of personality is always positively
regarded in Peacock, and an easy acceptance of the
spectrum of humankind spreads its warmth over everyone in the book. Melanghel and Angharad are in the
long line of Peacock's sturdy and independent women;
Melanghel bounds like a deer, and at the time of the
bursting of the embankment Angharad shows 'The spirit
of the Cymric female, vigilant and energetic in per-
il' (pp.32-3). Even the clergy are not dismissed
with Peacock's former acerbity. They are more misguided than actively hypocritical, and have a compensating gastronomic zeal to which he responds with
relish: 'The brethren of Avallon were the apples of
the church. It was the oldest monastic establishment
in Britain; and consequently, as of reason, the most
plump, succulent and rosy' (p.115).

    Uncertainties about the conduct of discussion
are a feature of most of Peacock's writings. Argument, and particularly prescriptive argument, is
frequently placed against actual experience and is
shown to be futile. In Chapter II, when Teithrin
tries to convince Seithenyn that something should be
done to repair the embankment, the different discourses of the two men clash and move parallel to one
another, and in the end nothing gets done. We know

from evidence given earlier in the book that Teithrin is right, and that the embankment is in a dangerous state, but Seithenyn is so animated, his justification of his indolence so coherent, that we are left with no certain impression of one side or the other having won or lost. No single, neat answer is permitted: instead there is an entertaining drunken chaos which provides us with a sense of remission if not of resolution: 'Some fell, in the first impulse, with the tables and benches; others were tripped up by the rolling bowls; and the remainder fell at different points of progression, by jostling against each other, or stumbling over those who had fallen before them' (p.20). The chapter involves, it has often been said, clever satire which is directed at the opponents of reform of Peacock's own day. But its irony extends more widely as well. What is demonstrated is really the inadequacy of argument to guide us properly, to help us in the practical business of our lives, or reliably to arrive at a 'truth' in which everybody can concur.

It is impossible, therefore, for Peacock to write fiction which does not question established orthodoxies. This book has a surer trust in the individual than do the conversation novels, but it shares with them, in an understated way, similar disenchanted views as to political or intellectual authority. Circumstances are subtly dramatized, and witty dislocations of what we expect surprise us out of habitual responses. Often the action is delayed: we read a passage and grasp each word, but full comprehension only comes later, with a sense of being fooled and given a new viewpoint. The direction of Peacock's feelings is more political in The Misfortunes of Elphin than in most of the other novels. Peacock is always suspicious of institutions, and has no truck with the impedimenta of society. He thinks that officials, and especially kings, almost invariably act with a total disregard for others: Melvas is only the best example in this book of a whole array of greedy oppressors who batten (albeit comically) on the lives of those subordinate to them.

In The Misfortunes of Elphin the characters associated with the state are rulers and functionaries, and to a lesser extent clerics. Peacock links kingship with duress, as well he might. Taliesin disappears from Caer Lleon because 'He knew the power and influence of Maelgon Gwyneth; and he was aware that King Arthur, however favourably he might receive his petition, would not find leisure to compel the liberation of Elphin, till he had enforced from

Melvas the surrender of his queen' (p.113;9). Even
the rhythm of this sentence, quite apart from the
greater vehemence of the words, channels our attention towards 'compel' and 'enforced'. We have a sense
throughout the novel that kings merely foist themselves on their subjects. Social and political organization is the principal target for Peacock's
irony, but there are also doubts as to the Church.
In a way that is simultaneously whimsical and
serious, Peacock feels that both state and Church are
guilty of trying to impose patterns of life upon
people who ought to be free. He indicates that there
has been a continuity of elites, one no better than
the other, and that all have had pernicious effects
on the mass of the population not involved in their
maintenance: 'The Druids were the sacred class of
the bardic order. Before the change of religion, it
was by far the most numerous class; for the very
simple reason, that there was most to be got by it:
all ages and nations having been sufficiently enlightened to make the trade of priest more profitable
than that of poet' (p.60). These sentiments do not
lead Peacock into any advocacy of revolution: his
novels encourage us to lucidity of vision and not to
direct political activity. His position is well
described by Payne Knight, the philosopher and pole-
micist with whose works he was well acquainted:
'Established authority, both in literature and art,
is so imposing, that few men have courage openly to
revolt against it'(10). The critical word here is
'openly': Peacock was, I think, just as distrustful
of entrenched power as were his contemporaries, but
he expresses his unease in a way that is oblique
rather then evident.

   The Misfortunes of Elphin is full of abductions
and imprisonments, and the main thematic prepossession of the novel is with the uncontrolled use of
authority. Even in the first chapter we are made
aware of the uncertain, and generally inverse, relationship between wordly power and true justice.
Those in positions of responsibility mostly abuse it:
kings, in particular, use violence to get their way,
and pay no heed to the rights of those who are hurt
in the process. Melvas, for instance, 'had a total
and most complacent indifference to every thing but
his own will and pleasure' (p.125). A contrast is
made between this regal persecution and the liberty
of Elphin's rustic community. The incarceration of
Elphin becomes a trial of the values of his clan,
and we note that captivity entirely fails to subdue
him. We come to see that force of arms only succeeds

in the short term, since what stands against it is a
central quality of human nature, the desire to be
free and happy—— a desire to which regimentation and
political double-talk are anathema.

This concern with the relation between duress
and liberty is given its sharpest exposition in
Chapter XIV, 'The Right of Might'. The function of
this chapter is ironically to dramatize the various
uses of the word 'right' and to demonstrate its amb-
iguities to the reader. The most incisive indication of the problem comes in Melvas's speech on the
Saxons, whom the abbot has described as 'spoilers' of
'a land in which they have no right even to breathe'
(p.131). The king replies,

> 'Have not you and I a right to this good
> wine, which seems to trip very merrily
> over your ghostly palate? I got it by
> seizing a good ship, and throwing the
> crew overboard, just to remove them out
> of the way, because they were troublesome.
> They disputed my right, but I taught them
> better. I taught them a great moral
> lesson, though they had not much time to
> profit by it. If they had had the might
> to throw me overboard, I should not have
> troubled myself about their right, any
> more, or, at rate, any longer, than they
> did about mine'.

The conflict here could hardly be wittier or more
clearly expressed, and is carried through in the rest
of the chapter in speeches setting 'might' against
'right' with great acuteness and ingenuity. The
foremost irony is that what Melvas says is in fact
correct; if we disregard the implication of fairness
called up by the word 'right', then he offers an
exact statement of the way such things operate in his
world. Everything is simple: if you want something,
you take it, and the only thing which might hold you
back would be the greater strength of someone else
who wanted it too. Peacock's cleverness comes in his
casting these sentiments of the jungle (or of life in
society) in an ethical vocabulary, and bringing the
notion of a 'moral lesson' to the reader's mind.
Melvas identifies 'might' with 'right': Peacock encourages us to set them apart. We cannot fail to
appreciate the distinction that is suggested as between the effectiveness of force, on the one hand,
and on the other the quite different matter of the
justification of one's actions. Force may work, at
least in some circumstances: but that does not mean
that it is 'right' or that it should proffer itself

as an instrument in our dealings with those around us
--the role of Elphin and his family is exactly to
illustrate the heartening obverse to such a buccan-
eering view of existence.

One of the best examples of Peacock's handling
of this topic is his treatment of Maelgon and Melvas.
Both use their position in a purely repressive way,
to satisfy their own wishes at the expense of other
people's rights. There are attempts to persuade
them to restrain their exactions in favour of the
general good, but these come to nothing. However, in
the end both kings come to grief. We see that those
who live by the sword will be reproved by the sword,
and that unless life is lived in a freedom tempered
by care and responsibility, and removed from the
world of politics, then it cannot be truly lived at
all. As it is, in a fallible civilization such as
Maelgon's (or our own), kings should be deterred
from too cruel an abuse of their powers: we see that
human desires must be curtailed when the person
nurturing these desires is egotistical and authoritarian. Peacock gives another twist to his development of this theme, for more and more he hints to us
not just that the might of the state is pernicious,
but also that it limits kings as much as it gives
them liberty. When Maelgon talks to the captive
Elphin, for instance, we have a stronger sense of the
burdens upon the king than of those upon his prisoner. As Maelgon explains the principle of "fitting-
ness" by which he lives, he increasingly shows himself to be in thrall to a model of kingly deportment
which destroys any possibility of liberty of action.
Thus, if Elphin is a prisoner in body, Maelgon is
more importantly a prisoner in spirit.

Peacock's purpose in The Misfortunes of Elphin
is deftly to balance the unillusioned insights which
I have been describing against the pastoral warmth
which is their antidote. This purpose is difficult
to achieve, and I have pointed out moments when
Peacock becomes strident or awkward; but his overall
success is considerable, and the seriousness of his
enterprise seems hard to dismiss. In Horne Tooke's
EPEA PTEROENTA, a book which he knew well, Peacock
could find the following exchange, which offers a
pertinent gloss on his aims in this novel:

    '(F.) Must we always be seeking after
           the meaning of words?
   (H.) Of important words we must, if we
           wish to avoid important error'[11].
After all, what word is more important than the word
'right'?

There is a glaring contrast between the general wisdom of The Misfortunes of Elphin and the way that immediate, contemporary remarks are addressed to the reader. On the one hand there is balanced consideration; on the other, ungainliness and bad temper. As in Maid Marian, Peacock becomes intemperate when he speaks unequivocally to the follies of his period, though he handles a wider dimension of political commentary with convincing lucidity. There seems no judgement, either aesthetic or argumentative, to the procedure Peacock adopts: simply, from time to time, a brusque and querulous paragraph, usually condemning the modern world by comparison with a better state of affairs in the past, erupts from his quietly ironic evocation of Welsh antiquity. Peacock has a pervasive distaste for his age, and is anxious to point out the harm it has caused: in Caer Lleon, especially, he sets its early glory sharply against the town's later decline. We know from the poetry how strong a hold this fear of transience had on Peacock's emotions: a powerful, elegiac disquiet is found everywhere in his work, and fuels the dialectic which gives it such quickness and energy.

But the problems which are entailed are considerable. Firstly, our perspective is troublingly elusive: mediaeval Wales is evoked with greater warmth than nineteenth-century England, but not always, and it is never systematically aggrandized as a Golden Age after which all else must be a disappointment. Quite often, in fact, 'then' and 'now' are shown to be suffering from the same difficulties, mainly as these regard the protecting of personal liberties, and the effect of this is to indicate continuities rather than to set the periods in opposition to one another. Thus Peacock comments of the Arthurians that, 'Of moral science they had little; but morals, without science, they had about the same as we have' (p.51), and sceptically detects in the Druidism of Taliesin an 'allegorical mummery' (p.56) which is characteristic of other religions as well. Even in this area, therefore, Peacock's distrust of absolute attitudes and simplified contrasts sometimes forces him to abate the vigour of his antipathy, and to perceive imperfections from which no era is exempt. But for the reader the conjunction of thoughtful relativism with single-minded contempt, often about the same topic, produces a fracture of tone which is not easy to accept. This leads us to the second and more serious of these problems: the disturbance caused to the stylistic fabric of the book by the interpolations I have been discussing.

Chapter VI, for instance, entitled 'The Education of
Taliesin', has little to do with Taliesin himself.
Much of it is given over to a leaden exposition of
historical material, and a great deal of the rest
consists of an overt, comprehensive attack, satiri-
cally couched, on pretty well every aspect of
Peacock's times. The failure of tact is underlined
by the muffledness and inelegance of the prose, as
Peacock crudely compares present with past:
> 'The science of political economy was
> sleeping in the womb of time. The advantage
> of growing rich by getting into debt and
> paying interest was altogether unknown: the
> safe and economical currency, which is prod-
> uced by a man writing his name on a bit of
> paper, for which other men give him their
> property, and which he is always ready to
> exchange for another bit of paper, of an
> equally safe and economical manufacture,
> being also equally ready to render his own
> person, at a moment's notice, as impalpable
> as the metal which he promises to pay, is a
> stretch of wisdom to which the people of
> those days had nothing to compare' (pp.50-1).

This is hard-hitting but also disruptive. It hurls
itself bluntly at the reader; no effort has been
made to assimilate it to the rest of the novel or to
harmonize it with the more celebratory side of Peacock's writing. Such hasty and ill-prepared assaults
cannot help but give us an impression of mismanagement, of an element in the book which the author has
not been able to subdue to his overall plan.

The sense of being chivvied is unusual in Peacock, and most of The Misfortunes of Elphin is urbane
and amusing. There can be no doubt about Peacock's
disaffection from his period and his need to discover
compensation for the futility of the world around
him. But one regrets that these feelings should show
themselves here with such exasperation.

All of Peacock's writing is a matter of different qualities set off against one another rather than
of synthesis. The Misfortunes of Elphin ends quietly
on a note of contentment, having told a comic story
with pleasing freshness, and also presented a number
of Peacock's habitual themes. The last few paragra-
phs give us a great deal of information, but they
have nothing of the adventitiousness and bald summary
which mar the same section in Maid Marian. Instead,
they briefly indicate the ascendancy of Elphin and
Taliesin and the discomfiture of their opponents, and

fill in the details we expect as to the endings of
the various narratives which make up the novel. There
is a sense of appropriateness and of things going
well: 'flourished' and 'ripeness' (p.152) are the
most significant words in the last sentence of all.
The reader is left cheerful and enlivened, and with
less unease than in Peacock's previous works. Of
course the book has flaws, as I have said; but as a
piece of story-telling which mingles celebration with
attack, a subdued but trenchant treatment of themes
of authority and individual freedom and an admirable
achievement of style, it is hard to equal in the rest
of Peacock's oeuvre.

CHAPTER VI

CROTCHET CASTLE

Critics have always been divided in their opinion of <u>Crotchet Castle</u>, the conversation novel which followed <u>The Misfortunes of Elphin</u> in 1831. More than any of the rest of Peacock's works, its tone and procedure have been a matter of debate. It appears straightforwardly to conform to the pattern set by <u>Headlong Hall</u>, and even repeats some of the matter and many of the techniques of the earlier novels. But its effect is disconcertingly different. In all of Peacock's previous books there are elements of struggle, and the author's optimism seems fragile or intermittent. In <u>Crotchet Castle</u> one detects little of this. As before, we have witty dialogues, amusing incidents and romantic episodes, all mingled with sceptical asides on the follies of the day. But nothing seems at risk; the mood is acquiescent, almost indifferent. Some critics have remarked on this and others not, but most have been aware of a special quality to the novel that needs to be explained and perhaps excused. In the course of his vigorous attack on what he sees as Peacock's triviality, Mario Praz calls <u>Crotchet Castle</u> 'a nerveless work'[1]; Douglas Hewitt accuses it of 'a frivolous and reactionary complacency'[2]; for Saintsbury, on the other hand, it is 'by common consent the completest and urbanest product of the author's genius'[3]. What I shall try to do here, in response to this disagreement, is to analyse what seems to me to be the different purpose of <u>Crotchet Castle</u>, by comparison with its predecessors, and to consider the pleasures it still offers to a sympathetic reader.

We have little evidence as to Peacock's life in the 1830's except what can be gleaned from reviews and music criticisms. There is no diary, few anecdotes exist, and no letter survives from the period between February 12 1827 and June 21 1838. <u>Crotchet</u>

Castle is the only novel that Peacock published between The Misfortunes of Elphin and Gryll Grange. He
shows even less energy in poetry than he does in
fiction: the Halliford edition records only two
poems, 'The Legend of Manor Hall' and 'The New Year',
from the decade 1830-1840, and neither is of any
great interest[4]. We know that Peacock was greatly
upset by the death of his mother in 1833 and that his
duties at India House took up a good deal of his
time, especially after he succeeded to the senior
post of Examiner in 1836. But his drift away from
literature remains striking. After all, Peacock
wrote rapidly, and he had often been busier in his
early life. I think we have no basis for suggesting
that outside pressures alone prevented him from
carrying on with his novel-writing during these
years. It is rather that he was unable or unwilling
--somehow, that he had lost impetus.

A sense of abeyance becomes more marked when we
look at Peacock's contributions to periodicals during
the early 1830's. The music criticism which he wrote
between 1830 and 1834 for the Globe and the Examiner
is fastidious with regard to standards of performance, but sometimes, also, curiously rapt. He says
of Beethoven's Fidelio that it 'combines the profou-
ndest harmony with melody that speaks to the
soul'[5], and comments that 'There is nothing perfect
in this world except Mozart's music'[6]. Although
there is solicitude in the review of Thomas Jefferson's Memoirs and the essay on a proposed new London
Bridge which appeared in the Westminster Review in
1830, Peacock seems less vivaciously concerned than
before. His inveterate dislike of artistic laxity
and biographical inaccuracy carries on in scathing
comments on Moore's Letters and Journals of Lord
Byron[7], but the public bearing of his remarks grows
less pronounced with time. Of course, on Jefferson
he makes plain his approval of the freedom and democracy of the young American state, and on London
Bridge he has much to say against needless upheaval:
'we do not like these sweeping changes, which give to
the metropolis the appearance of a thing of yester-
day, and obliterate every visible sign that connects
the present generation with the ages that are
gone'[8]. However, except for the attack on Moore,
there is a remote, mellow air to these writings.
They show a thoughtful interest in the world, but no
deep anxiety. Although their subjects are present-
day, their tenor is almost antiquarian. Even the
eulogy of Jefferson, which makes points of obvious
political relevance to the troubled 1830's in

England, has no feeling of immediacy.

The impression given by the work of these years is, therefore, one of withdrawal. The struggles of Peacock's early days are muted. We see him now as an established, successful man of affairs, somewhat preoccupied, and turning away from imaginative creation and a serious response to the problems of his period. Instead, seclusion at home in Lower Halliford, reading, music, work, and a limited, undemanding kind of authorship engross his attention.

The fact that Crotchet Castle is so much less apprehensive than Peacock's previous novels may give us a further clue to the slackening of his vigour during these years. It is plain that he saw things as sharply as ever, and Marilyn Butler has shown that the book is full of particular contemporary references and nods at most of the important and many of the minor controversies of its day. If anything, these were more intractable in 1831 than they had been at the time of Headlong Hall. As we see from the novel, and as we know from history, it was a period of intense upheaval. Political agitation was leading towards the Reform Bill of 1832. Economic instability generated widespread unease, and Peacock persistently rides a favourite hobby-horse in his attacks on paper money. Popular disturbances show themselves more clearly in this book than ever before: Dr Folliott is set upon by both body-snatchers and Charity Commissioners; Chainmail Hall is beseiged by a rabble; financial mismanagement is everywhere. Sceptical conversations touch on flaws in government, science, art, education, business, charity and monetary policy. Emotionally, Peacock was always drawn to deteriorationism, and in this novel he seems to feel that every facet of public life has grown more corrupt. There is a kind of wildness, but also weariness, in the way so many targets are yoked together, briefly assailed, and then dismissed. One cannot avoid a sense of disorder, a feeling that the author does not quite have his material clearly in focus. As a result, while the novel is not a collapse, it has no fight in it.

Thus, as Lorna Sage says, 'Like Meredith's Dr Middleton, Peacock...became expert at excluding from his consciousness anything that might pose a threat to his peace of mind or his digestion'[9]. His new reaction to strife--almost to anarchy--is to suppress its unpleasant implications. Crotchet Castle reflects the conservative, sequestered enjoyments of a man of cleverness and wit who knows perfectly what is going on in the world, and is perfectly determined

not to allow this knowledge to shatter the cossetted
equanimity of his existence. The book is almost
insolent, touching on every problem of the day, but
refusing to be deeply moved by any of them. It marks
the beginning of the Alexandrinism of Peacock's later
years, in which he turns away from the world and its
cares towards a soothing impassibility bolstered by
food and drink, music and the classics. In this
novel, however, the circumstance is difficult, for
although little is taken seriously, we are constantly reminded of real dilemmas: Peacock seems to be
fiddling while England burns.

Crotchet Castle contrasts with The Misfortunes
of Elphin. The romance, published only two years
previously, draws cordiality and warmth from the form
in which it is written, but remains an imperfectly
settled kind of book. Crotchet Castle uses the rest-
ive, relativist mode of works like Headlong Hall,
and frequently draws in material from a threatening
outside world. Also, it was probably written very
closely on the heels of The Misfortunes of Elphin,
though not published until later(10). Everything
leads one to expect a novel which is at least as
troubled as its predecessors, rather than much less
so. One cannot believe that Peacock's feelings could
change so radically in such a short time, or that he
could easily cast off the doubt which marks all his
earlier books. But critically, it seems to me, it is
impossible to ignore the remarkable fact that
Crotchet Castle is largely undisturbed. In general
terms, I have explained this change as being due to
a retrenchment on Peacock's part, as he copes with a
lessening of his imaginative impetus and an increasing remoteness from the society in which he was
living. But one must also suggest that it was deliberate. Between The Misfortunes of Elphin and
Crotchet Castle occurs a leap which can only have
been made by choice. The composure of Crotchet
Castle is not entirely unruffled, but it is willed.
My conclusion is that, in relation to fiction at
least, Peacock is laying down his arms in this book,
and looking for refuge. It has an air of pastime,
of imperturbable entertainment. It is Peacock's
violon d'Ingres, on which he plays farewell to the
stresses his previous conversation novels had expressed so well.

It may seem perverse that Peacock should choose
the form of the conversation novel rather than that
of the romance, when he is deliberately to reject
the disquiet that we associate with books such as
Nightmare Abbey. But this is not so if Crotchet

Castle is making a considered gesture of withdrawal
rather than merely playing with the techniques of the
earlier works. In fact, Peacock's methods are overt.
He takes unpalatable ideas and events, as in the
other novels, but repeatedly draws their sting. The
uneasiness of tone, the hedging of feeling, the reticence of judgement and point of view, the unresol-
vedness of the arguments in Headlong Hall and its
successors, are either mitigated or overturned. The
festive satisfactions of love, music and food and
drink, which provide a positive undertow in all of
Peacock's writing, here boldly rise to the surface.
There are references to pantomime, and reminiscences
of the circus; we feel that Peacock is quite aware
of what he is doing, and that his emasculating of the
conversation novel is carefully contrived. I think
we must see in this work an acknowledgement that his
efforts to find some responsible literary accommodation of the follies of the world around him could no
longer be maintained. Crotchet Castle is Peacock's
conscious vale to many of the prepossessions of his
younger life and in large part, also, to the imaginative efforts which they brought in their train.

    Even on the first page of Crotchet Castle we are
aware of a different tone from that of Nightmare
Abbey. Our impression is of orderliness and continuity, and a natural harmony which seems far from any
note of fracture. The Thames 'rolls a clear flood
through flowery meadows, under the shade of old beech
woods, and the smooth mossy greensward of the chalk
hills' (p.1), and Crotchet Castle itself stands 'on a
bold round-surfaced lawn, spotted with juniper, that
opened itself in the bosom of an old wood, which rose
with a steep, but not precipitous ascent, from the
river to the summit of the hill' (pp.1-2). Though
the brisk, flowing prose is ironically pointed, its
principal purpose is to establish a pattern of entertainment and easiness which the novel will subsequen-
tly follow. The exposition pokes fun at Ebenezer
MacCrotchet's nouveau riche social climbing, but
satire is not its main aim. Even the irony has no
edge: it indicates the truth without exciting either
passion or animosity. So, when MacCrotchet makes his
way to London, it is comically 'with all his surplus
capital, not very neatly tied up in a not very clean
handkerchief, suspended over his shoulder from the
end of a hooked stick' (p.2). Similarly under-
emphasized is the ruined Roman camp near the Castle,
whose genuine age and power point to the falsity of
fly-by-night pretensions like MacCrotchet's. In

every way there is less dash than we have come to
expect. Crotchet Castle, for example, has the
advantage of 'the visits of a number of hardy
annuals, chiefly from the north, who, as the interval
of their metropolitan flowering allowed, occasionally
accompanied their London brethren in excursions' (pp.
6-7), and Miss Crotchet is attractive 'to one or two
sprigs of nobility, who thought that the lining of a
civic purse would superinduce a very passable factitious nap upon a threadbare title' (p.10). This is
undeniably nice, but not thought-provoking; like the
whole of the first chapter, it seems low-key and
playful, as if it had no intention other than to
offer us agreeable amusement.
     The milieu of the novel reinforces this sense of
moderation and sang-froid. Crotchet Castle is almost
suburban; we feel that it is a part of the world,
and that the habits of living that it encourages are
no longer so cut off from everyday reality as they
were before. Despite the trip on the river, the
rustic interludes in Wales and the easy mobility of
the characters, the ambience of Crotchet Castle is
companionable and unified. Even Susannah's letters
from America, rather brusquely introduced in Chapter
XI, do little to disturb this impression. We infer
that America is a better place from the point of view
of social equality, but that injustice, and the curse
of paper money, flourish there as they do in England;
explicitly, Robthetill indicates that absolute values
are not to be found, and that the best one can hope
for are some variations in fairness as one moves from
place to place. Peacock could certainly have made
something of such views if he had wished, but in
practice the book does not invite comparisons between
life in England and life in America; instead it
keeps comment on the New World safely insulated in
these unexpected missives. The characters, too, are
more gregarious than in most previous novels. We see
them chatting amiably, or eating and drinking together; obsession is less pronounced, communication and
agreement simpler; they form a convivial group,
rather than a collection of individuals. As breakfast is succeeded by lunch, and lunch by dinner, a
notion of settlement is hard to avoid. Although we
are aware of the gap between the fashionable world
of London and Crotchet Castle, and the pastoral
serenity of the abandoned Susannah, it enforces no
qualification of the basic unity of the novel's
social compass. Susannah blossoms under the influence of 'occupation, mountain air, thyme-fed mutton,
thick cream, and fat bacon' (p.9), while her former

lover is left 'blighted, sallowed, and crows'-footed'
by 'the intense anxieties of his bubble-blowing days',
yet this contrast has little force. We accommodate
both the health and freedom of the Merioneth countryside and the empty exploits of the town, and they are
not set sharply in opposition to one another.
Partly, this is because the tone of Crotchet Castle
is so pliant, and because the characters act no
differently wherever they may find themselves. But
partly, too, it follows from the striking separation
of the Welsh episodes, with their air of romantic
fulfilment, from the action of the rest of the book.
Apart from passing notice in Chapter I, the celebration of Susannah's Celtic exile, and its termination
in marriage to Mr Chainmail, are pretty much confined
to Chapters XIII to XVI; and their effect does not
strongly radiate out to modify our response to the
other concerns of the novel.

This affable homogeneity of circumstance carries
through into the main activities which Crotchet
Castle describes. Crotcheteers like Dr Morbific and
Mr Toogood are as single-minded as ever, but are
relegated to the wings and form a mere comic chorus
to the antics of fully developed characters such as
Dr Folliott. Fantasy and extravagance remain, therefore, but are placed in the background of our attention. In the foreground is a mundane and recognizable
world where characters often have occupations, and
are concerned with making money and keeping their
heads above water. They are more exposed to the
facts of existence than in earlier books: fortunes
are made and lost, and Susannah is faced with the
unique necessity of earning her own living after the
disappearance of her once wealthy father. Even ari-
stocrats are not exempt from financial worries: Lady
Clarinda knows quite well that money is essential for
her happiness: 'I dare say, love in a cottage is
very pleasant; but then it positively must be a
cottage ornée; but would not the same love be a
great deal safer in a castle, even if Mammon furnished the fortification?' (p.37). This novel is
peopled by self-made men and figures from the middle
rank of society; its interests are the necessary
ones of making do and coping with difficulties.
Crotchet Castle itself is no great mansion, but
rather the modest 'castellated villa of a retired
citizen' (p.2), and most of the lords and ladies whom
we meet are all too willing to sell themselves in
return for a comfortable income. Much of the action
is occasioned by cash, or by the lack of it. The
book's purpose is to assert the value of love, and

of traditional festivity, as against the silliness,
but above all the materialism, of contemporary
England. As in the rest of Peacock's work, the
central romantic entanglements revolve around a clash
of true feeling and external obstruction: both for
Mr Chainmail and Lady Clarinda, it is worldly considerations that get in the way of the love-matches they
would really like. We almost have the feeling that
Crotchet Castle is drawn from experience, and reflects the author's own environment. Certainly it has a
more inclusive and everyday setting, and less imaginative enlargement, than any of Peacock's previous
novels.
     This brings us sharply up against the principal
critical difficulty of the book. For it is reasonable to assume that a novel which draws much of its
material from the public life of the time, involves
a larger, cooler view of the human condition, and is
less heightened in tone and fabling in manner, should
also be more directly engaged than its predecessors.
In fact, Crotchet Castle is close only to the surface
of things; genuine enquiry is further away than in
any earlier work. In the first chapter a rather
indigestible mass of topics, including paper money,
speculative schemes, financial intrigues and the new
science of political economy, is touched upon. All
of these, we know, were features of the modern-day
scene which moved Peacock to scorn. Yet here they
make brief appearances in a context of mild irony,
are given little explanation or elaboration, and are
swiftly scuttled by genial gourmandise under the
aegis of the attractive Dr Folliott. Witty playfulness is important in all of Peacock's fiction, but
here it seems paramount; notions are constantly
brought up only to be sent down again. This is not
just a matter of Peacock's use of farce and of the
dinner-table to defuse potentially serious discussions, for instance, or his maintenance of an easygoing tone. We also have a sense that nothing is
quite firmly grasped; the book has some thematic
direction, but around this central core dealing with
the relations of money and integrity is a diverse
grouping of subjects which are merely mentioned, and
then left dangling inconsiderately. A Jamesian
exactness of patterning is found nowhere in Peacock,
and we do not expect it here. But only in Crotchet
Castle is there such a refusal to follow through
distasteful implications. The long, brilliant arguments between optimist and pessimist in Headlong
Hall, or the clever speeches on might and right in
The Misfortunes of Elphin, are replaced in this novel

by lightweight sparrings which leave the reader with
no residue of anxiety, and no impression of anything
resembling the systematic consideration of a work
such as Melincourt. Thus, when 'paper prosperity'
(p.7) and 'the blowing of bubbles' are introduced, it
is half-hearted, and no real force of feeling fuels
the references to politics and economics which litter
almost every conversation.

One of the major differences between Crotchet
Castle and a novel like Melincourt lies in the quality of the discussions each presents. In the later
book, there is less sermonizing, and more desultory
chatting; grand argumentative bouts are rarer.
There is a new emphasis on activity and enterprise.
Characters spend more time doing and less time talking; they move around the countryside, take trips
on the river, or hurry to London on business like
Captain Fitzchrome; they even amicably transfer
themselves to Chainmail Hall at Christmas-time. Not
only are there fewer crotcheteering speeches, but
they are also usually briefer and more rapidly paced
than before. The whole conversational manner is
subdued, closer to the pattern of normal, sociable
talk. So, when Dr Folliott meets Captain Fitzchrome
for the first time, their exchanges seem unexcited
and familiar:
        'THE STRANGER. [Captain Fitzchrome]
        I beg your pardon, sir: do I understand
        this place to be your property?
        THE REV. DR. FOLLIOTT.
        It is not mine, sir: the more is the pity;
        yet is it so far well, that the owner is my
        good friend, and a highly respectable gentle-
        man.
        THE STRANGER.
        Good and respectable, sir, I take it, mean
        rich?
        THE REV. DR. FOLLIOTT.
        That is their meaning, sir' (p.29).
Even when the characters begin to broach their hobby-
horses, these do not generate the same high pitch as
in previous works. At an early point in the book,
Mr MacQuedy brings up the topic of civilization,
which Peacock can never bear to let pass. Mr Skionar
asks the initial question:
        'What is civilisation?
        MR. MACQUEDY.
        It is just respect for property: a state
        in which no man takes wrongfully what belongs
        to another, is a perfectly civilised state.

MR. SKIONAR.
Your friend's antiquaries must have lived
in El Dorado, to have had an opportunity
of being saturated with such a state.
MR. MACQUEDY.
It is a question of degree. There is more
respect for property here than in Angola.
MR. SKIONAR.
That depends on the light in which things
are viewed' (pp.34-5;11).

Not only is this a genuine debate, but it ends on a
note of reconciliation rather than being left up in
the air or annulled by a recall to dinner. Even the
liveliest arguments in Crotchet Castle do not
approach the single-mindedness and delirium of some
of the earlier novels; they are companionable and
jokey, and far from the frenzied vitality of figures
like Sir Patrick O'Prism.

The less extravagant characterization and calmer
progress of discussion in Crotchet Castle give an
unusually reasonable air to many of the remarks that
are made. There is no absolutely simple and approving point of view in this book, any more than there
was in its predecessors, but the more temperate
style of the speeches makes it hard for us not to
respond to their intermittent good sense. We have
notions here which are acute and often convincing,
and sharp observations which are not undermined. So,
in answer to Mr MacQuedy's complaint that, 'as to
your poetry of the twelfth century, it is not good
for much' (p.124), Mr Chainmail replies,

'It has, at any rate, what ours wants,
truth to nature, and simplicity of diction.
The poetry, which was addressed to the
people of the dark ages, pleased in prop-
ortion to the truth with which it depcited
familiar images, and to their natural
connection with the time and place to which
they were assigned. In the poetry of our
enlightened times, the characteristics of
all seasons, soils,and climates, may be
blended together,with much benefit to the
author's fame as an original genius' (p.125).

Equally, the comments on education, and the dialogue
between those stressing the importance of inborn
qualities and those the determining power of environment, are as much persuasive as they are wrong-
headed. Our impression of an apparent plausibility
is reinforced by the different handling of the argument: evidence is adduced, information is accepted,
and irrefutable propositions are not refuted. There

is a sense of give and take: even Dr Folliott, pressed hard on the subject of fish sauces by Mr MacQuedy, is forced wittily to concede, 'In their line, I grant you, oyster and lobster sauce are the pillars of Hercules' (p.50). We have a new feeling, particularly with the major figures, of a more recognizable kind of intercourse in which agreement is possible and some properly acceptable ideas and matters of fact may be accepted.

In this novel, then, crotcheteering comes more prominently than before to play second fiddle to chat and to the rendition of lower-pitched social circumstances. This is obviously a change, but not entirely a gain. One of the prime attractions of previous works was the precariousness and excitement that they generated. Crotchet Castle offers us a cooler world in which less is at risk, and this means that the novel itself is domesticated and rather diminished.

Speaking of Nightmare Abbey, Kiely says that, 'In the end, it is not the sanity of Peacock's humor which one admires, but its gaiety, its refusal to be serious in an age when frivolity was not the literary fashion'[12]. It seems to me that this is contentious when applied to the early novels, but appropriate for Crotchet Castle. This book operates within its society, but remains disengaged, whether galvanizing the Charity Commissioners into ironic stichomythia or expounding the pro and contra of nudity in art (with Dr Folliott pungently remarking, 'I must say that, if I wished my footman to learn modesty, I should not dream of sending him to school to a naked Venus', p.96).

A good deal of the novel touches on public affairs and a major topic is clearly that of finance, but questions of political economy or monetary impropriety seem more time-passing than thought-inducing. They are almost games, and like games are punctuated by recollections of the physical needs of the players - for 'a leg of that capon' (p.17), perhaps, or some 'Matchless claret' (p.73). More than in any previous book, Crotchet Castle is warmly responsive to these needs, and gives due weight to the variety of straightforward pleasures open to mankind. It is not just at Christmas and at Chainmail Hall that one thinks of Peacock's fondness for Old English virtues and the meals that go with them; here, 'punch and wassail' (p.211) spread their benign influence throughout the novel.

It is in the areas of money, and of comparisons between past and present, that this accommodation is

most striking. We see from Paper Money Lyrics that
Peacock was capable of the fiercest belligerence when
aroused by what he considered to be the root cause of
the financial instability of his times. Also, the
power of money to impede the progress of true love is
repeatedly noted in Crotchet Castle, and affects the
romantic entanglements of all of the novel's courting
couples: is even gives the story whatever slight
suspense it may have. The worldly concerns of the
first few chapters, with their disapproval of an insecure prosperity 'that has grown up like a mushroom'
(p.32), and the twin dangers of materialism and
status-seeking mooted from the start in the experience of Ebenezer MacCrotchet, thread themselves
constantly into the fabric of the book. Young
Crotchet, for example, considers marrying Susannah,
the daughter of the banker, Mr Touchandgo, 'when, one
foggy morning, Mr. Touchandgo and the contents of his
till were suddenly reported absent; and as the fortune which the young gentleman had intended to marry
was not forthcoming, this tender affair of the heart
was nipped in the bud' (pp.7-8). It is hardly necessary to point out the contrast in this sentence
between wealth and 'affair of the heart', or the way
in which Crotchet is said to be marrying 'the fortune' rather than the girl. Yet despite the profusion
and robustness of these references, their air is
whimsical. They are the kind of dismissals one might
expect from a crusty eccentric of a certain age, suggesting set habits,irascibility and fundamental ind-
ifference-- the last quality the most significant.
One feels, therefore, that there has been a lessening
in the energy even of habitual Peacockian crotchets
like this antipathy to the merchantile ethos and to
paper money, and that the author can only have conn-
ived in the process.
      In earlier books, especially The Misfortunes of
Elphin, direct contemporary references are generally
accompanied by a vexation of tone and harshness of
manner that disrupt the texture of the writing. However, this anger does not point consistently in any
one direction: the prospect of his own period seems
to call up in Peacock a knot of emotion that he does
not quite know what to do with. In Crotchet Castle
there is a residue of irritation in remarks on The
March of Mind and the Steam Intellect Society, and a
corresponding mild indulgence towards the twelfth
century as praised by Mr Chainmail and the Greek
paradise eulogized by Dr Folliott. But neither of
these is presented as a viable alternative to the
present-day world. Mr Chainmail is ironized as

someone who 'holds that the best state of society
was that of the twelfth century, when nothing was
going forward but fighting, feasting, and praying,
which he says are the three great purposes for which
man was made' (p.60), though he becomes more sensible
as the book progresses. Dr Folliott, too, is no
model held up for our unstinted admiration: he is
lively and agreeable, but his classical learning
sometimes degenerates into pedantry and in any case
seems to provide him with little more than a vast
stock of quotations. Peacock is too clever and
wordly-wise to believe that we can really live in
mediaeval Wales or fifth-century Athens as a counter
to our dissatisfaction with our own time. Here, his
attitude towards his age is more acquiescent than
formerly: he does not like what is going on around
him, but it no longer awakes in him such ambiguous
excitability. Even when the egregious Modern Athenian Mr MacQuedy asserts the richer culture of Edinburgh as opposed to the South, there is no violent
response; Dr Folliott calmly dismisses him with, 'I,
for one, sir, am content to learn nothing from you
but the art and science of fish for breakfast' (p.
16). Peacock seems more at ease with his surroundings, obnoxious though they are; there are no more
crude outbursts, and angst makes no appearance in his
discussions of modern folly. In part, this is due to
the novel's avoidance of stress and high pitch of
feeling. But it is also that its wider social grasp,
its nearness to its subject-matter, almost automatic-
ally involves more accepting views than in the past.
In The Misfortunes of Elphin the present is an intrusion, and is felt as such; in Crotchet Castle it
forms the fabric of the work.
    Van Doren says of Crotchet Castle that in it
'appear the evidences of a dignified retirement from
commotion'(13). This seems to me to be perfectly
fair with regard to the book's handling of the copious materials which it draws from the public life of
Peacock's day. The crotchets and controversies are
all there, but have undergone some calming sea-change
in their passage to this penultimate work. There is
less antipathy, and also less obliqueness of effect;
opinions which previously had been tetchy or subdued
now volunteer themselves with cheerful directness.
Only in Crotchet Castle do we meet a Peacock who has
scrutinized the world with care and then withdrawn
from doubt and responsibility into an easy-going
neutrality which can admit everything and be troubled
by none of it.

This shift towards tranquillity is particularly evident in Peacock's treatment of the more affirmative aspects of his novel. This is not simply a matter of a less harassed rendition of the relations of the characters. It extends generally: there are Wordsworthian moments which seem free from irony, and Rousseau, 'the philosopher of Geneva' (p.154), teaches Susannah the bliss and consolation of 'The society of children, the beauties of nature, the solitude of the mountains' (p.155). The whole novel is emotionally at rest, and emanates a mood of gratification it would be hard to equal except in Gryll Grange.

However, although the links between Susannah and Mr Chainmail, and Lady Clarinda and Captain Fitzchrome, are of importance in establishing this mood, the role of affairs of the heart in Crotchet Castle is underplayed. The characters are nicely developed, and their love pays heed to circumstances of wealth and status, yet somehow vigour does not result. For all the brightness surrounding Susannah and the contrasting, expedient argumentation of Lady Clarinda, there is little real force to the handling of love in the book: we recognize that no genuine risk is involved, so in spite of the detailedness of Peacock's presentation, and the thematic prominence of love's power over material constraint, we are not deeply touched. It seems that, as Peacock's perplexities have diminished, so too has the energy of his counsels to mankind. There is romance in plenty in Crotchet Castle; but in the love lives of the major characters it is no longer potent or moving.

This is a pity, since the novel toys with a clash of loyalties which is intrinsically of great significance. The literature of all periods is full of stories of true love hindered, and sometimes destroyed, by the conservative forces of money and position. One need only think of Jane Austen to see how vital a theme this could be for Peacock's own time. Yet in Crotchet Castle the personal conflicts and hard-won education which give Pride and Prejudice so much of its strength are largely absent; this too is a social comedy, but of a conciliatory kind. The course of Captain Fitzchrome's wooing of Lady Clarinda is obstructed by financial problems of which each clearly sees the implications. As Lady Clarinda says, 'I am out of my teens. I have been very much in love; but now I am come to years of discretion, and must think, like other people, of settling myself advantageously' (p.62). The couple discuss the matter with thoughtful good sense, and the situation of the soliciting of an urbane, materialistic woman

by a love-sick man has interest and freshness. In
fact the handling of Lady Clarinda's divided feelings
is altogether excellent; when the Captain goes missing after one of her sallies, for instance, she does
not doubt that he 'had gone away designedly: she
missed him more than she could have anticipated; and
wished she had at least postponed her last piece of
cruelty till the completion of their homeward voyage'
(p.132). As in the rest of Peacock's books, nobody
is in any doubt as to the worth of love and marriage.
But when the difficulties are as loosely treated as
they are here, and the resolution as summary, we can
have little sense of involvement. Thus, although we
recognize that Captain Fitzchrome's lack of fortune
and Susannah's lack of family may thwart their intended marriages with Lady Clarinda and Mr Chainmail,
and note that this is an important topic in the
novel, we are not encouraged to dwell profoundly on
their dilemmas.

One can have no sense of thinness, however,
when one comes to consider Peacock's treatment of
Wales. Whatever he might think about the Scots, his
attachment to the Welsh landscape and its people
remains constant throughout his fiction. In Crotchet
Castle, Merionethshire is a land of freedom, simple
pleasures and healthy satisfactions. From the start,
it is associated with the cheerful family life of the
Ap-Llymyry's, a matter not just of sensible occupation but also of mutton, cream, bacon, 'an occasional
glass of double X' (p.9), 'mead' and 'elder wine'.
The effect on Susannah, a girl of resilience and
wholesome instincts, is rapid: 'the poor deserted
damsel was flourishing on slate, while her rich and
false young knight was pining on chalk'. Her existence is energetic and contented; she does her work,
and wanders at will among the many beauties that lie
around her: 'Sometimes she descended into the bottom
of the dingles, to the black rocky beds of the
torrents, and dreamed away hours at the feet of the
cataracts' (p.156). Liberty and independence are
fostered; although 'more of the contadina of the
opera than of the genuine mountaineer' (pp.151-2),
Susannah in Wales seems an admirably Peacockian sort
of girl, active, unconstrained, and of conspicuous
sexual attractiveness - 'as plump as a partridge'
(pp 160-1), it is said.

However, Wales is not idolized as an Arcadian
alternative to the town. It offers no escape from
actuality, though its life may be richer and more
harmonious - after all, Susannah and Mr Chainmail
face similar problems in Wales to those encountered

by Lady Clarinda and Captain Fitzchrome in society.
Wales is not absolutely different, therefore; it is
only more salubrious, less complicated and further
away. There are parallels between Merionethshire
and London, and they are always to the city's disadvantage, but rustic soundness is not set up in
strident opposition to urban taint. When Susannah,
and later the Captain and Mr Chainmail, move to 'one
of the deep valleys under the cloudcapt summits of
Meirion' (p.133), they gain freedom and strength, but
with no overtones of culmination or metamorphosis.
In Wales, truths are clearer than in the outside
world, material constraint is less powerful and it is
easier for emotion to be unhindered. But Crotchet
Castle is too sophisticated to advocate any simplis-
tic retreat, even to a place as beautiful and untra-
mmelled as Wales is made to seem. The book permits
holidays, encourages them or finds them necessary,
yet in the end it accepts that we have no choice but
to make the best life we can within our proper sphere
--that is to say, in the city and the country houses
with which it is mostly concerned.
     A similar pragmatism governs Peacock's use of
food and drink in Crotchet Castle. The pleasures of
the feast are celebrated in almost every scene.
Partial, schematic attempts to tame the world's diversity are constantly subverted by reference to
communal satisfactions of the table which are unpoll-
uted by controversy and independent of financial
status. This is much more striking than in Peacock's
previous conversation novels, where such delights
provide only a subdued counterpoint to the hobby-
horsical rhetoric of most of the characters. Here,
the stratagem is boisterous, almost coercive; only
the book's unruffled manner prevents us from rebell-
ing against it. But we see the aptness of Peacock's
enthusiasm when we view it in the context of his
presentation of Wales and of love and his use of
music. These are the positive elements in the novel,
and combine to persuade us of the sufficiency and
attractiveness of the joys available to mankind. But
it is not merely that food and drink are gratifying,
or that they remind us that we have stomachs as well
as minds. They join Mr MacQuedy and Dr Folliott in
a discriminating parley on the subject of salmon, and
after the discord of Chapter VI, 'Theories', we end
with a song and universal agreement on the pleasures
of dinner. Their role, therefore, is to unify at the
same time that they give comfort. They recall disputants to a fellowship which may be forgotten in the
heat and emptiness of their theorizing. They

indicate that man's existence will be most satisfying
when he is together at table with his friends, chatting playfully, maybe, but never neglecting the real
business in hand which provides him with both an
actual and a metaphorical raison d'être. The last
word on this topic, and the wittiest, may be left to
Peacock himself: 'We have recorded, as historical
evidence, that the most incorruptible republicans
were austere and abstemious; but it is still a
question whether they would not have exerted a more
beneficial influence, and have been better men, if
they had moistened their throats with Maderia and
enlarged their sympathies with grouse'(14). Peacock
was a music-lover as well as a gourmet, and in
Crotchet Castle, as elsewhere, he associates singing
with eating and drinking, and clearly regards all
three in an approving light. Music is less assert-
ive here than in Gryll Grange, but it pervades the
novel. Mr Trillo has a significant function as the
book's chorus-master, awakening us to the power of
song and twice cheering the company with lively airs.
Susannah, when 'comforting her wounded spirit' (p.
133), turns to 'music, painting, and poetry', writes
a wan little song to her father, sings the robust
ballad of 'Ouf! di giorno' for the Ap-Llymyry children, and then wins Mr Chainmail's approbation with
'passages of ancient music' (p.168). Also, after a
first dance at Chainmail Hall, 'in which all classes
of the company mingled' (p.206), Susannah again plays
her harp and gives the gathering 'a song of the
twelfth century'. At the same Christmas party, other
guests 'sang in the intervals of the dances' (p.208),
and even Lady Clarinda is prevailed on to offer a
melancholy ballad:
        'Wiser were the lovers,
    In the days of old' (p.210).
However, Lady Clarinda is a cooler character than
Susannah, who remains the centre of the novel's
musical interest, playing 'without affectation' (p.
167) and possessed of a voice which 'had that full
soft volume of melody which gives to common speech
the fascination of music' (pp.163-4).
    Both in this book and in others, songs are used
to consolidate feelings of harmony, often over the
dinner-table, or to prompt a sense of community after
crotcheteering dissensions. But it seems to me that
music is contributory rather than primary in this
respect: it reinforces Peacock's other positive
values, but does not dominate them. Teyssandier, I
think, exaggerates this matter when he says that
Peacock's 'vision positive du monde' is 'exprimée

symboliquement par la musique et par la danse'(15);
more correct, because more inclusive, is his later
comment on 'la gaieté sonore d'un monde qui trouve
son unité dans le bonheur de vivre'(16).

One final aspect of <u>Crotchet Castle</u>, its habit
of extensive quotation from the classics, resists
firm linkage with the optimistic elements I have been
discussing. In this novel, as before, there are
epigraphs from Homer and Pindar and discussions of
ancient poets and playwrights and of the merits of
their works, and it is hard to avoid a sense of approbation. Peacock and his Dr Folliott would both
agree with Lord Monboddo that Greek is 'the language
the most perfect that I know, or, I believe, that is
known'(17). Although there is no downright statement
to this effect, the relish with which the classics
are handled, and their trenchant championship by Dr
Folliott, give one an impression of their abundant
worth. It is only with the slightest irony that,
when Mr Chainmail says he is for 'truth and simplicity' (p.126), Dr Folliott energetically replies, 'Let
him who loves them read Greek: Greek, Greek, Greek'.
From remarks such as these we may gather that the
function of the classical quotations is to conjure
up another and better time than the present, when
Peacock's criterion of 'truth to nature' (p.125) was
properly embodied both in art and in action. This
seems subtly and whimsically confirmed in Chapter
VII, 'The Sleeping Venus', which gives prominence to
the nobility and bodily freedom (and, by implication,
the sexual openness) of classic art, and encourages
the characters to follow their impulses and to
ignore the petty constraints of the society of their
day. It is not by accident, therefore, that the
Greek Venus is described as the epitome of 'truth and
beauty' (p.97). Yet the pointedness of this chapter
seems almost entirely absent from the Greek and Latin
verse and incidental references more generally scattered throughout the book. Given the status of the
Ancients and the records of Peacock's library, one
might expect lines from Homer or Vergil to offer
indices of conduct or to confer an ultimate authority
on one view as opposed to another. In practice, they
do nothing of the sort. Not only are they morally
inactive; even their role in underlining the feeble-
ness of the present by comparison with the greatness
of the past does not seem thoroughgoingly accomplished. Pindar is called to mind in a discussion of
breakfast, and Nonnus gives a heartfelt evocation of
the attractiveness of wine. They give weight to no
general view of the world, and ratify no neat rules

of behaviour. If anything, they may encourage us to
feel that dining has always been with us, and has
always given pleasure, but even this is not stressed.
Quotation thus becomes a branch of sociability and
eloquence rather than of debate; it provides
speeches with variety and piquancy, not proof[18].
So when Dr Folliott draws on his reading, it is not
for learning's sake, nor is it really an attempt to
bolster his opinions. It is a sign of his ebull-
ience, and its aim is to supply the connoisseur with
verbal delights of a cultivated and felicitous kind.
   Although it is low-key, Crotchet Castle is not
thin. The positive elements in the book produce a
gregarious warmth that is far from Peacock's earlier
disquiet. This is a work of easy entertainment, and
indicates how well a latter-day Peacock could heed
the excellent advice of Epicurus: 'We must then
meditate on the things that make our happiness, seeing that when that is with us we have all, but when
it is absent we do all to win it'[19].

   Crotchet Castle follows on from Nightmare Abbey
in its management of a more ordinary social orbit and
its fuller sense of personality and circumstance.
Even figures like Mr Firedamp and Mr Eavesdrop are
less heated than before, and no-one reaches the
heights of poetry and exaggeration exemplified by the
Hon Mr Listless. There is still the same pleasure in
human vitality which one finds in all of Peacock's
books, but here its forms are closer to our everyday
experience. Peacock's new openness and bonhomie are
best seen in the more substantial presentation of
his major figures, but a boyish exuberance remains
even to Mr Trillo and his peers, whose single
passions offer no real threat to the harmony of the
company. Here, a genuine sociability can be developed; it is not just the lovers who have the possibility of getting together in Crotchet Castle, it is
all their companions as well--and there are songs,
dances, parties, trips, trysts and dinners enough to
provide friendly encounters for even the most disparate of characters.
   Dr Folliott possesses the distinctive voice in
the novel, and has often been taken as the image of
his creator. He seems frequently to be right, and
his Rabelaisian personality singles him out as a
character rather than a mere guzzling, ecclesiastical
crotcheteer. Although he has weaknesses and blind
spots, he sets standards of lucidity and common sense
which cannot but give credence to what he says.
Also, he is closely linked with eating and drinking;

it is generally his ringing tones which call out for
wine or lamb, to cut short the disputes of his
fellow guests. Throughout the book he is a sturdy
and determined maître d'hôtel, offering pleasures,
allotting places and settling procedures, and
bringing to everything the same breezy Epicureanism.
There is no other work by Peacock where the sway of
a single figure is so marked. For it is not only in
social matters that Dr Folliott is commanding; he
can also act. He threatens Mr Eavesdrop with his
bamboo, defends himself stoutly when two ruffians
waylay him, and in the seige which concludes the
novel 'He clapped a helmet on his head, seized a long
lance, threw open the gates, and tilted out on the
rabble' (p.203); this is 'the church militant' (p.
202) indeed. Dr Folliott seems, therefore, straightforwardly to represent virtues of reasonableness,
vigour and good living which are habitually favoured
by Peacock in his fiction and which also form the
core of Crotchet Castle.
    Yet in the end Dr Folliott's presentation is
subtler than this might suggest. Despite the leisur-
eliness of Crotchet Castle, irony continues to lurk
in quiet corners, and Dr Folliott does not escape
its witty reproof. Even Dr Folliott's chief attractiveness, the rich delight of his gastronomy, is not a
matter of unhampered celebration; when he talks of
breakfast, for example, it is difficult not to
suspect the conscious rhetoric of his speech:
        'Chocolate, coffee, tea, cream, eggs,
        ham, tongue, cold fowl,--all these are
        good, and bespeak good knowledge in him
        who sets them forth: but the touchstone
        is fish: anchovy is the first step,
        prawns and shrimps the second; and I
        laud him who reaches even to these:
        potted char and lampreys are the third,
        and a fine stretch of progression; but
        lobster is, indeed, matter for a May
        morning, and demands a rare combination
        of knowledge and virtue in him who sets
        it forth' (p.15).
'Knowledge and virtue' is too much to be taken seriously even from Dr Folliott, it seems to me.
Equally, there is mockery of the solemnity of utter-
ance which gives him so much of his power:
        'THE REV. DR. FOLLIOTT.
        Now, Mr. MacQuedy, Achilles was disting-
        uished above all the Greeks for his inf-
        lexible love of truth: could education
        have made Achilles one of your reviewers?

MR. MACQUEDY.
No doubt of it, even if your character
of them were true to the letter.
THE REV. DR. FOLLIOTT.
And I say, sir--chicken and asparagus--
Titan had made him of better clay' (p.53).
This conversation forms part of the novel's debate
around the potentials of education, and its purpose
seems to be to cast oblique light on the fools who
try, by the pursuit of wealth or status, to cover up
their irremediable and intrinsic deficiencies. Its
wit lies in the placing of the 'chicken and
asparagus', which offers itself not just as Dr
Folliott's categorical answer to Mr MacQuedy but also
as a sly affront to his own orotund self-righteous-
ness.

However, alththough he is certainly not the pure
voice of truth, Dr Folliott is a figure of great
allure. His constant association with good humour
and with pleasure must encourage us to see him mainly
in a sympathetic light even if we cannot accept that
his role is, in any systematic way, to stand in for
the author himself.

Lady Clarinda is Dr Folliott's only peer. What
she has in common with him is a brisk, pragmatic
clarity of vision which sees the world as it is and
does not try to change it; instead, she makes the
best life she can within its limits. Like Jane
Austen's women, Lady Clarinda is only too aware of
material constraints, and at the end of the novel it
is a triumph of thoughtful consideration as well as
of romance when she agrees to marry Captain
Fitzchrome: not only does she feel 'partiality' (p.
212) and 'gratitude', she also knows that the fortune
she shares with him is humbler 'but less precarious..
than that to which she had been destined as the price
of a rotten borough'. Throughout Crotchet Castle we
have been impressed by her verve and cleverness, and
the perspicacity of her assessment of her own circumstances. Admiration is generated by this realistic
self-knowledge, especially when it is expressed with
such sharpness and wit: 'Respectable means rich, and
decent means poor. I should die if I heard my family
called decent' (p.38). Lady Clarinda operates, as
Marilyn Butler has said, as 'a genuine focus of
intelligence'[20]; she is our most dependable comm-
entator on the social mores of the book, and her
commanding stance and poised discrimination make it
hard to withhold assent from what she says. However,
she is no frigid blue-stocking intent merely on
clinical analyses of her milieu; we may approve of

her mind, the most incisive in the novel, but we also
warm to her emotions. Peacock is careful not to give
her too relentlessly mastered a position. Despite
herself, her feelings break through, and her true
affection for Captain Fitzchrome refuses to be subdued; she always shows him 'a certain kindness of
manner' (p.130), and when he leaves the travelling
party in despair 'she missed him more than she could
have anticipated' (p.132). She is the latest
Peacockian herione to combine sagacity with sentiment: able on the one hand authoritatively to crit-
icize her fellow-guests, but on the other to leap
thankfully into the arms of her faithful lover at
the close of the book.

The other figures need little comment. I have
already remarked on the fresh self-possession of
Susannah, and the balanced, energetic nature of her
character. Young Mr Chainmail develops wisdom under
Susannah's influence, and takes on substance as the
book progresses; her love changes his crotchets into
good Old English virtues, and leaves him an affable
husband rather than a deluded enthusiast. Captain
Fitzchrome complements his lady's sophisticated
decisiveness with ingenuousness and adoration; he
is a buffeted lay-figure, never required to be more
than a gallant foil to Lady Clarinda's dominance.
The surprise in Crotchet Castle comes from the
Crotchets themselves; after the first chapter, they
are not much called to mind, and never acquire the
officiating and organizing roles of their predecessors in Headlong Hall or Nightmare Abbey. Perhaps
old Mr Crotchet represents what is wrong with the
present day, even down to the discreet anti-semitism
which tinges the presentation of his wife and daughter, but I do not think that this leaves a very significant mark on the reader's mind. Possibly in a
novel like this any cheery direction like Squire
Headlong's would seem out of keeping; all that is
needed is a first, brief impetus, a setting, and
the convenient collapse of young Crotchet's firm at
the end, and that is all we are given. The leading
parts in this book are taken by the guests, and there
is no inevitable, controlling recall to the host and
his problems, as there always was with Squire Headlong or the Glowries.

Peacock is rarely concerned with tightness of
plot; all his books have an air of impromptu. But
Crotchet Castle has almost no recognizable structure
at all; although it encompasses two love stories, a
great deal of talking and a number of themes, it is

really composed entirely of interludes.

Marilyn Butler calls the novel 'a dispersed panorama'(21), and this seems completely appropriate. Something is always going on, in a wide range of locales, and we seem far from the stasis of Headlong Hall. Crotchet Castle operates on a basis of expansiveness, not of concentration. There is conversation, as there always is in Peacock, but it is interpersed with more action and more changes of scene than in the other conversation novels (Melincourt being the evident exception). The movement, from Crotchet Castle onto the river, to Wales and finally to Chainmail Hall, has an unforced vivacity of effect. The same is true of Peacock's language: felicitous, clever and expert, it offers constant jokey delights from which ominous undertones have mostly been expunged. Nothing goes on for too long, and the more rapid flow of dialogue and events ensures that there is always something new to distract us. We never have the sense in this book, as with Mr Flosky in Nightmare Abbey, that the author has misjudged the interest of his characters or the span of our attention.

Crotchet Castle is a work less of contemporary anxiety than of loco-descriptive complaisance; the stresses and upheavals of the 1830's figure in its texture, but do little to ruffle its tenor. Like a pantomime (or a banquet), it does not progress but simply carries on, and pleases us by its various set-pieces rather than by its uniformity. Its effects are individually amusing, but they are loosely inter-related; one episode does not follow on necessarily from another, nor build on what has gone before. Only its themes--such as they are--and its grouped characters prevent the book from falling apart into a series of independent units: Dr Folliott's role as a genial major-domo is an essential one, if Crotchet Castle is not to seem fragmentary beyond redemption. As it is, there are good-natured fits and starts of incident, the characters tread their agreeable paths and time passes until we arrive at the Christmas festivities which conclude the novel. Crotchet Castle never descends into boredom; as entertainment, it is as lively as anything Peacock ever wrote.

The Christmas celebrations at Chainmail Hall provide a wily culmination to the novel. The keynote is set by feasting, music and dancing. Everything is subordinated to the relish of traditional, Old English joys: Peacock seems determined

resoundingly to end his book with communal satisfactions of the table, and with the marriages which have
been impending for so long. Thus in the 'spacious
and lofty' (p.193) hall there is a 'stupendous fire',
'on which blocks of pine were flaming and crackling';
Susannah is 'the picture of a happy bride, rayonnante
de joie et d'amour' (p.194); the dishes of the
banquet are brought in 'in grand procession' (p.197),
to the sound of a harp; they include a boar's head
'garnished with rosemary, with a citron in its
mouth', 'an enormous sausage, which it required two
men to carry', 'the ancient glory of the Christmas
pie, a gigantic plum-pudding, a pyramid of minced
pies, and a baron of beef bringing up the rear';
'Ale and wine flowed in abundance' (p.198); and
there are 'Christmas gambols', and singing and dancing in which everyone participates. Even the conversations are hearty and convivial; good humour and
playfulness seem paramount. The stage is set, we
feel, for Crotchet Castle to offer the most celebratory conclusion of any of Peacock's works.
     In fact, it does so, though not without interr-
uption. As the guests are enjoying themselves and
their dinner is passing off 'merrily' (p.198), suddenly there is 'tremendous clamour' outside. Dr
Folliott optimistically suggests that this may be due
to mummers, but 'a chorus of discordant voices' (p.
199) identifies itself as coming from '"Captain
Swing"'(22). There follows a brief discussion of
popular discontent, terminated by Dr Folliott's
virile call to arms: 'Let us get rid of the enemy'
(p.200). With varying degrees of zest and bravery,
his fellows gather round him, and the terms of the
combat become clearer. This is not mere thuggery
like the earlier attack on Dr Folliott, nor can it
quite be reduced to a conflict between good sense
and 'the march of mind' (p.199). Mr Chainmail defends his hearth as 'the fortress of beef and ale'
(p.201), and Dr Folliott leads the men into battle
'Pro aris et focis! that is, for tithe pigs and
fires to roast them!' (p.203). Their opponents, on
the other hand, are a 'rabble-rout' and scatter
feebly 'in all directions' at the first sign of resistance. The party at Chainmail Hall then sets itself to revelry again, with even greater gusto than
before, and ends the day with 'punch and wassail' (p.
211) before dropping off one by one 'into sweet for-
getfulness'. This incident has an almost disdainful
swagger; it is hard not to see it as a deliberate
sloughing off of some of the major problems of the
day.

However, the incident is more troubled than it seems. It has much comedy, especially at the expense of Mr Philpot, who 'had diluted himself with so much wine, as to be quite hors de combat' (p.203), and of Mr Toogood, who becomes trapped in his suit of armour 'like a chicken trussed for roasting'. But more striking are the ironies which undermine the allegorical simplicity of its message. These ironies commence with an epigraph from Rabelais protesting that ignorance, 'mere de tous maulx' (p.193), is opposed but still permitted by the 'Vous autres' apparently in authority. This is impossible exactly to pin down, but the implication must surely be that the rabble which attacks the Hall is not entirely responsible for its actions--and that the carousers inside, as representatives of the forces of wealth, learning and position, must bear some of the blame both for the dilemma they find themselves in and for the unimproved state of the mob by which they are beseiged. Subversive feelings such as these seem confirmed as the chapter proceeds: with some gravity, Mr Chainmail attributes the Jacquerie(23) and 'the march of mind' (p.199) to the same brutalizing 'poverty in despair'; equally, it is with accuracy and sarcasm that he notes, 'The way to keep the people down is kind and liberal usage' (p.201). Much of this goes against the general tenor of the book, and it is difficult to reconcile it with the overall direction of this chapter as I have already outlined it. I think one clue to Peacock's intentions may be gathered from his insistence on the word 'old', which he ubiquitously couples with each anticipated element of the life at Chainmail Hall: 'Old hospitality, old wine, old ale--all the images of old England; an old butler' (p.190). The whole world-order of Mr Chainmail and Dr Folliott, joyous and stable as it may seem, therefore, contains the seeds of its own destruction: its celebration of old things, in this shadowed context, gives warning of decline. What we feel here is that Old England, a sunny concept to which Peacock is determinedly faithful, is painfully at risk; with some ambiguity, it seems to be rescued and vindicated--but for how long, we may ask?--and what will happen next time? One cannot avoid an impression of confusion in these veerings of attitude. I think that what happens is that, despite his denial of the urgent issues of his time in Crotchet Castle, and his reaching out towards phlegm and festivity, Peacock is in the end unable to view things quite as neatly as he might wish. So, while the outline of this assembly at Chainmail Hall is

relatively lucid, its undertones are far from being
either congruent or easy.

It is useful, but may also be misleading, to see
Crotchet Castle in the light of its predecessors. It
seems so plainly to be the same kind of novel as
Headlong Hall and Nightmare Abbey that it appears
reasonable to expect it to give us the same enjoyments that those books do. We may therefore approach
it as a comic fable in which certain powerful doubts,
particularly as to the effects of prescription and
the value of institutions, will be sharply exposed to
view. In practice, it uses the techniques of the
conversation novels, but purges their concern. It is
a work of repudiation; with the exceptions I have
noted, it turns its back on anxiety, and in its place
praises the delights of the table, of the countryside, of music and of love. We miss the excitement
of earlier books, but we have the compensations of
amusingness and vivacity. And yet, especially at the
end of the novel, it is hard not to be rather shocked
by Peacock's abnegation of former responsibilities.
I would not agree with what Steuert says about
Peacock's books in general, but he comments appropriately on Crotchet Castle and offers a due qualification of its integrity and success: 'For all
[Peacock's] clear-sighted appraisal of what his age
had lost and what it needed again for its essential
balance and health, there is a certain obtuseness or
rather readiness to leave off worrying which suggests
a half-conscious compromise with Philistinism'(24).

CHAPTER VII

GRYLL GRANGE

There are not many authors who would care to leave a
gap of nearly thirty years between two works, or who
would attempt an elaborate and original novel at the
age of seventy-five. Peacock, unexpected and idiosyncratic to the last, does both. Gryll Grange, the
last and richest of his books, appeared in Fraser's
Magazine from April to December, 1860 in serial form,
and was republished the next year as a bound volume.
Evidently, after the immense period that separates it
from Crotchet Castle, and issuing quixotically so
late in Peacock's life, to crown a time of reduced
and lesser literary activity, Gryll Grange must have
the air of an after-thought, of a work called forth
specifically to meet new and perhaps pressing circumstances. Certainly it is different in manner and
technique from its six predecessors, and easier and
more romantic than any of them. The result of this
is that the novel has been rather undervalued;
critics have tended to sentimentalize it, or to see
it dismissively as the mere subdued, mellow adieu of
a writer whose best work had been done almost half a
century before. In fact, as I shall try to show,
Gryll Grange is worthy of the closest attention and
of high praise. It represents a change from Peacock's established patterns; it is remote from the
public world, warm in feeling and direct in approach;
it lacks the fraughtness and risk of Melincourt or
Nightmare Abbey. But this implies no relaxation of
artistic control. Gryll Grange is anything but
facile: although long, it is one of the most assured
and perfectly achieved pieces of writing that Peacock
ever produced. It needs no excuses, and can stand
comparison, from the point of view of artistry, with
anything in his oeuvre.
      As we investigate the events of the last decade
of Peacock's life, the genesis of Gryll Grange

becomes easier to understand. Peacock retired from
the East India Company in 1856, and was rewarded with
a substantial pension for his thirty-seven years of
distinguished service. He looked forward to a quiet
existence at Lower Halliford, surrounded by books,
family and friends, and well able to indulge his
tastes for good food and good wine. We know that his
reading continued unabated, and that he carried on
with his Greek studies and spent much time with
Italian epic poets such as Boiardo and Ariosto; in a
letter to his friend Lord Broughton, dated September
10 1856, he records, 'I have just read through, for
the seventh time, Orlando Innamorato'(1). But in
fact Peacock's later years were far from unruffled.
His wife, long valetudinarian, had died in 1851, and
his retirement was disrupted by a series of distress-
ing personal problems. His daughter Rosa Jane died
in 1857. His son Edward, who had married against his
father's wishes, like Rosa Jane, gave him nothing but
disappointment. Most important of all, his brilliant
and wayward daughter Mary Ellen, the favourite of all
his children, left her husband, the novelist George
Meredith, in 1858, and eloped to Capri with a painter
named Henry Wallis. In 1859 she returned alone and
in disgrace, and died two years later at Weybridge.
After the death of his mother in 1833, Mary Ellen had
become Peacock's confidant and occasional collabora-
tor, and he was deeply pained by her folly and the
sufferings it brought in its train. Something of his
concern can be gauged from a letter he wrote to
Broughton in 1861, in which he comments with unchara-
cteristic weariness that 'I have struggled in vain
against the double weight of mental depression and
physical fatigue'(2). Only Mary Rosewall, his
adoptive child, really offered Peacock sympathy and
support in this time of stress. Even alleviated by
material well-being and the resources of friendship
and a well-stocked library, the last years of
Peacock's life cannot have been happy. Gryll Grange
is his response to these circumstances of gloom. It
derives from genuine anguish, and its aim is to
assert the life-giving virtues which appeared to
Peacock to be most in danger at this time.
    After the publication of Crotchet Castle, Pea-
cock produced no fiction for twenty-nine years and
comparatively little writing of any kind. If he
wrote at all it was for the Reviews, or an incidental
piece of verse; mostly, his literary activity was
critical rather than imaginative. Essays that he
contributed to Fraser's Magazine during the 50's bear
Peacock's habitual stamp of scholarship and sharp

intelligence, but retreat from bold interpretation
towards a reserved, inward-looking concentration on
academic minutiae. Three rather staid pieces on the
classical drama offer little that is fresh, though
they indicate a high estimation of Aristophanes,
whose Old Comedy seems to Peacock to have 'abounded
with poetry of the highest order'(3). The review of
the Müller and Donaldson History of Greek Literature
occupies itself largely with cool exposition; however, a note of superior reproof is sometimes heard
as well. Much more interesting are the essays on
Demetrius Galanus's Greek translations from the Sans-
krit and on the Oeuvres of the charming, lively travellers, Chapelle and Bachaumont, in both of which one
detects undertones of regret and nostalgia, the sentiments of a discontented old age. The 'Memoirs of
Percy Bysshe Shelley', which extended over three
issues between June, 1858 and March, 1862, is more
vigorous in approach but remains profoundly retros-
pective in content. In addition, there was a resurgence not just of writing, but of fictional writing,
from about 1858 onwards: several unfinished stories
date from these years. But of greater significance
than any of these are three lesser-known works which
have a direct bearing on the mood and themes of
Peacock's last novel.
The first is the unpublished, fragmentary 'Dialogue on Friendship after Marriage', which is water-
marked 1859 and must therefore be close in date to
the composition of Gryll Grange. The subject of the
dialogue is the relation between 'reality' and 'ideality'(4) in marriage, and the way in which husband
and wife either can or should be accommodated one to
the other. Clearly, given the experience of Mary
Ellen's flight to Italy, and his disapproval of Rosa
Jane's and Edward's marriages, this is a matter which
would be much in Peacock's mind during this period,
and it figures prominently in Gryll Grange. However,
Peacock was not content with this sketchy version,
and shortly afterwards returned to the topic in a
fuller second draft, this time entitled 'A Dialogue
on Idealities'(5). Here he draws in a good deal of
material he was also to use in his novel, and makes
plain both the importance he attaches to 'true
happiness in marriage'(6) and the difficulty of rec-
onciling this with 'practical life'(7). These dialogues give us a valuable clue to the impetus behind
Peacock's unlikely return to fiction in Gryll Grange.
They pick up the threads of his personal anxiety over
the married lives of his children, and weave them
into the tentative, questioning fabric of brief

symposia. But this form, though it underlies most of
Peacock's fiction, is unsatisfactory here: their
subject may be interesting, but the dialogues themselves seem insufficient. They point to a problem of
some intractability, whose exploration might require
the larger sphere of a novel, as dilemmas of political authority and private oppression had done in
previous years.

The third piece which I have in mind is a plan-
gent short essay on 'The Last Day of Windsor Forest'.
This was probably written in 1862, but was not published during the author's lifetime. It is beautifully composed, reflective and elegiac; its evocation
of the enclosure of the forest flows easily into a
deep-seated regret for past beauty and past joys. As
Peacock says, with the fencing of once open land,'the
life of the old scenes was gone'(8). Here the writer
seems sadly conscious of his age and apartness; he
feels that the best of life has departed, and that he
needs some refuge from the emptiness of his everyday
existence. Dejectedly, he concludes, 'I think it
best to avoid the sight of the reality, and to make
the best of cherishing at a distance
        The memory of what has been,
        And never more will be'(9).
A couple of years before, Gryll Grange had already
demonstrated the power of Peacock's feelings on the
subject of enclosure. An introductory note warns
that: 'In the following pages, the New Forest is
always mentioned as if it were still unenclosed.
This is the only state in which the Author has been
acquainted with it. Since its enclosure, he has
never seen it, and purposes never to do so' (p.[xi]).
In contrast, and with a clearly admonitory intention,
Gryll Grange itself is presented as an image of old-
fashioned rustic wholesomeness, situated 'on the
borders of the New Forst, in the midst of a park
which was a little forest in itself, reaching nearly
to the sea, and well stocked with deer, having a
large outer tract,where a numerous light-rented and
well-conditioned tenantry fattened innumerable pigs'
(p.13). Quietly, throughout the novel, we have a
sense of the dangers which menace the beauties of the
landscape and the natural order of country living. It
is only in Gryll Grange, with something of the fear
and impotence of declining years, that Peacock's
enduring affection for the countryside shows itself
with such awareness of risk. The outside world is
held at bay in this book, but the prospect of enclosure still stimulates Peacock to strong feeling. Dr
Opimian points out to his new friend, Mr Falconer:

'here is a charming bit of forest scenery. Look at that old oak with the deer under it; the long and deep range of fern running up from it to that beech-grove on the upland, the lights and shadows on the projections and recesses of the wood, and the blaze of foxglove in its foreground. It is a place in which a poet might look for a glimpse of a Hamadryad' (p.32), but the latter can only gloomily reply: 'The admiration of sylvan and pastoral scenery is at the mercy of an inclosure act, and instead of the glimpse of a Hamadryad you will sometime see a large board warning you off the premises under penalty of rigour of law' (p.33).

By this time Peacock was an old man, and thoughts of death must often have come to his mind; several of his friends as well as members of his family had died at the end of the 50's. When he writes to Broughton, he quotes desolating lines from Béranger:

'Encore une étoile qui file,
File, file, et disparait'(10).

When one is no longer young, thoughts of dying and teasing memories of long-gone pleasures can hardly fail to pose disturbing new threats to the hard-won assurance of maturity. Like the question of marriage, the fate of England's countryside was much on Peacock's mind at this time, and both topics were exacerbated by the intimations of mortality which we may draw from his correspondence. All these problems point insistently towards some restatement or development of the easygoing synthesis which seemed, in Crotchet Castle, to signal the end of Peacock's career in fiction.

It is by putting together some of the material I have presented here that one can best understand the reasons for Peacock's resumption of his novelist's mantle, this time as a Victorian, in Gryll Grange. From about 1857 we see that problems became increasingly pressing, and that Peacock's suffering was principally caused by the deaths of people close to him and by the difficulties of his children in love and marriage. He must have felt his values more at risk than at any time since his young manhood; the festive acquiescence and calm withdrawal celebrated in Crotchet Castle,which had fostered his happiness for years, must now have seemed vulnerable, if not entirely dissipated. Peacock's answer to these stresses is the same as it had been in the Regency, when he also faced intransigent dilemmas both in society and in himself. It is the answer of art, and of art as respite and accommodation. He writes Gryll

Grange, therefore, a book of rounded emotional assurance which addresses itself to the particular issues
of his seniority and strengthens and clarifies some
of the notions with which he has approached the world
for so long. In rebuttal of the hazards of sudden
death and marital discord, and in a context of
healthy country living, he sets out the antidotes by
which he has fought off pessimism for much of his
adult life. In circumstances of classical warmth and
physical pleasure, he gives a final vindication of
the importance of true love and of the necessity of
savouring to the full life's joys of music, wine,
conviviality and the dinner-table. The public world
impinges little on the private, romantic compass of
Gryll Grange. Instead, the novel is intimate and
domestic, focussing exactly on the personal relationships about which Peacock must have been most uneasy
at this time.

It seems plain, then, that Gryll Grange is intended as a literary response to the harassments that
had accumulated for Peacock during the late 50's.
Like his other books, its purpose is amusement and
consolation; it looks for compensation, and tries to
bring things into a clearer perspective. And, as
time has passed, Peacock has grown more lucid. This
last work is purer in outline and more coherent in
tone than any of its predecessors. Its feelings are
distilled and powerful; its confronting of mortality
and strife has a ring of necessity but also of tranquil understanding.

The mood of Gryll Grange is established in
Chapter I, and carefully maintained throughout the
novel. A telling epigraph from Petronius sets up the
atmosphere within which the action is to evolve: 'Ego
sic semper et ubique vixi, ut ultimam quamque lucem,
tamquam non redituram, consumerem' (p.1;11). After
this we move immediately and pointedly to the first
of the book's many friendly dinners, and a discussion
of Palestine soup ('A very good thing', p.2) between
the Reverend Dr Opimian and his companion Squire
Gryll. The talk is unpressed, and ranges freely over
matters of scholarship and gastronomy and the cultivated gossip of the day. We feel ourselves to be in
the presence not of crotcheteers but of urbane old
gentlemen who know what they like, and are used to
getting it. This cheerful first impression is also
appropriate to the rest of the novel, though it is
not the complete truth; the situation is more complex and finely balanced than it seems. Thoughts of
death, and of the need to live one's short life to

the full, have already been aroused by the quotation from Petronius; Mr Gryll, in addition, voices disapproving views of the 'world of misnomers' in which the two men live. Clearly, their Epicurean contentment is not perfect; fears of mortality, and a distaste for the follies of a misguided contemporary society, hedge it in. But satire is not much on Peacock's mind in this novel; the references to the outside world are unassertive, and carry no strong charge of irritation. When there are asides on the telegraph or on ballooning, or the achievements of modern science, they convey no vigorous sense of ironic qualification. Even politics is productive more of jokes than of the committed enquiry of a work like Melincourt. From chance remarks, one sees that Peacock's notions have not changed; it is just that his whole outer sphere of interest has become subordinated, in Gryll Grange, to more urgent, personal anxieties. This is a book in which death plays a considerable part, and where it intensifies and consolidates the romantic and festive delights which always provide the positive element in Peacock's writing. Gryll Grange is a novel of retirement even more than Crotchet Castle had been, of an impelled, clear-sighted withdrawal from the arena of public affairs and into the surer warmth of private life, buttressed by music, the classics, food and drink and above all by love. The stress on pleasure is emphatic; in no other book known to me is there such a profusion of dinners, or so genial a concentration on the felicity of young people falling in love. Although there are contrary feelings which cast a hortatory shadow over the whole enterprise, it is this reassurance which seems central. Gryll Grange cooly excludes almost the entire refractory range of the disagreeable social and political problems of its day, and instead creates a world in which affirmation is given its head and humanity is shown to withstand death and delusion by the power of its physical and amatory satisfactions. We might even apply to the novel what Peacock's friend Buchanan, somewhat sentimentally, said of the author himself: 'the secret of his beautiful benignity lay deeper. "L'amour a passé par là!"'(12).

From the very beginning of Gryll Grange, and not just about Palestine soup, salmon and Madeira, Dr Opimian and Mr Gryll are in agreement; the latter's attractive young niece, Morgana, adds the accord of a younger generation to that of her elders. In spite of mild flurries of discord, expressed with polite, even-toned self-possession, our impression is of a

rare degree of unanimity. The personal relationships
in this novel are conducted in a setting of ripe con-
currence, where amity, ease and harmony inform each
character's dealings with the others. The only significant opposing note comes from Mr Falconer, whose
Christian coldness is broken down in the course of
the story by a more human, and also more pagan,
passion for Morgana. Crotcheteering is softened
almost out of existence. Monomaniac tirades are replaced by the elegant, sociable attunement of a group
very much at one over its preponderant concerns.
Conversation, with Peacock's usual freight of wit and
erudition, takes on cordiality and collaboration;
genuine feeling is communicated, and there is a new
sense of interchange to mitigate the vivid separateness of the characters in Headlong Hall or Melincourt. So, in the first chapter, there is room for
different viewpoints, but at the same time a possibility of give and take, and a conclusion by which
each friendly interlocutor may be satisfied. For the
Christmas celebrations at the Grange, Dr Opimian
suggests 'a tenson of the twelfth century' (p.9); Mr
Gryll prefers an updated 'Aristophanic comedy' (p.
11); and Morgana's enthusiasm, in keeping with the
book's complaisance of outlook, gleefully combines
both proposals and adds a spice of satire: 'I should
so like to hear what my great ancestor, Gryllus,
thinks of us: and Homer, and Dante, and Shakespeare,
and Richard the First, and Oliver Cromwell' (p.12).
Given the obliging common sense of these figures,
their calmer and more ordinary speech, and the purposes and views which they share, one comes to see
Gryll Grange as a very different kind of work from
the earlier conversation novels. Its core of interest lies in romance and its mood is serene and approving; it is much more given over to festivity and
the delineation of complex emotions than any of its
predecessors. As Kjellin says, it 'differs... in
particulars only from the novel of manners'[13]. The
concomitant of this is that the investigative function of Peacock's fiction, which is so marked in the
political questioning of Melincourt and the literary
unease of Nightmare Abbey, is muted. Certain topics
are brought into the open and clarified as they were
before, but in general our attention is directed more
at love-affairs than at polemical debates. What the
book engenders is pleasure and alleviation; it does
not focus upon doubt. The Divorce Court, the Peace
Society, Pantopragmatism and competitive examination
may thread their way through the novel, the source of
much fun and mild irony, but they no longer dominate

its texture. For the first time, in Gryll Grange the celebration of romantic love is absolutely ascendant over the negative voice of Peacock's criticism. As in Crotchet Castle, but more forcefully, this gives charm to Peacock's prose. I noted in the earlier book that it was hard not to miss the tightness and flourish to which Peacock had accustomed us from Headlong Hall onwards. But here there is no sense of lack. The writing is given potent appeal by the wealth of feeling which it registers with sympathetic directness. Thus, after Lord Curryfin and Miss Niphet have agreed on their engagement and he has kissed her hand, 'He sealed his claim again, but this time it was on her lips. The rose again mantled on her cheeks, but the blush was heightened to damask. She withdrew herself from his arms, saying, "Once for all, till you have an indisputable right"' (p.315). Elsewhere in the novel, Peacock is as sharp and sceptical as ever; but here he achieves a tender simplicity of effect which it would be hard to match in his previous work. This passage is graceful and lightly handled; its wistful tone is of the sort one might expect from a widower for whom love offered life's prime illumination and whose youth had been (on his own admission) an endless succession of affairs. But that this widower should be Peacock, the sophisticate to whom ironic obliqueness was second nature, points cogently to the gulf which separates this book from its predecessors.

Gryll Grange is a latter-day mirror-image of Melincourt, from which it borrows a good deal of material and several situations. In the earlier novel, Peacock's attempt to set off Italianate allegory against contemporary mockery never really establishes itself, and we are left with an excess of carping and little that is affirmative to put against it. Here Peacock makes no mistakes; his command of tone and unity is sure, and the hopeful elements of the book are presented with convincing balance and ease. It is not just from the atmosphere of Gryll Grange, but also from its organization and from the literary references neatly implanted in its text that we are soon apprised of its romantic and fairy-tale nature. Its avoidance of the world is evident, its air of legend no less so. The gods and goddesses of classical times, the epic poetry of Italy, the writings of Athens's golden age, the soothing rituals of music and gastronomy, all contribute to the novel's visionary detachment from the modern period. From the start, Bacchus looms larger than the Christian God, and characters and incidents are associated

with classical myth rather than Christian teaching.
The long, chivalric poems of Tasso, Boiardo and
Ariosto are often called to mind, and Morgana, 'reading what I have often read before, Orlando Innamorato' (p.202), finds a kindred spirit in her would-be
lover, Mr Falconer. The literature of Greece, especially in Peacock's pastiche, 'Aristophanes in
London', gives a constant heightening to the action.
Music, food and drink spread pleasure and harmony
wherever they appear. The use of music, in particular, is more extensive than in the other books; it
appears not only as communal song, a way of joining
people cheerfully together, but also as a metaphor
for the human concord which Peacock wishes to display
and approve. These yea-saying elements of Peacock's
are to be found in book after book, fulfilling app-
roximately the same function as in Gryll Grange; I
have already pointed out their extra prominence in
Crotchet Castle, by comparison with its precursors.
But nowhere are they so persuasive and so reverber-
ating as here. Only in Gryll Grange do they constitute the main fabric of the novel, and support so
unhindered a belief in the ultimate value of romantic
love. As a result of this, the book conveys the
warmth of Peacock's sentiments with extraordinary
richness and power; of all his works, it is the one
which best demonstrates the resilience of his attitude towards mankind, which in previous novels is
disturbed by unconquerable doubts and insecurities.
     The dreamy Hellenization of nineteenth-century
England which Peacock is attempting in Gryll Grange
gains poignancy from the epigraphs by which each
chapter is begun. By David Garnett's count, 'Of the
thirty-five chapters, sixteen are headed with quotations concerned with love, thirteen with death or
old age, and ten with wine. Some quotations combine
thoughts of all three'[14]. This is not accidental:
the effect of these epigraphs is to dramatize the
conditions which called the book into being, and to
establish the terms of Peacock's balancing of life
with death in this final work. A dialogue is set up:
on the one hand, inevitable fears:
     'To-day we live: none know the coming morn'
     (p.140),
on the other, the joys of wine-drinking:
     'Where wine is not, no mirth the banquet
          knows:
     Where wine is not, the dance all joyless
          goes' (p.86),
and of marital love:
     'No greater boon from Jove's ethereal dome

Descends, than concord in the nuptial
    home' (p.369).
The consistent use of these epigraphs in Gryll
Grange is clearly pointed by Peacock himself, who
describes them as apposite 'frequently to the general
scope, or to borrow a musical term, the motivo of the
operetta' (p.[xi]). It seems plain from this that
his intentions are indeed consolatory in this novel,
and that it is devised specifically to offer bulwarks
against the threats of mutability by which he had
always been troubled, and which recent events had
brought more violently to his mind. These bulwarks,
reinforced by a firm emotional commitment, gather
together the elements of life in which Peacock had
always placed his trust. First, there is wine, and
with it a copious assemblage of sensuous pleasures
which encourage us to make the most of our bodies
and to reject the futile metaphysical questionings
and ideological controversies of the public world.
Second, and closely associated, is love, which in
Peacock's view is a matter of personal fulfilment
and freedom of choice, and relates not to money or
class but to passion. In both these areas, though
his quotations may be Classical, his feelings are
Romantic. And certainly the weight of emotion that
attaches to them in Gryll Grange, and the vigour of
their conflict with the forces of mortality, give the
book a more piercing grasp on our sympathy than mere
straightforward predication would have done. This
grasp is tightened by two additional aspects of the
novel. One correlative of the Greek epigraphs that
Peacock often uses is the importation of a characteristic, intensifying sense of time passing, and of
the necessity of living to the full while one can:
    'Rejoice thy spirit: drink: the passing day
    Esteem thine own, and all beyond as Fortune's'
    (p.41).
As in Shakespeare's sonnets, this enhances our feelings of urgency, and of the significance of decisions
from which there may be no later recourse. As in the
sonnets, too, it encourages us to think not only of
ourselves, but also of our children: Gryll Grange is
a book full of older men and women, looking to a
younger generation for energetic continuance and
proofs of joy. Even the weather and the seasons make
well-judged contributions, for the novel advances not
towards summer but towards winter, and much of the
love-making occurs against a warning backdrop of
chill and whiteness.
    I hope that in this introduction to Gryll Grange
I have gone some way towards justifying Marilyn

Butler's description of it as 'a finely articulated performance'(15). What I should like to do now is to discuss some aspects of the book in more detail, and to pay particular attention to its adroit execution and subtlety of design.

The fact that Gryll Grange is sited at several removes from actuality, and establishes an unperturbed, romantic sphere judiciously separate from the outside world, does not mean that its ambience is totally without stress, or that hints of the follies of public life are not permitted within its easy precincts. There are both personal problems concerning the characters, and glancing asides at some of the controversies of the day. It is simply that these are assimilated into the novel's positive texture, and that fierce positions are not taken up: there is recognition, but it is quiet and unantagonistic. We see from Chapter I that things are not quite as they should be; the two old gentlemen complain, for example, that labels confusingly contradict the objects they refer to: 'A Sympathizer would seem to imply a certain degree of benevolent feeling. Nothing of the kind. It signifies a ready-made accomplice in any species of political villany' (pp. 2-3). There are sallies against new-fangled inventions and supposed improvements, and Dr Opimian leads a languidly ingenious attack on the 'triumphs' of modern science. In its handling of Harry Hedgerow's courting of Miss Dorothy the book even accommodates a sense of class suitedness, just as Jane Austen does. It is evident that the contemporary civilization largely excluded from Gryll Grange has hardly improved, in Peacock's view: the contrary, if anything. But his earlier antipathies, though they reappear in this work, are now subordinated to a surer concentration on love and festivity. Even the Scots, invariable targets of irony in previous books, are represented here by the buoyant, agreeable Mr MacBorrowdale, who refuses to join in debates and calmly opts instead for wine and spectatorship. We do not feel that Peacock's prepossessions have suddenly altered in Gryll Grange, or that the political notions of a lifetime have disappeared. As a matter of choice, but of necessity as well, Peacock has shifted his focus in this novel away from the health and concerns of man and society, and towards the life of the individual. The satire on the public world, with its authoritarianism, its merely fashionable values, its self-seeking and oppressiveness, still lingers on in Gryll Grange, but it is less emphasized than in any previous work. Instead of might and right, or the wrongs of the English electoral system, our attention in this book is directed at the intimate realm of love and the personal struggles of four attractive young people. In his usual, deliberative way, it is Dr Opimian who best speaks for this happiness which is to be found in the sociable compass of a family or a group of friends, but not in solitude or in the hustle of the beau monde: 'A hermit reading nothing but a newspaper might find little else than food for misanthropy; but living among friends, and in the bosom of our family, we see that the dark side of life is the occasional picture, the bright is its every day aspect' (p.62).

There clings to Mr Falconer some of the deteriorationism with which Peacock regularly endows at least one figure in each of his novels, and most of his peers would agree with the weary disillusion of his perspective on the contemporary scene and the rationale of his retreat to the harmonious seclusion of his Tower in Hampshire. Although he is opposed by the energetic and enterprising Lord Curryfin, who is always ready for something new, Mr Falconer receives due support from Dr Opimian and Mr Gryll, who second a number of his complaints and originate several more of their own. But these remain incidental to the main business in hand; they never amount to a real, pertinacious commentary on affairs. In this respect, the manner of the book can be gauged from an exchange between Mr Falconer and Dr Opimian:

'MR. FALCONER.
I look with feelings of intense pain
on the mass of poverty and crime; of
unhealthy, unavailing, unremunerated
toil, blighting childhood in its blossom,
and womanhood in its prime; of "all the
oppressions that are done under the sun."
THE REVEREND DOCTOR OPIMIAN.
I feel with you on all these points;
but there is much good in the world;
more good than evil, I have always
maintained.
They would have gone off in a discussion on
this point, but the French clock warned them
to luncheon' (p.92).

The contrast here is a triple one: first, we have the inflated rhetoric of Mr Falconer's declamation; then the common sense of Dr Opimian, the cardinal voice of the novel's optimism and vivacity; and finally, the clinching recall from outer reference to inner man, with the summons to luncheon overwhelming

even Mr Falconer's 'intense pain'. This seems to me
neatly to demonstrate in little the approach of <u>Gryll
Grange</u> at large. To start with, although they cast
shadows, '"all the oppressions that are done under
the sun"' are not rendered powerfully or in detail;
they are a matter of occasional reference or oblique
remark, and that is all. There is no attempt in this
book to be true to an outside world and its problems:
they are not ignored, but they are a matter largely
of fun and denigration to the witty banqueters at the
Grange. Here, as elsewhere in Peacock, the comments
on science or competitive examination can be under-
stood best as elaborate conceits or metaphors signifying the absurdity of 'outside', and in no way as a
comprehensive evocation of the life these lucky hed-
onists have left behind them. The people in Peacock's novels are like travellers who have had a long
and arduous exposure to the great world,and bring
back strange reports of its curious habits: stories
which are exciting, distorted, partial, with a grain
of truth exaggerated into fantasy. So, despite the
fact that one notices the presence of controversial
material in the book, it is hard not to feel that
Peacock has consciously made light of it so that his
more positive feelings can have a purer effect on
the reader.

    In <u>The Broken Column</u>, Harry Levin considers the
Hellenism of the Romantic period in England, and
reaches conclusions that seem apposite to Peacock's
practice in <u>Gryll Grange</u>. 'Perhaps', he says, 'it
was the real secret of the Greeks that, instead of
practising a cult of far-fetched aestheticism, they
managed to invest the daily and commonplace concerns
of life with a certain beauty and symmetry'(16).
<u>Gryll Grange</u> includes much scholarly discussion that
has an air of mild pedantry, though its whimsical
relaxation of context prevents us from suspecting
instruction rather than entertainment. As is usual
in Peacock, the classics are also suggested as models
of 'nature and simplciity' (p.141), the two qualities
he most sought for in art and praised in life. The
whole company agrees in preferring the chastity and
expressiveness of the older literature and music as
against modern perversities, and Dr Opimian is their
authoritative spokesman: 'Therein is the essential
difference of ancient and modern taste. Simple
beauty--of idea in poetry, of sound in music, of
figure in painting--was their great characteristic.
Ours is detail in all these matters, overwhelming
detail' (pp.132-3). But, more importantly, the

classics have a role in shaping the structure of the
book, and are integral to the success of its tone.
     Almost every event and person in Gryll Grange is
coloured by some classical reference. Morgana is
Circe; Dr Opimian draws his name from a celebrated
Roman wine; Mr Falconer is compared to Numa, and the
seven sisters who attend him, 'the regulating spirits
of the household' (p.45), to the Vestal Virgins and
the Pleaides; Mr Gryll is descended, he thinks, from
Gryllus, one of the Greeks whom Circe transformed
into swine; and one of the central incidents of the
novel is a version of Aristophanes brought up to date
and set ironically in modern-day London. This
'Aristophanes in London' is a zestful charade with an
unstressed charge of meaning. Although it has a
certain significance in terms of plot (it gives the
characters further opportunities for meeting and developing their relationships), its subordination to
the romantic theme is emphasized by its comparative
brevity and by the fact that so much of it is given
in summary. We have no impression that it is a
committed work, or that it really intends to take
account of the fads such as spirit-rapping with which
it is concerned. It is robust and amusing, if not
very Aristophanic, and it does not take itself seriously:
     '"Shadows we are, and shadows we pursue:"
     But in the banquet's well-illumined hall,
     Realities, delectable to all
     Invite you now our festal joy to share' (p.291).
Other examples are too numerous to note: the texture
of the book is dense with parallels between the
present and the classical past, and this is not a
matter only of tags like those profusely spouted by
Dr Folliott in Crotchet Castle. Here, deliberate
identifications are made, and the point seems inter-
pretative, not ornamental. The secluded contemporary
existence led at Gryll Grange and at Mr Falconer's
Tower is given breadth and richness by the veil of
classical allusion through which it is seen. For
once in Peacock, the characters of England take on
the gloss and charisma of the legendary heroes and
heroines and charming, sportive deities of Greek and
Roman lore. As in Melincourt, but with much greater
assurance, Peacock's aim seems to be to import the
largeness and nobility of ancient life into a present
from which they are sadly lacking. Like poetry,
painting and music, the characters are considered in
the light of criteria of truth to nature and 'simplicity' (p.141); they are judged in terms of their
fidelity to the core of real experience, and not by

reference to mere external elegancies. The intention
is transformation, and the introduction of the enchantress Circe, qua Morgana, is not accidental. The
classics here are a source of genuine, needed power,
and Peacock uses them to bolster up every element of
his story. As a poetic stroke, this is extraordinary: the mundane world, rebarbative as ever, is
eclipsed by an encouraging vision of the splendour of
the past. Thus, in a setting of the material
progress of mid-Victorian England, enchantresses,
paladins and celestial beings walk the earth; Hampshire becomes Arcadia; a pagan joy informs the
polite match-making of affluent, upper-class couples.
The effect is of liberation and discovery. First,
the bonds of orthodoxy are loosened, and a far wider
range of free and satisfying activity is opened up
for the characters. Second, there is solace: the
misguided may be set upon the proper path, and even
in 1860 an impression of the truer pleasures of the
past, and of their continuing availability in the
present, may be obtained. Thematically, then, the
role of the classics is crucial in Gryll Grange;
without their succour, Peacock could never have
achieved the uplifting warmth for which he was
seeking. But even more significant artistically is
the imaginative sheen that they give to Peacock's
daring, original scheme in this book.

If the word 'daring' seems too strong, one
should bear in mind that Peacock is thoroughgoing in
Gryll Grange, and that a Christian God can hardly be
the creator of a classicized world. I think a distaste for the established church, its doctrines and
institutions, is to be found everywhere in Peacock's
work. But nowhere else is it so evident as here,
presented with such sly wit, or set so unflatteringly
in opposition to the fulfilment offered by Bacchus or
Venus. Roman religion, in particular, is omnipresent
in the novel; it is associated with Dr Opimian, the
soi-disant Christian divine, who 'propitiated his
Genius by copious libations of claret, pronouncing
high panegyrics on the specimen before him, and
interspersing quotations in praise of wine, as the
one great panacea for the cares of this world' (p.
88); '"Jupiter himself"' (p.331) is said to have
arranged the fortuitous settling of Lord Curryfin
with Miss Niphet; and at Christmas, a jubilant
occasion in the book, we are regaled not with carols
and tales of the infant Jesus, but with folkish ghost
stories from Miss Niphet and Mr MacBorrowdale, the
insipid 'The Legend of St. Laura' from Mr Falconer
and--in first place--two incidents from the most

hedonistic and unillusioned work in Latin literature, the Satyricon of Petronius. Above all, at the end of the novel, after Mr Falconer's undue devotion to the ideal of continence represented by St Catharine has been overturned, our envoi is in terms of no Christian apologia, but emphasizes the virtues of classical gods instead. Dr Opimian is the toastmaster: 'Let all the corks, when I give the signal, be discharged simultaneously; and we will receive it as a peal of Bacchic ordnance, in honour of the Power of Joyful Event, whom we may assume to be presiding on this auspicious occasion' (p.377). Both comedy and irony are derived from the feline paganism of Gryll Grange, but it is more than just a joke. It is in this book more than any other that Peacock's disapproval of Christian asceticism, and preference for the emancipated bodily pleasures nourished by the mythologies of Greece and Rome, come boldly and convincingly to our notice.

Although the classics are used in Gryll Grange in a more functional way than before, we also find pleasing residues of Peacock's usual, self-taught pedantry. The long discussions of Greek music and of the tonsorial habits of Greek and Roman womenfolk point to the continued vigour of Peacock's taste for the minutiae of scholarship, and are handled in circumstances of such easy, cultivated conversation that it is hard not to savour their oddity and learning. The conditions for this acceptance are much better organized in Gryll Grange than in earlier novels, where one often felt that information was being obtruded upon the text in a way that harmed the continuity of Peacock's writing. But here the academic musings are mostly propounded by the jovial, sympathetic figure of Dr Opimian, and take on the quaint colour of his personality. The point of Dr Opimian's lengthy deliberations as to whether or not the Vestals wore their own hair is a double one: we have a fine pageant of antiquarian delight and bravura, but we also have an utilitarian conclusion which places such erudition in the light of the everyday: '"I shall let well alone"' (p.40) is the doctor's sensible decision. In Chapter XXIX the discussion is resumed, in bizarre relation to the bald Venus or 'Venus Calva' (p.294) of the Romans. This is a kind of joke even more than the earlier reference had been: Peacock is establishing the distance between the rarefied, donnish concerns of the parental generation, and the passionate love, the sense of immediate female beauty, of their juniors. In fact, this whole chapter tellingly counterpoints

the talking of the old against the intense activity
of the young. Thus, in Gryll Grange, apparent
digressions on remote topics of classical controversy
can still be put to use: the tone of the novel is
relaxed, and can accept something of the indulgent
display of connoisseurship and abtruse punditry that
we find in Athenaeus--though there is nothing in
Peacock quite as outré as Athenaeus's remarks that
'Even the wise Socrates was fond of the "Memphis"
dance, and was often surprised in the act of dancing
it'(17) or that 'Aeschylus wrote his tragedies when
drunk'(18).

Gryll Grange is a fable of the perfecting of
contentment, and owes much of its success to the
sunny Helenism of its texture. But this Hellenism
does not remain single; it is associated with pursuits such as eating and singing which mingle together in producing the heightened warmth which is so
much more plausibly created here than elsewhere in
Peacock's oeuvre. Peacock's classicism has an important role, but is assisted by references to Italian
poetry, and especially by the identification of
Morgana with her name-sake in Ariosto and Boiardo,
where she appears as a bewitching figure who dispen-
ses the treasures of the earth: a 'sister enchantress' to Circe, 'who had worked out her own idea of a
beautiful garden, and exercised similar power over
the minds and forms of men' (p.17). Also, partly as
a result of Peacock's casting of his story in terms
of classical deities and romantic heroes, notions of
magic give a fairy-tale aura even to the commonplace:
the loves of yeoman farmers acquire the same elevation as those of lords and ladies. An air of romance
spreads evocatively over every concern: if Mr
Falconer '"might be Sir Calidore himself"' (p.23),
and the chivalric love of the Italian poets finds
echoes in contemporary hearts, then it seems just
that the sorceress, Morgana, should be endowed with
supernatural charms to which all men respond. This
has a feeling of poetry and legend which is unalloy-
edly appealing. The courtship between Morgana and
Mr Falconer and Miss Niphet and Lord Curryfin takes
on almost mythic dimensions: we see it not merely
as a pleasing fiction but as a vivid confirmation of
man's resilience and hopefulness and of the proper
ordering of young people in any society--in pairs, in
love, and, eventually, married.

The rich consistency of this novel, and its
affect on the spirits of a well-intentioned reader,
are a sufficient proof of the maintenance and growth
of Peacock's skills as a writer. Its gathering

together of former joys and their illumination in the
steady, optimistic light of the classical past are
indices not just of artistic fruition; they point to
a consummation of Peacock's personal strivings as
well.

In The Symposium love is defined by Socrates as
'"desire for the perpetual possession of the
good"'(19). Peacock was a scholar of Plato's dialogues, but we have no reason to suppose that his own
feelings about love would be derived only from literary sources. In book after book we sense a sturdy
commitment to the notion of true love freely given
between two young people; in Peacock's world, it is
the guarantor of contentment, and is awarded with
regularity at the end of each of his novels, though
more forcibly to the sensitive and aware than to the
merely modish and eager. In Gryll Grange it is
brought quickly to our attention, and is never
allowed to fade from the centre of the scene. As the
cynosure of interest, and the most powerful positive
influence in the book, it concentrates the emotion
called up by Peacock's classical, gastronomic and
musical enthusiasms and expresses it in the courting
between Morgana and Mr Falconer and Miss Niphet and
Lord Curryfin, the fascinating relationships around
which the novel revolves.

Throughout Gryll Grange, love is in the air:
characters, from the plaintive Harry Hedgerow to the
matchmaking Dr Opimian, are concerned with little
else. Both in discussion, and by example, a natural,
simple love is accorded the highest praise. Miss
Ilex, witty and perceptive though she is, gives warning of the dangers of spinsterhood; with comic animation, Dr and Mrs Opimian demonstrate the real give
and take of married life and cast proper doubt on
'vows of celibacy, and inward spiritual grace'(p.55);
even Nature seems favourably inclined, and apt to
bring would-be lovers together at propitious moments
--when Lord Curryfin and Miss Niphet dance the polka,
'It seemed as if Nature had pre-ordained that they
should be inseparable' (p.233). Of all the aspects
of the novel, it is love which Peacock most opens to
aristocrat and commoner alike, in promise of a culminating fulfilment of their deepest human needs.

In a subdued way, this had also been true for
Peacock's earlier books. But in Gryll Grange it is
more compelling because Peacock's emphasis is single-
minded, and the novel more collectedly drawn around
this core than was ever the case with its tenser,
more disparate predecessors. This shows itself in

the fuller psychological development of the lovers. The creation of genuine personality, which had surfaced in Nightmare Abbey, is taken much further in Gryll Grange. Characters are delineated with fullness and conviction; veerings of attitude, and particularly the slow, difficult growth of love, are recorded with sympathetic exactitude. The climate of feeling in this novel is both finer and more substantial than in any of Peacock's previous books. In Headlong Hall, there was something factitious, almost jokey, about the marriages by which the book was concluded. Here, however, the solicitude and warmth of Peacock's observation increase our involvement and give us a vital sense of the importance of what is at stake.

In Gryll Grange, too, a strange conspiracy is at work. It is not just that the characters are impelled into love by their human nature; external forces help them along. We have the feeling that it is by the will of the Gods that Morgana and Mr Falconer are drawn into their first meeting, and that what lures one to the other is not only affection, but also something more like magic: when Mr Falconer is on his way to the Grange, he passes 'into the full attraction of the powerful spell by which he was drawn like the fated ship to the magnetic rock in the Arabian Nights' (pp.209-10). At the opposite end of the social scale, the unidealistic man of the earth, Harry Hedgerow, though apparently 'fortified by beef and ale against all possible furrows of care' (p.49), proves equally vulnerable: 'Cupid's arrows had pierced through the aes triplex of treble X, and the stricken deer lay mourning by the stream'. This gives us a curious impression that the whole universe is hopefully engaged with the lovers, and makes us feel that their unions are necessary as well as desirable, as if they were the completion of some cosmic plan for mankind.

In terms of story Gryll Grange is far from static. The movements of advance and retreat, and the gradual emergence of basic preferences among the four young people principally concerned, are treated subtly and at length. The book is more than just a marriage-go-round to celebrate the joys of love. We are always aware of the gap between the old and the young, and it is plain that Peacock sees youth as the time of decision, of choices on which the whole of one's subsequent happiness may depend. There are impediments in the paths of all the characters, and these must be removed or obviated before the wished-for weddings can take place. In the case of Lord

Curryfin and Miss Niphet, these impediments belong
to the orthodox treasure-house of romantic fiction:
on the one hand, a previous, polite attachment, on
the other, a cool, shy demeanour. But the obstructed progress of Mr Falconer's wooing of Morgana has a
good deal of thematic significance in the novel. Mr
Falconer is presented as a figure of altruism opposed to the looser compromises of the real. He plays
a main part in the debate in Gryll Grange as between
the varying advantages, and even the feasibility, of
these two positions. Both from his own mouth, and
by implication, we see that his life at the Tower is
a monument to 'the purity of ideal beauty, as developed in St. Catharine' (p.71), and that he is governed largely by 'an intense desire of shutting up
myself' (p.33). As Peacock is aware, this is
counter-productive, and must exact a hardening and
restriction of one's experience; he is always on the
side of a practical accommodation with reality,
rather than its mere avoidance or repression. So he
introduces the troubling power of love into Mr
Falconer's tranquil, withdrawn existence, and watches
as it destroys and then recreates his joie de vivre.
As for Mr Falconer, 'He felt that his path was now
crossed by a disturbing force, and determined to use
his utmost exertions to avoid exposing himself again
to its influence' (p.99). But to no avail: love is
not only natural, it is also irresistible; its
siren-call to a fuller, sunnier life is one which
nobody can withstand. Dr Opimian, as usual, conclu-
sively voices this truth: 'Every man must be subject
to Love once in his life' (p.102), he says, and
again, 'It is vain to make schemes of life. The
world will have its slaves, and so will Love' (p.
103). So, by the end of the book, reality triumphs
over ideality--not by obliterating the notions which
Mr Falconer holds, but by incorporating them into
circumstances which are closer to the actual and more
responsive to authentic needs.
  The direction taken by Mr Falconer's drive towards the ideal is an interesting one, and carefully
chosen. In Peacock's fiction we have frequent,
underlying impressions of sexuality, though they do
not manifest themselves directly. The women in his
novels are notably physical in their appeal, and are
clearly bound to their menfolk by passion as well as
by a more evident congruity of partialities and antipathies, but the sexual aura of their attractiveness
is not quite openly expressed. It is as if only
obliqueness were available to Peacock before he came
to write Gryll Grange, and even here the sexual

feeling is subdued. Nevertheless, not only is it
present, it is also more pronounced than elsewhere.
For Mr Falconer's prime crotchet is his devotion to
St Catharine, whom he describes as 'the type of ideal
beauty--of all that can charm, irradiate, refine,
exalt, in the best of the better sex' (p.72), and it
is not by chance that it is his bedroom which he sets
up as a shrine to this chaste patroness. Now St
Catharine, of whom it was said that 'in a beatific
vision the Saviour of the world placed a ring on her
finger, and called her his bride' (p.73), combines
three qualities of which Peacock was especially disapproving. She was a devout Christian; being the
spouse of Christ she was, like a nun, forbidden the
love of mortal men, and therefore embodied the so-
called virtue of virginity; and she faced life not
pragmatically, but with a fervent rigidity of outlook
that eventually led to a protracted martyrdom at the
hands of the Emperor Maxentius. The role of Morgana
is to change all this by awakening Mr Falconer to the
sounder life from which his continence is an
unhealthy escape. In the first few chapters of Gryll
Grange, nothing important seems lacking--nothing,
that is, except the married love of a younger generation which would complete the pattern of its world
and ensure that it continued blithely into the
future. The context is classicized and sensuous, and
we cannot but feel that St Catharine, with whose
history even the learned Dr Opimian is 'not very
familiar' (p.72), hinders rather than helps the
pleasures which Peacock is offering his characters.
And in fact, in the course of the book, it is St
Catharine's influence which is expunged and that of
Morgana, leading Mr Falconer towards the nobler
delights of love and marriage, which flourishes.
What we learn from the novel is that no real happiness can be enjoyed in an existence given over to a
stern discipline of abstinence, rather than in the
satisfying fulfilment of man's innate desire for
love. It is a message which is contained in all of
Peacock's writing, but in Gryll Grange it achieves
its utmost relish and authority.
     Although there are several ways in which one
might trace changes and developments in Peacock's
work, one of the most illuminating would be to follow
through the different treatment of love as between
Headlong Hall and Gryll Grange, a period covering
forty-five years and seven novels. In the earliest
books, romantic entanglements are much less striking
than the wit of crotcheteering and an insidious
irony; love is present, but is not so deeply felt.

By 1860, however, it has usurped the major role in
the novel and has come to signify Peacock's greatest
hope for a mankind which he sees disenchantedly as
subsisting within a social framework about which few
prospects of amelioration can be entertained.

If the handling of love becomes richer as we
move from Peacock's first book through to his last,
so too does his creation of character. In Gryll
Grange a considerable variety of figures is animated,
studied in detail, particularized in speech and sentiment, and led through changes in themselves and in
others to a conclusion every bit as moving and well-
rounded as those in novels of the mainstream. With
Dr Opimian, Morgana, Mr Falconer and their peers we
have a full, sympathetic sense of personality to
replace the dramatic silhouettes of Headlong Hall.
Gryll Grange is a book about feelings, and requires
an ampler human complexion than its predecessors:
after all, love cannot be persuasive unless lovers
are persuasive too. So, without sacrificing clarity
or incisiveness, Peacock gives us a greater impression of depth and mystery: Morgana talks of 'inexpl-
icable affinities' (p.307), and Peacock takes care
that these are rendered with sensitivity. Morgana,
Mr Falconer and Miss Niphet, especially, convey the
sense of living a more complex and shifting life than
we expect in Peacock; they are as vital as Mr
Asterias or Dr Folliott, but more substantial and
closer to everyday experience. Each is treated with
fellow-feeling; it is not just that their world is
easier and their behaviour less extreme, it is that
they themselves are more approved by the author.
They are no longer crotcheteers, and point to no
general follies of their society; they are characters who fall in love, are forced to come to terms
with this pleasant, engrossing state of affairs, and
who achieve an anticipated happy marriage by the end
of the book. Thus their lives are like ours; they
assimilate experience, learn from their mistakes, and
pursue goals that are attractive to them, exactly as
we do. Altogether, there is subtlety, completeness
and accessibility to the characters in Gryll Grange
which is not matched (and perhaps does not need to
be matched) anywhere else in Peacock's oeuvre.
Since even minor figures like Miss Ilex and
Harry Hedgerow are so much less separate and extravagant than before, and express themselves in conversation rather than by diatribes, the social setting
of Gryll Grange is relatively unstressful. There is
a real community in this novel, and it is

distinguished by the facility with which relationships are formed and the concord about essential
matters which underlies its contentment. The excitement of crotcheteering debate is blunted, but in its
place we have the quieter charm of well-observed
affiliations among a group of recognizable figures.
Fantasy and declamation are avoided: the characters
talk more simply, and with less rhetorical pointing
and intensity of pitch, than before. Even Mr
Falconer, Gryll Grange's exemplar of Peacock's
habitual deteriorationist, speaks in a much more
reasonable way than any of his predecessors.
Although disappointment may be his hobby-horse, he
sounds almost sensible on the subject, and that can
rarely be said of Mr Escot in Headlong Hall or Mr
Forester in Melincourt. As he says: 'We may be
disappointed in our every-day realities, and if not,
we may make an ideality of the unattainable, and
quarrel with nature for not giving what she has not
to give. It is unreasonable to be so disappointed,
but it is disappointment not the less' (p.32).
      However, conversation is also easy in Nightmare
Abbey and Crotchet Castle; the unique feature of
Gryll Grange is that it is the only one of Peacock's
books in which we have an awareness of growth in the
characters. We see Mr Falconer, for example, initially living a life of orderly serenity, tended by his
Vestals; when fate throws Morgana in his path, his
balance is disturbed, and he moves towards retreat;
yet her seductiveness is so great that he cannot but
respond to it; then comes the problem of Lord Curryfin's prior understanding with Morgana, and the
jealousy this causes him; after that is cleared up
and he is sure of her affection at last, there is
still the dilemma of the attendant Vestals to be
resolved and the long period of waiting before his
proposal to be endured. The tracing of Mr Falconer's
emotions is beautifully done: the conflict within
him between chastity and love, the ideal and the
real, the present and the future, is handled with
insight, and by the end of the novel we feel that he
is an altered and wiser man, and a fitting partner
for the sorceress he is to marry. Clearly, in a work
of this kind, some impression of psychological development is essential, for otherwise the love it is
concerned to celebrate might seem merely theoretical.
I think that Peacock successfully creates this
impression, and that this also reveals to the full
the sympathetic perceptiveness which is more cloaked
in his other books.
      One reason for this may be that in Gryll Grange

he abandons the linking of his characters to real-
life exemplars which he had sometimes employed in the
past. In this novel it is difficult to see that any
of the figures is convincingly taken from life; each
is an individual, and operates freely on its own.
Although the characters are still organized into
pointed and symmetrical groups (the active Lord
Curryfin contrasted with the contemplative Mr
Falconer, for instance, or the passionate Morgana
with the marmoreal Miss Niphet) they have more flexi-
bility than any of their predecessors. Their separation from the inhabitants of the real world has done
them no harm; on the contrary, it has done them
good--they are richer and more alive than ever
before.

Gryll Grange is the only one of Peacock's novels
in which a large cast is handled to such effect; it
is also a book in which little irony is directed at
the major characters. This leaves open the possibility of presenting a plausible community, and also
permits the emergence of spokesmen who bear a much
higher charge of authorial approval than had previously been the case. Foremost among these, and the
novel's chief mediator, marriage-broker and comment-
ator, is Dr Opimian. He has many similarities to
earlier incarnations of the gourmet clergyman such as
Dr Folliott, but differs from them all in the straightforward manner of his treatment. Only the slightest qualification seems to attach to his jolly
activities; he is an important positive agent in the
book's structure, and encourages love, music and good
eating and drinking with the same openhearted
bienveillance. In addition, his evident virtues of
optimistic common sense and realism of outlook give
him great usefulness as the novel proceeds: he is
not only an informant and scholiast, but also
fosters the healthy qualities which conduct the
book's plot to its cheerful marital conclusion. The
four young lovers stand apart from Dr Opimian, the
hearty father-figure who regards them with such
indulgence. Morgana combines Peacock's usual female
excellences of independence, learning, beauty and
sharp sight with a potent admixture of fairy-tale and
magic, and creates a lasting impression of the exalt-
ed strengths he felt women to possess. At first
contrasted with Morgana, but later growing towards
her, is Mr Falconer. Apart from Messrs Minim and
Pallet, whose part in the action is infinitesimal, he
is the nearest thing in the novel to an old-style
crotcheteer, with his relentless pessimism, his blind
idealism of approach and his absurd chastity.

However, he burgeons as an old-style crotcheteer never could, and we warm to him as he is roused and freshened by the sorcery of love that emanates from Morgana. A similar process occurs with Lord Curry-fin; we see him first as a foolish lecture-giver of little interest, but watch with sympathy as the affection of Miss Niphet transforms him into a lively, agreeable young man largely cured of eccentric enthusiasms. It is in Miss Niphet that one of the most remarkable changes in the book takes place. In the beginning, she is a repressed and chilly creature, but love, and the outdoor pursuits she shares with her lover, soon advance her to the 'almost surprising degree of physical presence'[20] which has been noticed by Marilyn Butler. The connecting factor between the experiences of the four lovers in Gryll Grange is that all are subject to growth: even the enchantress Morgana, whose Circean charms play such a powerful role in the novel's action, is herself transformed from rejecting spinster to accepting wife. This emphasis on metamorphosis chimes nicely with the classicism of Gryll Grange and also with the overriding forcefulness of Peacock's notion of love: the three together combining energetically to give dramatic substance to the author's belief that love can transmogrify even the most obdurate of figures and set them on the path to happiness.

Even if one gives credit for the originality and animation of characters like Scythrop, Anthelia and Lady Clarinda, in earlier works by Peacock, all must seem pallid by comparison with their well-rounded peers in Gryll Grange. This last novel is a major achievement, and a prime contribution to its quality is made by the vigour, mobility and variousness of the characters Peacock has created to give life to its purposes.

In general, action in Peacock's books is sporadic. We are aware of a need for diversity by which they are governed, and we know that romantic intrigues will end in marriage, but it is hard to discover a precise rationale for each incident and every conversation. Themes are developed and expressed, but their articulation is not completely systematic: a degree of gratuitousness is always permitted. Nightmare Abbey and The Misfortunes of Elphin are partial exceptions to these remarks; Gryll Grange is another. In this novel, there are few of the wide-ranging episodes which are frequent in Melincourt or the mediaeval books, but an

elaborately circumstanced story of the growth of
feeling is handled with poise and concentration. The
work begins with a leisurely, dinner-time conversation full of curious learning, and by gradual, friendly accretion evolves characters and plot and establishes tone. The progress of the story is slow, and
we have no impression of strain; rather, a convincing density of exposition is marshalled around the
characters, and we are led to relate closely to their
plight and to follow their movements with sympathy.
Complications such as the bond of duty which Mr
Falconer feels towards the Vestals, and Morgana's
unconsidered flirtation with Lord Curryfin, are
introduced without fanfare into the easy advance of
the action in the linked directions of the staging of
'Aristophanes in London', the Christmas festivities
and the nine triumphant weddings which follow them.
And, when those weddings take place, it is with glee
but with no inconsequentiality; the entire novel has
led measuredly up to this event, and it is with a
unique feeling of completeness that it ends. Already
children have appeared miraculously as heralds of the
future, to indicate the continuance of the human
cycle, and we have a prospect--the old at cards, the
young dancing, the youngest in the wings--which
movingly embodies Peacock's principal hopes in this
book. Even the ghost stories have implications beyond their value as entertainment. They convey an
old, pagan view of Christmas, and are a means of
getting rid of the past before sway is assumed by the
novel's young, loving and corporeal couples, hasten-
ing towards marriage. The motif of Gryll Grange is
perhaps 'L'amour vient sans qu'on y pense' (p.160),
and the idea is given a final emphasis in Mr Falconer's tale of St Laura, with its obvious applicability
to his former, self-denying life in the Tower: 'a
dream too much above mortal frailty, too much above
the contingencies of chance and change, to be permanently realized' (p.374). Of Peacock's works, this is
the only one that leaves us with an achievement of
consummation; all of the others are awkward, or in
some way subverted; Gryll Grange alone brings
decisively to a resolution the enquiry into human
love and happiness with which it is concerned.

     J.B. Priestley is right to call Gryll Grange 'an
ideal envoi'(21). It is the most accomplished of
Peacock's books, and a fitting conclusion to his
literary life. It highlights the joys of love and
the festive pleasures of the flesh, but I hope I have
shown that this is not trivial or escapist. Instead,

it offers a vision of a world which can be transformed by love, and in which the major problems of
relationships and of living itself may be soothed
and brought cheerfully to a close. The context of
this vision is a sense of mutability, of fears of
death and the fracture of the links between men and
women on which a good life depends. The aim of the
novel is consolation, therefore, and it seems to me
that it fulfills this aim with immaculate art but
also with a directness of feeling of which one would
hardly have thought Peacock capable. <u>Gryll Grange</u>
is 'our comedy' (p.375) and presents us, as Mayoux
has said, with 'la vie, la courte vie des mortels,
jugée à la sortie'(22). But it does this without
sentimentality, and with no diminution of the clear
sight and subtle intelligence which are the hall-
marks of Peacock's fiction.

CHAPTER VIII

CONCLUSION

I hope that in the preceding chapters I have adequately pointed to both the uniformity and the variety of Peacock's writing. In the simplest sense its variety is undeniable, for Peacock produced good work in a number of forms, and deserves to be remembered for some of his poetry and for his sharp periodical essays as well as for his novels. However, interesting and sometimes excellent though his non-fiction may be, Peacock's reputation must always rest with his novels. These books present to the reader a facade which is curious and enticing but also rather misleading. Apart from the two romances, they constitute a group which has every appearance of homogeneity. Their concentration on dialogue, their high comedy, the fabling nature of their effects, their wit and irony and the slightness of their story-telling and characterization all set them apart from the mainstream of contemporary fiction. Not only are they unlike the works of other writers of Peacock's own time, formally at least: they are also unlike most books that have appeared before or since. Their organization is unique, and, in order to refer to them, we have to invent a classification of 'conversation novel' in which we can convincingly admit only Peacock as author. Evidently, the fact that these works bear such limited and sometimes perverse similarities to other works which we also call novels has encouraged us to see them as a unity, offering us clever variants on a single, unchanging pattern. In some ways, this is correct. The ingredients and most of the techniques are not strikingly different as between Headlong Hall and Gryll Grange, although in time they span almost half a century.

But one of the things that has become plain to me is that the unity of Peacock's conversation novels cloaks a surprising diversity and development in

219

feeling and procedure. Their themes remain fairly
constant, but these are dialectical works, putting
doubts into motion and revolving nervously around
contrasting poles of optimism and pessimism.
Frequently, Peacock's festive cheerfulness is subdued: in a book like Melincourt it seems overwhelmed.
However, it always makes itself felt, and always
suggests some counterbalance to his fears of mutability and constraint. Even in a world largely given
over to oppression, misdirection and folly, he can
perceive hope, especially in love, in Nature, in
freedom, and in the pleasures of music, food and
wine. In the later novels, from The Misfortunes of
Elphin onwards, it is this hope which predominates,
though a due sense of difficulty and a distaste for
the most disagreeable manifestations of the public
life of the time accompany it to the end. Thus, if
Peacock's career in fiction begins with the frail
joviality and hectic glitter of Headlong Hall, it
concludes with the reasserted warmth and solace of
Gryll Grange.
One should resist the impulse to derive too neat
a pattern from any oeuvre, no matter how small, and I
hope I am not being unduly systematizing here. But
it seems to me that it is hard to avoid an impression
of roundedness when one looks at Peacock's writing as
a whole, and not to see it in terms of a greater
comic richness and a more charged emotional involvement than it has often been seen in the past. In
addition, I find that Peacock moves towards a fuller
rendition of character and circumstance than one
might expect from the fabling quality of his materials, and that in Nightmare Abbey and Crotchet
Castle, but above all in Gryll Grange, he creates an
ambience that may not unfairly be compared with those
in more orthodox novels of his time.

Peacock has been mistakenly presented as a
tranquil Epicurean whose accomplished art merely
applies the chaste standards of the Augustans to the
intemperacy of the Romantic period. In fact, everything about him is bound up with the problems of the
age in which he lived. Political and economic
unrest, the growth of a radical new literature and
the rapid erosion of certainties incumbent upon a
time of change all influenced him as profoundly, if
not as directly, as his contemporaries. As Kiely
has said, the Romantic novel, the form most immediately engaged with the dilemmas of its world, 'at best
and at worst, is an almost continuous display of
divisive tension, paradox, and uncertain focus'(1).

CONCLUSION

In earlier chapters I have had occasion to compare
Peacock with Jane Austen, the greatest novelist of
the early nineteenth century in England, and to
remark on the gulf which separates them in spite of
their shared concern with social health and personal
concord. But although they are very different,
comparable doubts underlie their books and give notice of the disturbing circumstances of which both
writers are the product. An attentive reading of
either Pride and Prejudice or Nightmare Abbey could
produce no impression of serenity; the success of
Jane Austen and Peacock rests not upon security but
upon an engrossing accommodation with anxiety. I do
not pretend that Peacock achieves this with Jane
Austen's extraordinary pertinacity and technical
expertise, but it seems to me that his novels respond
as freshly as hers to the problems not only of their
own time, but of all times. They are taut and
moving; they may be diversions, but they have a
serious point; they do not evade pressing difficulties, but manage them subtly and pleasingly, at one
remove; above all, they are works of conflict, not
repose. Mayoux, I think, captures them precisely
when he says, 'Il y a quelque chose de contradictoire
--c'est le centre de force de Peacock'[2].
  Given his dislike of the society he saw around
him, his lack of religious belief and his susceptib-
ility to feelings of transience and alienation, it
is obvious that Peacock would need powerful compensations if he were not to produce books of undiluted
gloom and ill-omen. He finds the strongest of these
compensations in the notion of love, which becomes
for him a guarantor of the freedom and fulfilment
which his own world signally failed to provide. All
his novels end with weddings, among the sophisticated
as well as the simple, and we feel these to be hopeful portents for the future; they indicate that man
and woman may still achieve liberation from the mood
of fracture by which the books are often governed.
In Headlong Hall the love element in the story is
slight, and our interest is directed more at crotcheteers than at sweethearts. In succeeding novels,
its encouraging counterpoint to the follies of public
life grows in importance and affect. In Nightmare
Abbey, emotions take on a human charge and the major
characters are developed with fullness and sympathy;
as a result, romantic intrigues acquire both vigour
and depth. This process advances in Maid Marian and
The Misfortunes of Elphin, where the lovers are seen
in a legendary light which adds greatly to our sense
of the representative, torch-bearing quality of their

situation. It is consummated in <u>Gryll Grange</u>, a
book saturated with romantic feeling and one in which
love is brought to stand nobly against the forces of
death and disruption. Associated with love are the
power of Nature, and the delights of food, drink and
music which are regularly used by Peacock to recall
his characters from separateness, prescription and
obsession to the truer satisfaction of their
communal, sensuous natures. In every novel, music
produces harmony, and eating and drinking cut short
disputes and import cheerful gratification into the
companionable groupings that they foster. This is a
matter of comedy and a relish for the good things of
life, especially as these are seen, like love, to
offer prospects of camaraderie far more attractive
than the empty systems-making of figures such as Mr
Escot or Flosky. Although beef, Madeira and Old
English songs are to be found from first to last in
Peacock, and always engagingly perform the reassuring function I have ascribed to them here, one
notices again that their significance increases, and
their incidence becomes greater, as one moves to
<u>Crotchet Castle</u> and <u>Gryll Grange</u>. In these latter-
day works of retrenchment and consolidation,
Peacock's concentration on music and dinners is
expressed with extravagant insistence; it is as if,
towards the end of his life, his need for alleviation was even stronger than before. Also, it is only
in <u>Gryll Grange</u> that the recondite classicism of
Peacock's reading is thoroughly organized for an
artistic purpose. Previously, it was an omnipresent
constituent of texture, conducted an unstressed,
nostalgic campaign against the modern world, and
injected curious enjoyments into his prose. But, in
this final novel, references to Greece and Rome add a
visionary perspective to the love stories with which
he is dealing,and we come to feel the real romantic
warmth, nourished by Petronius, Lucian and Apuleius,
which underlay their earlier, quiet use. When we
unearth the positive elements of Peacock's books, as
I have done here, it is hard not to feel that their
basic congruity is more striking than their superficial disparity. Together, they give an impression
that mankind's happiness is to be discovered principally in the joys of the flesh, broadly conceived, and
in circumstances far from the constraint of the
public and fashionable spheres of life. Peacock dis-
trusts our civilization and all its manifestations
both personal and institutional; in his writing, he
moves out among the beauties of the countryside and
to country-houses largely segregated from the town,

and there he builds up his imaginative celebration of the private, liberated, loving and sensuously satisfied existence which he valued above all others. Peacock's conviction, which in one way or another is shared by many of his contemporaries, is that an existence such as he evokes is not only natural to man, but would also free him from the bonds in which he has been trapped by his society. The basis of Peacock's approach lies in his Old English, but at the same time Romantic, trust in man's innate capacity for a life of love and pleasure. In some respects this is primitivistic and pastoral, and very much of its time, and it certainly relates Peacock to Wordsworth and Scott as well as to the Jacobin novelists and Utilitarian thinkers(3) with whom he is commonly associated. Although its context is dreamy, this is neither trivial nor evasive; in most of his books, it is not that he is fleeing a public world of which he disapproves, but rather that he is seeking to accommodate and redeem it in the easier alternative realm of his fiction. His works cope with difficulties not directly but by amusing, consoling obliquity; in the face of disorder, they assert as best they can the affirmative, comic values of love, kinship and bodily delight. As Able says, Peacock's is a serious interest in the human spirit, 'whose cultivation he saw increasingly neglected in an age devoted to a mere material progress'(4). But with his hopefulness goes an inescapable scepticism as to the possibility of an actual change for the better. I do not think that his novels express any immediate, reforming urge, except in the case of Melincourt; they expose our true natures and indicate the misdirection of many of our efforts, but they do not urge us towards revolution. Instead, they offer refreshment, and return us to everyday life with a surer trust in our more resilient selves and a sharper awareness of the forces of pro and contra in our experience. Their aim is clarification and compensation; they encourage us not to act but to understand.

It must be evident from what I have said that Peacock, except perhaps in Crotchet Castle, is not at all concerned with giving indulgent triumphs to the positive elements in life and neglecting the more threatening, contrary aspects of his world. In fact, he shows a distaste not just for his own society, but for many features of society tout court; corrupt institutions and authoritarian procedures are detected and opposed as keenly in the Arthurian Wales of The Misfortunes of Elphin as in the present-day literary milieu of <u>Nightmare Abbey</u>. I think it is a mistake to restrict the satirical application of Peacock's fiction merely to overt, contemporary targets, though these are clearly important. He goes out of his way to demonstrate that most of the follies about which he complains are to be seen in all civilizations, only the Greek offering a partial exception. He really has no faith in the state or in the systems by which man attempts to regulate and organize his behaviour; acutely, Able compares him with de la Rochefoucauld, 'persuaded that the selfish interest of the individual is...the cause behind every social institution'(5).

In view of the turmoil and rootlessness of his period and his own disenchantment with public life, it is easy to imagine that Peacock would suffer from no shortage of targets at which to direct his irony. I think there are four main ways in which his scepticism is felt by the reader. First, there are the Peacockian crotchets casting aspersions on Scotsmen, paper money and the universities which reappear in book after book. There is a substratum of censure to these remarks, but in principle they affect one in a playful, jokey way rather than as requiring solemn consideration. They are almost aspects of character and tone instead of theme; it is as if they were pointing out Peacock's own good-natured identification with the crotcheteers in his fiction, and inviting us to extend to him the same tolerance he reaches out to them. These are entertaining matters of texture, I suggest, and need not be taken <u>au sérieux</u>. Second, in most of his novels Peacock occasionally casts aside the clever relativism and refraction of his approach, and speaks openly to some question in hand. This is particularly the case in <u>The Misfortunes of Elphin</u>, where crude, high-pitched belligerence sometimes juts through the urbane indirection of the prose, with disastrous effects on the usually elegant ordonnance of Peacock's writing. I see this as evidence both of the strength of his disapprobation of certain features of his own age, and of the necessity of subtle stratagems for the mastering and expression of this feeling. Certainly it disrupts the tone of the books, and I can see no way in which we could regard this as other than an error of tact on Peacock's part. Third, we have the vivid, and intermittently not so vivid, crotcheteering for which Peacock is best known. Figures like Mr Asterias are creatures of a single obsesssion around which they try to arrange their whole experience of the world; they are reductionists, replacing multifariousness

and liberty with singleness and authority. In
general, these figures have a pronounced contemporary
colouring; their hobby-horses may derive from the
controversies of Peacock's day, or they may incorp-
orate features of characters who attracted the auth-
or's attention during the composition of his novel.
It is only rarely, it seems to me, that the crotcheteers can be taken as simple, parodic transpositions
from life into literature. Mostly, they put together
material cunningly annexed from different sources,
and rearrange it in the interests of artistic vivacity rather than of convincing, authentic commentary.
Mr Cranium, for example, is a charming creation whose
relevance goes far beyond a mere ironic rebuttal of
the claims of craniologists. Thus, although the neat
systems by which they operate are shown to be unnatural impositions on the diverse fabric of life, and
their energetic discussions, inevitably futile, get
them nowhere near agreement or conclusiveness, the
crotcheteers are far from negative. Their fads and
prescriptions do not work, but they themselves are
treated with indulgence; as producers of comedy and
animation, they are superb. There is no bitterness
in their handling; they are in error, as we all may
be, and Peacock is tolerant of quirks which give so
much pleasure and so rich a liveliness and brio.
Some, such as Mr Cypress and the Hon Mr Listless,
also reach heights of poetry and extravagance whose
effect is almost purely attractive, and which compensate for the leadenness of figures like Flosky. The
problem with Flosky, I think, as with Mr Forester
and a number of others, is that they exist in a disconcerting state mid-way between developed character
and satirical marionette, and that it is difficult
for a reader to accommodate the veerings of presentation that this involves. But in principle Peacock's
crotcheteers are hard to fault, combining criticism
with amusement in a way that had not previously been
well explored and has not since been used with anything like equivalent success. Fourth, and encompassing and arising from the forms of reproof which I
have just been describing, is the larger political
and ethical dimension of Peacock's antipathies.
Although his works are full of contemporary reference, it seems to me that their vision is more universal than particular; they are comedies, not only
satires. They are really about mankind in general,
about the problems which it has always faced and will
go on facing in the future: the follies of his own
time provide Peacock with impetus and example, but
his substance comes from a wider-ranging, cool

perspective on the activities of man. Peacock has a
constant preference for the freedom of the
individual, and constantly rejects authoritarianism
and constraint, in public and private matters alike.
If there is a single core to Peacock's thematic
concerns it is this attack on the brash,
prescriptive patterning which impedes the joy, openness and warmth that ought to form the true kernel
of existence.

Peacock's opposition to the sway of prescriptive theories and smothering institutions shows
itself throughout his novels, in all the areas of
their activity. In argument, his scepticism is
plain from the irresolution and undercutting which
attend each discussion of the crotcheteers, though
this diminishes after the romances and is quietened
to a more ordinary, conversational give and take in
Cortchet Castle and Gryll Grange. Not only is
argument in Peacock a matter of jeux d'esprit rather
than of proof or convincing exposition, so that no
agreement can ever be obtained about the parallel
monologues of which it is mostly composed. Also, it
is repeatedly concluded and upstaged not by superior
reasoning, or by irrefutable fresh evidence, but by
the unchallengeable lure of the dinner-table. It is
only in Peacock, I think, that argument so consistently gets one nowhere, and that its procedures seem
so empty by contrast with the bodily pleasures to
which they are set in opposition. Even logic takes
on freakish overtones of fantasy and unreliability:
everybody can argue anything with plausibility, and
it is only by dogged analysis, if at all, that we
can disentangle true premisses from false and point
to fallacies concealed in insidiously self-confident
rhetoric. But, when this is done, we are left with
no residue of demonstration or any clear indication
of the author's own opinion of the matter in hand.
It is rather that Peacock has inculcated a powerfully
felt mistrust of narrowly systematic ratiocination,
especially as this is exhibited in the dogmatic
theorizing of obsessives, and has favourably put
against it the securer joys of love and sensuous
delight. In some ways, I think, although I would not
press this very hard, Peacock's practice in his
fiction amounts to a misgiving not just about systems
of ideas, but even about the realm of ideas itself. I
certainly believe that the sphere of life about which
he was most deeply concerned was that of feeling, not
of thought, and it seems to me that this is reflected
in the growth in his books from the frantic crotcheteering of Headlong Hall to the poignancy of Gryll

<u>Grange.</u>

Socially, Peacock's antipathy to imposed values is evident in his attacks on merely fashionable standards of worth. He is always aware of fundamental qualities and inescapable needs, and he sees these traduced by the pursuit of transient novelties whose aim is frivolous effect and not true satisfaction. Thus in art he opposes trickeries of ornament and affectation, and endorses the nature and simplicity which he sees best embodied in the music of Mozart and the literature of the Greeks, and in conduct he condemns the regimen of status, wealth and <u>bon ton</u> which for too many of his characters prevents a proper expression of honest emotions. Clearly, Peacock's distaste for fashion does not exist in isolation from other aspects of his world view. It connects with his uncertainty about 'civilization' and his inclination towards a pastoral retreat from the world rather than an engaged presentation of marriage à-la-mode. It marks his rejection of surface forms and his trust in the more satisfying urges that lie beneath; it is a part of his Romantic credo that, far from the town and in circumstances of freedom and festivity, man could achieve a completer joy than any that might be offered by the metropolis.

In politics, Peacock repudiates all the oppressive institutions of the modern state, together with the machinery of self-seeking, corruption and chicanery by which they are supported. This viewpoint continues unaltered from Peacock's first novel to his seventh, and is maintained in his essays as well as his fiction. It was encouraged by friendship with Shelley, and reaches its culmination in <u>Melincourt,</u> the book which was the poet's favourite <u>and which</u> mounts a vociferous offensive against the entire English political system. However, in both general tenor and particular comment, it is a feature of every novel Peacock wrote. It provides an undertone to the concerns of the earlier and later books, but perhaps has its subtlest and wittiest expression in the romances. Here, in a context of folk-tale and remoteness from the everyday, Peacock's political freethinking takes on quiet amplitude of statement and he is able to point lucidly at the authoritarian injustice, revolving around king and clergyman, which seemed to him most inimical to man's natural freedoms. I think that Peacock's political stance is very much of a piece with his other enthusiasms and antipathies, and that it confirms one's impression of the powerful feeling that motivates his urge towards a liberation of the delight that the state too often suppresses.

Dyson writes disapprovingly of Peacock, but accurately captures the tenor of his art: 'To enjoy the present,' he says, 'to swallow up foreboding in geniality, to feast and to celebrate--these are Peacock's gifts as a writer'[6]. This does not pay sufficient attention to Peacock's unease, nor to the honest struggles of which most of his novels are the record. Overall, it is fair only to Crotchet Castle, which is in fact the focus of Dyson's comments, though it gives an evocative, partial notion of one area of Peacock's sensibility. In the light of this quotation and of my remarks on the themes of his fiction, it seems hard to deny Peacock a place among the Romantics who were his contemporaries. Like them, he is profoundly suspicious of external constraint and in favour of innate, liberating human springs of love and pleasure, though he avoids sentimentality by the irony and sharpness of his effects.

Given the drama, conflict and irresolution of Peacock's writing, it is evident that the mood of his novels cannot be simple or single. Since in most cases its basis is not bland assertion but rather a complex balancing of forces, each doing battle with the others for supremacy, the result can only be a matter of dividedness and shifting half-tones of feeling. In his best work, Peacock marvellously presents the poignant strivings towards happiness and truth which are characteristic of his time, and in a context which does justice to the unsettlement of his circumstances. He is far from the frivolous escapism and classical tranquillity of which he has been accused, and his Epicurean accommodation of the problems of his time is anything but irresponsible. It is important that so much of his writing derives from the tradition of the debate; composure or predication is neither its aim nor its effect. A note of disturbance is heard throughout, and it is about this core of anxiety, this long-term collision between the claims of hopefulness and despondency, with its attendant qualities of animated equivocation and restlessness, that the books are organized. As I have said, there are variations between the novels, as in any process of change there would have to be. Melincourt is the blackest, its Italianate romance submerged in political satire and direct attack; The Misfortunes of Elphin has the most jovial bonhomie; Crotchet Castle is agreeable, but determinedly supine; Gryll Grange has the greatest charge of emotion and the fullest rendering of the power of love.

A wide range of moods is found in Peacock's works, from the warmth of satisfied love through the comic tautness of crotcheteering to the exasperation of political complaint, and our overall feelings are mingled and intricate. Absolute affirmation or negation does not exist; every element of every book is presented with a subtle threading of approval and disapproval. The consequences of this is that straightforward views and complacent acceptances are thoroughgoingly forbidden the reader; he is not permitted to sit back in conventionality and ease. Instead, alertness is enjoined at the same time that witty entertainment is provided. Peacock is humorous but sceptical, and prevents us from tolerating black and white notions or from looking thoughtlessly on any topic that comes within his purview. I have often had occasion to compare Peacock with Diderot in the course of this book, and it is Mayoux who best defines their similarity when he talks of them as 'deux esprits dialectiques, incapables de se tenir à une position sans apercevoir la force de la position inverse, et donc incapables d'orthodoxie'[7]. Thus, Peacock's irony is not just a matter of witty qualification: it is the necessary instrument of a probing sensibility alive to contrariety and nuance more than to the reassurance of simple outlines. A limp acquiescence in the status quo is allowed nowhere in his writing, apart perhaps from Crotchet Castle; his fiction is open-eyed and mercurial and, with the exception I have noted, emanates risk and liveliness rather than settlement. I think this awareness of fracture, this sense of the refractory nature of experience, is central to the success of Peacock's novels. It is what gives the lie to complaints about the evasiveness of his treatment of important notions. In fact, Peacock is a writer of serious concern and ingenious cleverness as well as a great entertainer, and, as I hope I have shown, the value of his work derives substantially from the fusion within it of anxiety and reassurance to produce a comedy which pays proper heed both to the gloomy and to the more hopeful aspects of the world he presents.

I have so far been describing the tenor of Peacock's novels as a whole, and have not registered the changes that occur between Headlong Hall and Gryll Grange. In principle, teasing doubts and hesitancies make room, over the decades, for surer optimistic feelings, but there is no schematic progression from first book to last. In the

earliest novels good cheer is more vulnerable than
later, though an elegant balance and clarity is
achieved in <u>Nightmare Abbey</u>. The romances move
towards a freer enjoyment of positive emotion, though
it is shadowed by a powerful undertone of political
disquiet. <u>Crotchet Castle</u> and <u>Gryll Grange</u> cast off
the cares of the outside world and pass concentrate-
dly towards a celebration of love and pleasure from
which the most burdensome import of the public sphere
and its activities has been expunged. As I have
said, I think there may be doubts about the integrity
of the former of these novels, but of the latter,
none: it is a genuinely noble piece of writing and
loses nothing from the comparative narrowness of its
scope and the personal quality of its regard.

Peacock's work is, then, less static than it may
seem, and offers a range of feelings which alter from
book to book but in which a pertinacious general
direction may be seen. Equally, in every work,
though in a framework of comedy, he is at pains to
sharpen our minds to the ambiguity of experience and
to prevent us from sinking gullibly into a mere submission to received opinion. In his career <u>in toto</u>,
one therefore sees Peacock simultaneously true to a
central core of interest, and exploring this core in
different and developing ways, and one can hardly
fail to be impressed by the richness of this process.

Clive Bell has written well and appreciatively
about Peacock, but concludes his discussion on a
downbeat note, remarking that 'He had stood for many
great causes but for none had he stood greatly'(8).
In this ringing apophthegm I would take exception to
the implication of the words 'great' and 'greatly';
it does not seem to me that the heroic endeavour they
appear to predicate is a necessary, or often even a
desirable, quality for the fostering of literary
success. In fact, I have several times noted situations in which Peacock's attempts to cope with the
problems of his day are half-hearted or rather comp-
romising. I do not think that he was at all gladia-
torial in his relations with the difficulties he saw
both particularly around him and also attendant on
life in general. But this does not detract from the
high intelligence, entertainment and acute enquiry
of his novels. Their merit is the cool, witty way
in which they accommodate at one remove certain fears
which are relevant to the novelist and to the world
at large; they are not grand, and do not need to be.
Their essence is better caught by Price, I think, who
says of Peacock that 'He has his own world as much as

Dickens, a fantastic place, strangely unreal, and yet
strangely serious'(9). That mention of Dickens is
apposite, and Price is fair to the cunning blend of
comedy and satire which only Peacock has achieved so
well. He does not seem to me to be a writer of
major stature, but I hope I have given good reasons
for estimating him very highly and that in doing this
I have not diminished the humour which has made his
comic fables enduringly attractive.

NOTES AND REFERENCES

All quotations from Peacock's writings are taken from
The Works of Thomas Love Peacock, the Halliford
edition, ed. H.F.B. Brett-Smith and C.E. Jones, 10
vols. (London and New York, 1924-34); this edition
will henceforth be referred to simply as _Works_.

Chapter I: Introduction;Headlong Hall
All page references in the text are to _Works_,
Vol. I (1934).
1. _Works_, Vol.VI (1927), p.8.
2. C.V. Deane, _Aspects of Eighteenth Century
Nature Poetry_ (Oxford, 1935), p.46.
3. _Works_, Vol.VI, p.[186].
4. _Works_, Vol.VII (1931), p.272.
5. _Ibid._, pp.29-30.
6. _Works_, Vol.VI, p.271.
7. 'Horae Dramaticae', _Works_, Vol.X (1926),p.3.
8. 'Biographical Introduction', _Works_, Vol.I,
p.cxiv.
9. _Works_, Vol.VII, p.332.
10. _Ibid._, p.331.
11. These authors, often described as English
Jacobins, are well summed up in Gary Kelly, _The
English Jacobin Novel 1780-1805_ (Oxford, 1976), p.7:
'They opposed tyranny and oppression, be it domestic,
national or international, spiritual or temporal;
they were against all distinctions between men which
were not based on moral qualities, or virtue; and
they were utterly opposed to persecution of individuals, communities, or nations for their beliefs on
any subject. Most important of all, they saw
history, both past and present, as an account of the
efforts of some men to establish the rule of reason
against its enemies, which were not imagination and
feeling, but error and prejudice'.
12. 'French Comic Romances', _Works_, Vol.IX

(1926), p.261.
    13. Marilyn Butler, Peacock Displayed (London, 1979), p.25.
    14. 'French Comic Romances', pp.258-9.
    15. Ibid., p.258.
    16. Ibid., p.262.
    17. Denis Diderot, Oeuvres, texte établi et annoté André Billy (Paris, 1935), p.280.
    18. Giorgio Manganelli, 'T.L. Peacock', Il Paragone, 5 (1954), 31.
    19. James Spedding, 'Tales by the Author of Headlong Hall', Reviews and Discussions Literary, Political and Historical 'not relating to Bacon' (London, 1879), p.128.
    20. Olwen Ward Campbell, Shelley and the Unromantics (London, 1924), p.48.
    21. 'Introduction', Peacock The Satirical Novels, ed. Lorna Sage (London and Basingstoke, 1976), p.12.
    22. Samuel Butler, Hudibras, Part I, Canto I, ll. 149-50.
    23. Sage, p.16.
    24. Diderot, Le Rêve de d'Alembert, ed.cit., p.684.
    25. Peter Garside, 'Headlong Hall Revisited', Trivium, 14 (May, 1979), 110.
    26. Jean-Jacques Mayoux, Un Epicurien anglais: Thomas Love Peacock (Paris, 1933), p.191.
    27. Epicurus, The Extant Remains, ed. and trans. Cyril Bailey (Oxford, 1926), p.89.
    28. Nicholas A. Joukovsky, 'A Critical Edition of Thomas Love Peacock's Headlong Hall and Nightmare Abbey with some Material for a Critical Edition of Melincourt', Vol.I (Unpublished D.Phil., University of Oxford, 1970), p.202.
    29. William Drummond, Academical Questions, Vol. I (London, 1805), p.39.
    30. Clive Bell, 'Peacock', Pot-Boilers (London, 1918), p.56.
    31. Edmund Wilson, 'The Musical Glasses of Peacock', Classics and Commercials (London, 1951), p.407.
    32. Mayoux, p.149.

Chpater II: Melincourt
    All page references in the text are to Works, Vol.II (1924).

    1. 'Memoirs of Percy Bysshe Shelley', Works, Vol.VIII (1934), p.99.
    2. Works, Vol.VIII, p.209. Letter to Shelley, dated November 29 1818.

3. Ibid., p.193. Letter to Shelley, dated May 30 1818.

4. Nicholas A. Joukovsky, 'The Composition of Peacock's Melincourt and the Date of the "Calidore" Fragment', English Language Notes, Vol.XIII, No.1 (September, 1975), 22-3.

5. Works, Vol.VII (1931), p.279.

6. Epicurus, The Extant Remains, ed. and trans. Cyril Bailey (Oxford, 1926), p.115.

7. Kingsley Amis, 'Laugh When You Can', Spectator, No. 6614 (April 1 1955), 403.

8. Carl Dawson, His Fine Wit (London, 1970), p.194.

9. Marilyn Butler, Peacock Displayed (London, 1979), p.86.

10. Håkan Kjellin, Talkative Banquets (Stockholm, 1974), p.65.

11. Butler, p.85.

12. Ibid., p.68.

13. Ibid., p.99.

14. E.L. Cloyd, James Burnett, Lord Monboddo (Oxford, 1972), p.vii.

15. The Letters of Percy Bysshe Shelley, ed. Frederick L. Jones, Vol.II (Oxford, 1964), p.244. Letter to Peacock, dated November 8 1820.

16. Ibid.,Vol.I, p.518. Letter to Hunt, dated December 8 1816.

17. PEACOCK 'L'Abbaye de Cauchemar' (Nightmare Abbey), 'Les Malheurs d'Elphin' (The Misfortunes of Elphin), traduits et préfacés Jean-Jacques Mayoux, (Paris, 1936), p.xli.

18. Hubert Teyssandier, 'T.L. Peacock et le récit satirique', Les formes de la création romanesque à l'époque de Walter Scott et de Jane Austen 1814-1820 (Paris, 1977), p.223.

19. Butler, p.77.

20. Cited in Teyssandier, p.221.

21. Leo J. Henkin, Darwinism in the English Novel, 1860-1910 (New York, 1963), p.35.

22. Butler, p.78.

23. Ibid., p.79.

Chapter III: Nightmare Abbey

All page references in the text are to Works, Vol.III (1924).

1. Johann Peter Eckermann, Conversations with Goethe, trans. John Oxenford, ed. J.K. Moorhead (London and New York, 1971), p.305.

2. The Letters of Percy Bysshe Shelley, ed. Frederick L. Jones, Vol.II (Oxford, 1964),p.244. Letter dated November 8 1820.

3. Works, Vol.VIII (1934), p.193. Letter dated May 30 1818.

4. W.E. Peck, 'A Note on Shelley and Peacock', Modern Language Notes, XXXVI (June, 1921), 371-3.

5. Jean-Jacques Mayoux, Un Epicurien anglais: Thomas Love Peacock (Paris, 1933), p.135.

6. Shelley, Letters, Vol.I, p.569. Letter to Hogg, dated November 28 1817. Apuleius, author of the lively satire The Golden Ass has often been seen as a Latin influence on Peacock's novels.

7. Works, Vol.VII (1931), p.54.

8. Works, Vol.VIII, p.204. Letter dated September 15 1818.

9. Shelley, Letters, Vol.II, p.6. Letter dated April 20 1818.

10. Ibid., p.27. Letter dated July 25 1818.

11. Idem.

12. Works, Vol.VIII, p.195: 'I have finished Nightmare Abbey'. Letter to Shelley, dated June 14 1818.

13. Ibid., p.203. Letter to Shelley, dated August 30 1818.

14. Ibid., p.193. Letter dated May 30 1818.

15. A. Martin Freeman, Thomas Love Peacock. A Critical Study (London, 1911), p.259.

16. 'Müller and Donaldson's History of Greek Literature', Works, Vol.X (1926), p.225.

17. Mayoux, p.267.

18. Shelley, Letters, Vol.II, p.98. Letter, June [20-21] 1819.

19. 'Memoirs of Percy Bysshe Shelley', Works, Vol.VIII, p.39.

20. Ibid., p.40.

21. Works, Vol.IX (1926), p.71.

22. Edmund Wilson, 'The Musical Glasses of Peacock', Classics and Commercials (London, 1951), p.408.

23. The most exhaustive study of this matter appears in Nicholas A. Joukovsky, 'A Critical Edition of Thomas Love Peacock's Headlong Hall and Nightmare Abbey with some Material for a Critical Edition of Melincourt' (Unpublished D.Phil., University of Oxford, 1970). Joukovsky's conclusion (Vol.II, p.31) is worth quoting: 'There are, then, many Shelleyan analogies in Scythrop's situation--so many, in fact, as to suggest that Peacock could hardly have hit upon a more psychologically appropriate basis for his plot. But to concentrate on similarities in detail, or to insist on identifying living models for the two young ladies, is to lose sight of Peacock's intention. For in transforming Shelley into Scythrop, he

was not writing a veiled biography but creating a
living psychological portrait'.

24. Shelley, Letters, Vol.II, p.98. Letter to
Peacock, June [20-21] 1819.
25. Augustus Henry Able, George Meredith and
Thomas Love Peacock: A Study in Literary Influence
(Philadelphia, 1933), p.103.
26. Aldous Huxley, Antic Hay (London, 1923),
p.172.
27. Shelley, Letters, idem.
28. John Horne Tooke, EPEA PTEROENTA or the
Diversions of Purley, new ed. revised and corrected
Richard Taylor, 2 vols. (London, 1829). EPEA PTER-
OENTA is a serious work of 'philosophical grammar',
Vol.I, p.10, which has nothing to do with love,
although its title translates into English as 'Winged
Words'.
29. Works, Vol.VIII, p.204. Letter dated
September 15 1818.
30. Shelley, Letters, idem.
31. Robert Kiely, 'Nightmare Abbey', The Romantic Novel in England (Cambridge, Mass., 1972),p.175.
32. Works, Vol.VIII, p.275.
33. Ellen Moers, The Dandy Brummell to Beerbohm
(London, 1960), p.19.
34. Shelley and his Circle 1773-1822, Vol.VI,
ed. Donald H. Reiman (Cambridge, Mass., 1973), p.549.
Letter from Peacock to Hogg, [April 15-27] 1818.
35. Ibid., p.755. Letter dated November 18 1818.
36. Percy Bysshe Shelley, The Complete Works of
Percy Bysshe Shelley, ed. R. Ingpen and W.E. Peck,
Vol.VII (London and New York, 1930), p.115.

Chapter IV: Maid Marian

All page references in the text are to Works,
Vol.III (1924).
1. 'The Four Ages of Poetry', Works, Vol.VIII
(1934), p.11.
2. Idem.
3. Works, Vol.VIII, p.202. Letter to Shelley,
dated August 30 1818.
4. Statius was the author of the Thebaid, a
Latin poem in twelve books on the subject of the
Seven against Thebes.
5. 'Diary', Works, Vol.VIII, p.440. Entry for
August 6 1818.
6. Works, Vol.VIII, p.209. Letter to Shelley,
dated November 29 1818.
7. Idem.
8. Idem.
9. Denis Diderot, Oeuvres, texte établi et

annnoté André Billy (Paris, 1935), p.272.
    10. J.R. Planché, The Recollections and Reflections of J.R. Planché (London, 1872), p.46.
    11. 'Biographical Introduction', Works, Vol.I (1934), p.ccvi.
    12. Lionel Madden, Thomas Love Peacock (London, 1967), p.53.

Chapter V: The Misfortunes of Elphin
    All page references in the text are to Works, Vol.IV (1924).
    1. Cambrian Quarterly Magazine, I (April,1829), 240.
    2. Literary Gazette, XIII, no.633 (March 7 1829), 155.
    3. 'Biographical Introduction', Works, Vol.I (1934), p.cxl.
    4. Westminster Review, X (April, 1829), 428.
    5. Peacock glosses 'Gwenhidwy' on this page as 'Used figuratively for the elemental power of the sea'.
    6. Robert Kiely, 'Nightmare Abbey', The Romantic Novel in England (Cambridge, Mass., 1972), p.176.
    7. 'Awen' is poetic inspiration.
    8. Timothy Webb, The Violet in the Crucible (Oxford, 1976), pp.57-8.
    9. King Arthur's wife is being held captive by Melvas.
    10. Richard Payne Knight, An Analytical Enquiry into the Principles of Taste (London, 1805), p.5.
    11. John Horne Tooke, EPEA PTEROENTA or the Diversions of Purley, new ed. revised and corrected Richard Taylor, Vol.II (London, 1829), p.3.

Chapter VI: Crotchet Castle
    All page references in the text are to Works, Vol.IV (1924).
    1. Mario Praz, 'Thomas Love Peacock', The Hero in Eclipse in Victorian Fiction (London, 1956),p.99.
    2. Douglas Hewitt, 'Entertaining Ideas: A Critique of Peacock's Crotchet Castle', Essays in Criticism, Vol.XX No. 2 (April, 1970), 209.
    3. George Saintsbury, 'Peacock: Maid Marian and Crotchet Castle', Prefaces and Essays (London, 1933), p.219.
    4. Marilyn Butler, Peacock Displayed (London, 1979), p.213, also notes the satirical poem on Lord Brougham which 'was published in the Examiner of 14 August 1831, and reprinted as a footnote to Dr Folliott's remarks for the first time in the Collected Edition of 1837'. The Paper Money Lyrics,

though issued in 1837, were largely written in 1825-
6.

5. Works, Vol.IX (1926), p.433.
6. Ibid., p.430.
7. This piece also appeared in the Westminster Review in 1830.
8. 'London Bridge', Works, Vol.IX, p.219.
9. 'Introduction', Peacock The Satirical Novels, ed. Lorna Sage (London and Basingstoke, 1976), p.22. Sage does, however, go on to say: 'it was not this mood that created Nightmare Abbey or Crotchet Castle'.
10. 'Biographical Introduction', Works, Vol.I (1934), p.cxlv: 'Crotchet Castle was already well advanced by the beginning of 1829, though it did not appear till the latter part of February 1831'.
11. The conversation has been begun by Mr MacQuedy, who reports a friend's opinion that men commence the study of antiquities only when they are saturated with civilization.
12. Robert Kiely, 'Nightmare Abbey', The Romantic Novel in England (Cambridge, Mass., 1972), p.176.
13. Carl Van Doren, The Life of Thomas Love Peacock (London and New York, 1911), p.200.
14. 'Gastronomy and Civilization', Works, Vol. IX, pp.400-401.
15. Hubert Teyssandier, 'T.L. Peacock et le récit satirique', Les formes de la création romanesque à l'époque de Walter Scott et de Jane Austen 1814-1820 (Paris, 1977), p.201.
16. Ibid., p.218.
17. James Burnet, Lord Monboddo, Of the Origin and Progress of Language, Vol.IV (Edinburgh, 1787), p.25.
18. Compare the comment of Douglas Bush, Mythology and the Romantic Tradition in English Poetry (Cambridge, Mass., 1937), p.11: 'we ask if the classics in the eighteenth century were a guide to life or only a hall-mark of gentility'.
19. Epicurus, The Extant Remains, ed. and trans. Cyril Bailey (Oxford, 1926), p.83.
20. Butler, p.210.
21. Ibid., p.183.
22. 'Captain Swing' was an imaginary figure to whom was attributed various attacks, in the early 30's, on farmers employing agricultural machinery.
23. The Jacquerie was an insurrection of the peasants of Northern France in 1358.
24. Dom Hilary Steuert, 'Two Augustan Studies', Dublin Review (January-March, 1945), 73-4.

Chapter VII: Gryll Grange
    All page references in the text are to Works,
Vol.V (1924).
    1. D.N. Gallon, 'T.L. Peacock's Later Years:
the Evidence of Unpublished Letters'. Review of English Studies, New Series, Vol.XX, No.79 (1969), 317.
    2. Ibid., 319. Letter dated November 21 1861.
    3. 'The "Flask" of Cratinus', Works, Vol.X
(1926), p.86.
    4. Works, Vol.VIII (1934), p.448.
    5. Nicholas A. Joukovsky, '"A Dialogue on
Idealities" : An Unpublished Manuscript of Thomas
Love Peacock', Yearbook of English Studies, Vol.7
(1977), 133-40.
    6. Ibid., 140.
    7. Idem.
    8. Works, Vol.VIII, p.154.
    9. Ibid., p.148.
    10. Ibid., p.251. Letter, [1860 or 1861].
    11. This is translated by Peacock on the same
page: 'Always and everywhere I have so lived, that I
might consume the passing light, as if it were not to
return'.
    12. Robert Buchanan, 'Thomas Love Peacock: A
Personal Reminiscence', New Quarterly Magazine, IV
(April, 1875), 239.
    13. Håkan Kjellin, Talkative Banquets (Stock-
holm, 1974), p.32.
    14. The Novels of Thomas Love Peacock, ed.David
Garnett (London, 1948), pp.770-1.
    15. Marilyn Butler, Peacock Displayed (London,
1979), p.235.
    16. Harry Levin, The Broken Column (Cambridge,
Mass., 1931), pp.71-2.
    17. Athenaeus, The Deipnosophists, trans.Charles
Burton Gulick, Vol.I (London and New York, 1927), p.
91. Athenaeus is mentioned on p.126 of Gryll Grange.
    18. Athenaeus, p.97.
    19. Plato, The Symposium, trans. W. Hamilton
(Harmondsworth, 1951), p.86.
    20. Butler, p.256.
    21. J.B. Priestley,Thomas Love Peacock (London,
1927), p.93.
    22. Jean-Jacques Mayoux, Un Epicurien anglais:
Thomas Love Peacock (Paris, 1933), p.509.

Chapter VIII: Conclusion
    1. Robert Kiely, 'Introduction', The Romantic
Novel in England (Cambridge,Mass., 1972), p.17.
    2. Jean-Jacques Mayoux, Un Epicurien anglais:
Thomas Love Peacock (Paris, 1933), p.280.

3. Peacock's social views are evidently influenced by Utilitarianism, defined crisply by the OED as 'the doctrine that the greatest happiness of the greatest number should be the guiding principle of conduct'.

4. Augustus Henry Able, George Meredith and Thomas Love Peacock: A Study in Literary Influence (Philadelphia, 1933), p.60.

5. Ibid., p.57.

6. A.E. Dyson, 'Peacock: The Wand of Enchantment', The Crazy Fabric (London, 1965), p.71.

7. Mayoux, p.606.

8. Clive Bell, 'Peacock', Pot-Boilers (London, 1918), p.71.

9. J.B. Price, 'Thomas Love Peacock', Contemporary Review, No. 1038 (June, 1952), 369.

SELECT BIBLIOGRAPHY

This is a bibliography of some annotated editions of
Peacock's works which I have found especially useful,
and of essays and books which are of major critical
interest. It omits a good deal of background reading
and a large number of articles, especially early
reviews, which concern themselves with textual matt-
ers or from which I have derived little assistance.
There is a very useful enumerative bibliography by
Bill Read: Part I, Bulletin of Bibliography, Vol.24,
No. 2 (September-December, 1963), 32-4; Part II,
Bulletin of Bibliography, Vol.24, No.3 (January-
April, 1964), 70-2; Part II, continued, Bulletin of
Bibliography, Vol.24, No. 4 (May-August, 1964), 88-
91. This is substantially complete up to 1963,
though the earlier period needs the appendix of
William S. Ward, 'Contemporary Reviews of Thomas Love
Peacock: A Supplementary List for the Years 1805-
1820', Bulletin of Bibliography, Vol.25, No.2 (Janu-
ary-April, 1967), 35. In addition, Lionel Madden has
an excellent 'A Short Guide to Peacock Studies',
Critical Survey, 4 (Summer, 1970), 193-7.

(i) Primary Texts

The Works of Thomas Love Peacock, ed. H.F.B. Brett-
        Smith and C.E. Jones, 10 vols. (London and New
        York, 1924-34). The standard edition, covering
        the poetry, plays, essays and incidental writ-
        ings as well as the novels; textually inval-
        uable, but without annotation of Peacock's many
        allusions, references to other writers, etc.
The Novels of Thomas Love Peacock, ed. David Garnett
        (London, 1948). Includes all the novels, with
        pleasant, brief introductions and the fullest
        easily available annotation
Novels of Thomas Love Peacock, ed. Barbara Lloyd

Evans (London, 1967). Includes Headlong Hall, Nightmare Abbey, The Misfortunes of Elphin and Crotchet Castle, sparsely but usefully annotated and with a good introduction by J.B. Priestley

Peacock, Thomas Love Nightmare Abbey Crotchet Castle, ed. Raymond Wright (Harmondsworth,1969). With useful notes

Peacock's Four Ages of Poetry, Shelley's Defense of Poetry, Browning's Essay on Shelley, ed. H.F.B. Brett-Smith (Oxford, 1929). A very convenient and well-annotated edition

Joukovsky, Nicholas A. 'A Critical Edition of Thomas Love Peacock's Headlong Hall and Nightmare Abbey with some Material for a Critical Edition of Melincourt' (Unpublished D.Phil. University of Oxford, 1970). Offers rich and thoroughgoing annotation to Headlong Hall and Nightmare Abbey and rather less to Melincourt; invaluable

(ii) Critical Works

Able, Augustus Henry George Meredith and Thomas Love Peacock: A Study in Literary Influence (Philadelphia, 1933). Offers some of the acutest criticism available, and much wider in scope than its title suggests

Amis, Kingsley 'Laugh When You Can', Spectator, No. 6614 (April 1 1955), 402-4

Bell, Clive 'Peacock', Pot-Boilers (London, 1918), pp.50-71

Burdett, Osbert 'Peacock the Epicurean', Critical Essays (London, 1925), pp.78-103

Bush, Douglas Mythology and the Romantic Tradition in English Poetry (Cambridge, Mass., 1937). Includes a full, sympathetic study of Peacock's poetry, especially of Rhododaphne

Butler, Marilyn Peacock Displayed (London, 1979). Much the soundest and best-informed study of Peacock's milieu and of his relationship with it, and a major contribution to the intellectual history of the Romantic period

-----'Myth and Mythmaking in the Shelley Circle', ELH, Vol. 49, No.1 (Spring, 1982), 50-72. An illuminating study of the uses of myth, especially in the poetry of Peacock

Campbell, Olwen Ward Thomas Love Peacock (London, 1953). A brief, judicious attempt to combine biography with critical appreciation

Dawson, Carl Thomas Love Peacock (London, 1968). A collection of extracts with a sharp critical

commentary; one of the best introductions to
Peacock's work.
-----His Fine Wit (London, 1970). Comprehensive and
thoughtful, but more valuable as a compendium
of information than as a work of criticism
Draper, John W. 'The Social Satires of Thomas Love
Peacock, Part I', Modern Language Notes, Vol.
XXXIII (December, 1918), 456-63
-----'The Social Satires of Thomas Love Peacock, Part
II', Modern Language Notes, Vol.XXXIV (January,
1919), 23-8
Dyson, A.E. 'Peacock: The Wand of Enchantment', The
Crazy Fabric (London, 1965), pp. 57-71. A well-
argued case for viewing Peacock merely as an
entertainer
Garside, Peter 'Headlong Hall Revisited', Trivium, 14
(May, 1979), 107-26. A very good introduction
to this novel and to the uneasiness of tone of
Peacock's works as a whole
Hewitt, Douglas 'Entertaining Ideas: A Critique of
Peacock's Crotchet Castle', Essays in Criticism,
Vol.XX, No. 2 (April, 1970), 200-12. An anti-
pathetic study which stresses Peacock's trivial-
ization of ideas in Crotchet Castle
Jack, Ian 'Peacock', English Literature 1815-1832
(Oxford, 1963), pp.213-24. A sensible short
estimate of both Peacock's poetry and his
fiction
Kiely, Robert 'Nightmare Abbey', The Romantic Novel
in England (Cambridge, Mass., 1972), pp.174-188.
A superb, sympathetic analysis of the function-
ing of Peacock's comedy
Kjellin, Håkan Talkative Banquets (Stockholm, 1974).
A well-researched, lucid study which emphasizes
the dialectic of past and present in Peacock and
the development of his fiction towards comedy
and away from satire
Klingopoulos, G.D. 'The Spirit of the Age in Prose',
From Blake to Byron, ed. Boris Ford (Harmondsworth, 1982), pp.187-208. Includes an interesting brief study of Peacock
Ludwig, Jack Barry 'The Peacock Tradition in English
Prose Fiction' (Unpublished Ph.D. dissertation,
University of California, Los Angeles, 1953).
Casts its net too widely, but full of interesting remarks on Peacock's ancestors and followers
Mackerness, E.D. 'Thomas Love Peacock's Musical Crit-
icism', The Wind and the Rain, IV (Winter,1948),
177-87
Madden, Lionel Thomas Love Peacock (London, 1967).

Clear, full and sensible; one of the best
introductions to Peacock's work

Manganelli, Giorgio 'T.L. Peacock', Il Paragone, 5
(1954), 28-36. Excellent, especially on Peacock's politics

Mason, Ronald 'Notes for an Estimate of Peacock',
Horizon, IX (April, 1944), 238-50. Emphasizes
the classical rigidity of Peacock's satire

Mayoux, Jean-Jacques Un Epicurien anglais: Thomas
Love Peacock (Paris, 1933). Still by far the
richest and most suggestive critical book on
Peacock

PEACOCK 'L'Abbaye de Cauchemar' (Nightmare Abbey)
'Les Malheurs d'Elphin' (The Misfortunes of
Elphin), traduits et préfacés Jean-Jacques
Mayoux (Paris, 1936). Mayoux's long introduct-
ion to this translation offers brilliant in-
sights into Peacock's art

Mills, Howard Peacock: his Circle and his Age (Cambridge, 1969)

Moody, H.L.B. (ed.) A Peacock Selection (London and
New York, 1966). Moody's brief introduction is
a model of sharpness and good sense.

Praz, Mario 'Thomas Love Peacock', The Hero in
Eclipse in Victorian Fiction (London, 1956), pp.
87-102. In general, gives an unsympathtic view

Price, J.B. 'Thomas Love Peacock', Contemporary
Review, No.1038 (June, 1952), 365-9

Prickett, Stephen 'Peacock's Four Ages Recycled',
British Journal of Aesthetics, Vol.22, No.2
(Spring, 1982), 158-66. Prickett finds wit to
be the central quality of the 'Four Ages', which
he also describes as a genuine defence of poetry
against the menace of contemporary frivolity

Priestley, J.B. Thomas Love Peacock (London, 1927).
Remains one of the most sensible and sympathetic
estimates of Peacock's work

Rodway, Allan English Comedy (London, 1975). Includes an interesting, detailed comparison between
Peacock and Jane Austen

Sage, Lorna (ed.) Peacock The Satirical Novels (London and Basingstoke, 1976). An essential book,
with a good introduction by Sage, which reprints
some of the best available writing about Peacock
and includes a translation of material from
Mayoux, Un Epicurien anglais

Saintsbury, George 'Peacock', Prefaces and Essays
(London, 1933), pp.210-72. Leisurely and fond,
but often acute

Salz, Paulina June 'Peacock's Use of Music in his
Novels', Journal of English and Germanic

Philology, Vol.LIV, No.3 (July, 1955), 370-9

Spedding, James 'Tales by the Author of Headlong Hall', Reviews and Discussions Literary, Political and Historical 'not relating to Bacon' (London, 1879), 121-52. The best-balanced nineteenth-century study, and still an excellent introduction

Stewart, J.I.M. Thomas Love Peacock (London, 1963)

Teyssandier, Hubert 'T.L. Peacock et le récit satirique', Les formes de le création romanesque à l'époque de Walter Scott et de Jane Austen 1814-1820 (Paris, 1977), pp.195-250. Gives excellent studies of Headlong Hall and, especially, Melincourt

Tillyard, E.M.W. 'Thomas Love Peacock', Essays Literary and Educational (London, 1962), pp.114-30. Stresses the seriousness of Peacock's comedy and its defence of important civilized values

Wilson, Edmund 'The Musical Glasses of Peacock', Classics and Commercials (London, 1951), pp.404-11. Suggestive and highly appreciative, this short essay finely evokes the mood of Peacock's novels

Woolf, Virginia 'Phases of Fiction', Granite and Rainbow (London, 1958), pp.93-145. Has some acute comments on Peacock.